Dream Sequences in Shakespeare

This book takes a new approach to Shakespeare's plays, exploring them as dream-thought in the modern psychoanalytic sense of unconscious thinking.

Through his commitment to poetic language, Shakespeare offers images and dramatic sequences that illustrate fundamental developmental conflicts, the solutions for which are not preconceived but evolve through the process of dramatisation. In this volume, Meg Harris Williams explores the fundamental distinction between the surface meanings of plot or argument and the deep grammar of dreamlife, applied not only to those plays known as 'dream-plays' but also to critical sequences throughout Shakespeare's oeuvre.

Through a post-Kleinian model based on the thinking of Bion, Meltzer, and Money-Kyrle, this book sheds new light on both Shakespeare's own relation to the play and on the identificatory processes of the playwright, reader, or audience. *Dream Sequences in Shakespeare* is important reading for psychoanalysts, playwrights, and students.

Meg Harris Williams is a writer, literary critic, and artist. She has published many books and papers on the relation between literature, aesthetic experience, and psychoanalysis, specialising in a post-Kleinian perspective. She teaches internationally and is a visiting lecturer at the Tavistock Clinic, an honorary member of the Psychoanalytic Center of California, and editor for the Harris Meltzer Trust. Her books include *Inspiration in Milton and Keats*; *The Apprehension of Beauty* (with Donald Meltzer); *A Strange Way of Killing*; *Five Tales from Shakespeare* (for children); *The Vale of Soulmaking*; *Bion's Dream*; *The Aesthetic Development*; *Hamlet in Analysis – A Trial of Faith*; *The Becoming Room*; and *The Art of Personality*. Website: www.artlit.info.

'Understanding Shakespeare's plays as aesthetic objects that transcend the limitations of time and space, Meg Harris Williams follows the dream logic of their aesthetic form. Her readings illuminate the transformative processes of Shakespeare's imagination, and her psychoanalytic perceptions yield insight after insight into Shakespeare's theatrical worlds. Her book is a welcome counterpoint to current historical and political readings.'

– Murray Schwartz, Professor Emeritus, Institute for Liberal Arts &
Interdisciplinary Studies at Emerson College

'In these "second thoughts" on Shakespeare's "dreamscape," Harris Williams invites us to accompany her in discovering latent elements of the plays through her own "counterdreaming" – Meltzerian form of "reverie" – that facilitates an experience-near exploration of how the characters handle the contrary emotions of love and hate that set in motion forward-moving, or regressive, "anti-thought" developmental sequences, while also prompting us to question our own openness to uncovering what we don't yet know. In so doing, she elucidates the "reparative possibility" of engaging with internal objects, not just for the protagonists and playwright himself, but in turn the reader – that to more intimately step-in, the reader, artist, much as analysand and analyst, is potentially granted access to the "poetic deep grammar" of emotional life that "enriches our own becoming," thereby affirming the transformative power of art, alongside psychoanalysis. This journey we are taken on is an eye-opening, inspirational one, steeped in the marriage of Harris William's scholarly knowledge of Shakespeare and her "deep rooted" appreciation of the Bionian-Meltzerian oeuvre, driven by her own desire to listen to the internal muse.'

– Vivienne Pasieka, Psychoanalyst, Toronto

Dream Sequences in Shakespeare

A Psychoanalytic Perspective

Meg Harris Williams

LONDON AND NEW YORK

First published 2021
by Routledge
2 Park Square, Milton Park, Abingdon, Oxon OX14 4RN

and by Routledge
52 Vanderbilt Avenue, New York, NY 10017

Routledge is an imprint of the Taylor & Francis Group, an informa business

© 2021 Meg Harris Williams

The right of Meg Harris Williams to be identified as author of this work has been asserted by her in accordance with sections 77 and 78 of the Copyright, Designs and Patents Act 1988.

All rights reserved. No part of this book may be reprinted or reproduced or utilised in any form or by any electronic, mechanical, or other means, now known or hereafter invented, including photocopying and recording, or in any information storage or retrieval system, without permission in writing from the publishers.

Trademark notice: Product or corporate names may be trademarks or registered trademarks, and are used only for identification and explanation without intent to infringe.

British Library Cataloguing-in-Publication Data
A catalogue record for this book is available from the British Library

Library of Congress Cataloging-in-Publication Data
A catalog record for this book has been requested

ISBN: 978-0-367-63551-0 (hbk)
ISBN: 978-0-367-63549-7 (pbk)
ISBN: 978-1-003-11962-3 (ebk)

Typeset in Bembo
by Apex CoVantage, LLC

Contents

Acknowledgements	vi
Preface	vii

1	The individual and the group: *Richard II* and *Julius Caesar*	1
2	The reason of love objects: *A Midsummer Night's Dream*	19
3	Dreamlife and adolescent identity in Hamlet and Ophelia	30
4	Dreams of dark corners: legalism at play in *The Merchant of Venice* and *Troilus and Cressida*	46
5	Explorations in minus K: *Macbeth* and *Othello*	59
6	The turbulence of aesthetic conflict: *King Lear*	78
7	Love and the evolution of thought: *Antony and Cleopatra*	93
8	The organ of consciousness in *Cymbeline*	107
9	A dream of reparation: *The Winter's Tale*	121
10	The birth of ideas: *The Tempest*	136
	Epilogue	152

Appendix: Dream-life in the post-Kleinian model of the mind	155
References and bibliography	164
Name index	169
Subject index	171

Acknowledgements

Wilfred Bion lamented how difficult it was to come by 'austere criticism' as distinct from 'complacent hostility' or 'fantastic admiration'. The author would like to give special thanks to Adrian Williams, Irene Freeden, and Neil Maizels for reading the chapters of this book as it progressed with close attention, for helpful critical comments, and above all for huge encouragement.

Publication acknowledgement

The author would like to thank the editors and publishers for permission to reprint sections from 'Cleopatra's Monument' in *The Vale of Soulmaking* (Karnac, 2004) and from 'The True Voice of Feeling: Lear's Pilgrimage' in *Psychodynamic Practice* (2011), 17(2), pp. 141–158.

Preface

In offering to the market yet another book on Shakespeare in ecologically conscious times, I feel the need to try to justify my literary aims, so this preface is by way of a brief personal apologia. Inevitably the material presented here goes back many years, with constant rewriting in my head and sometimes via the printed page. Although I have continued to take an interest in the current evolution of academic scholarship, I have found that the critics or writers whose approach remains most vivid in my mind are those whose immersion in poetic diction and dramatic structure best evokes the dreamscape of the plays, and that the type of criticism I most value consists in the description of a particular reading experience – the written equivalent of a theatre performance, reliant more on expressiveness than on debate.

While theatre productions show no sign of getting less entertaining and awe-inspiring, the plays remain not easy to read. Can literary criticism actually help, or add anything to what we may gain with so little personal effort by going to the theatre, where all the work of mediation has been done for us, and those black marks on paper are flooded with colour, movement, and sound, in the guise of recognisable people having recognisable interactions? It is so much more apprehensible to the senses, and if we follow a Platonic orientation, that means that the underlying essence of the drama is also so much more easily accessed – we are taught and delighted at the same time. We hardly know what we have learned. Is there ever anything to be added to an audience's appreciation by writing about the play, given the demands made on the reader?

This book explores Shakespeare's plays as dream-thought in the modern psychoanalytic sense of unconscious thinking. Through his commitment to poetic language the playwright discovers images and dramatic sequences that illustrate fundamental developmental conflicts whose solutions are not preconceived but evolve through the process of dramatisation.

I imagine the book as written for readers who enjoy going to the theatre, not seeking for a definitive production but hoping to re-apprehend the core features of a play that they know well, captured in the light of an idiosyncratic and selective lens. Shakespeare is infinitely interpretable, but without such a lens there is no commitment and no art form. In criticism, too, it is not so much a problem of having the experience but missing the meaning, but of fixing something otherwise transitory: to enrich existing knowledge by drawing attention to those latent or implicit elements that may not always be visible but that nonetheless have a logical foundation in the structure of the play itself. These elements are not invented but they are discovered subjectively. This type of criticism cannot claim to be authoritative, any more than a play production, except in the sense of aiming to clearly convey its author's meaning and experience.

Much as I value genuine social history, I am aware that my interpretations will be considered as naively presuming the existence of an ahistorical essence known as human nature or 'the mind'. This focus on the mind is not so much a universal claim as a mode of perception. Social and political critics will approach Shakespeare from a different vertex, looking for different aspects, and often what is branded psychoanalytic criticism is in fact political criticism. At its most dogmatic, this political-psychoanalytic approach denies that the mind or personality exists except to the extent that it is a cultural construct. This is actually anti-psychological and is based on the assumption that the mind and its mysterious internal operations can be explained away by an external frame of reference which is not in itself definitive but merely a transitory cultural application.

In the Appendix to this book, I have written more about the psychoanalytic ideas that I use and the model of the mind from which they derive. These ideas, being long and deeply rooted, have always existed in parallel to my literary reading. Unfortunately, but unavoidably, this explication involves the use of some special terms and jargon. The 'post-Kleinian' model is well suited to the analysis of artworks, as it links with philosophical concepts about symbol-formation and aesthetic appreciation and puts dream-life at the heart of the processing of emotional experience that is now considered to be 'thinking' in the developmental, rather than didactic, sense. Perhaps I can at this point borrow the quote from Lionel Trilling with which A. D. Nuttall prefaces his book *Shakespeare the Thinker:* 'It must puzzle us to know what thinking is if Shakespeare and Dante did not do it.' Where Nuttall analyses Shakespeare's deep and unobtrusive familiarity with, and manipulation of, the philosophical issues of his day, this book tries to identify the underlying patterns of the dream-thought through which Shakespeare realised and conveyed the implicit ideas about personality development that made him a poet not of his age but for all time.

Chapter 1

The individual and the group:
Richard II and *Julius Caesar*

In this chapter I would like to discuss two plays about the adolescent mind. By this I do not necessarily refer to young adults of a certain era in a certain social context, but to a particular state of mind. The adolescent state of mind is that which marks a turbulent turning-point in the evolving mentality of an individual who is emerging from a quiescent or latent condition. *Richard II* and *Julius Caesar* are both concerned with the adolescent's relation to his 'group' and attempt to grow from its shelter into an individual, to develop a sense of personal rather than group identity. The challenge for the adolescent, in Meltzer's view, is to suffer the paradoxical feeling of moving backwards into dependence on internal objects in the face of the hormonal and societal pressure to progress 'ruthlessly' to success:

> The adolescent thinks that what leads him forward into the adult world is in reality regressive, while what he experiences as the thing which pushes him back, to the point of making him into a child again, is in reality the very thing which makes him an adult . . . should he be ruthless, inflicting suffering on others in order to achieve success, or should he turn backwards and be the one to suffer?
>
> (Meltzer & Harris, [2011] 2018, p. 27)

When the 'dreaminess becomes too painful', the adolescent who finds the sense of helplessness intolerable may retreat into this march for success.

In *Richard II* and in *Julius Caesar*, we see different dramatisations of the conflict between success (leadership) and internal reliance in relation to the surrounding group.

Richard II: a dream of deposition*

Richard II is the king who deposes himself in a dream of moving from a narcissistic (paranoid-schizoid) to a depressive object-related vertex, with a sense also of moving from homosexual to heterosexual values. His self-deposition appears

---

* This section enlarges on a shorter analysis in *The Chamber of Maiden Thought* (Williams & Waddell, 1992).

2 The individual and the group: Richard and Julius

to be imposed by his group – the aristocratic society of his upbringing – but is in fact engineered by himself. It illustrates the fundamental Kleinian developmental shift of values. Essentially it is a story of growing up and out from within the adolescent group whose basic assumptions he is too intelligent not to perceive. In disposing of his 'kingship', his figurehead role of pseudo-divinity at the head of the group, he appears he is one of those 'aloof' adolescents. The loss of the crown is a dream of deposition – deposition of these basic assumptions.

In the process he moves from player-king to poet-king, as he was originally dubbed by Walter Pater, who described the entire play as a 'lyrical ballad' ([1889] 2016, p. 211). The background imagery of the play in which his story is set forms an intricate medieval tapestry of significant emblems: crown, sun, green land, tree circulating blood. This tapestry reminds us of the hierarchic structure of England as the idealised mother country of all the characters, which like an organism demands the harmony and obedience of all its components in accordance with the basic assumption of Divine Right. Like all basic assumptions (in Bion's definition), this is known by everyone to be a lie but is supposed to be necessary for social stability and protection from enemies. It was a lie in fact of Shakespeare's day, not of the historical Richard's, underlining that this was probably Shakespeare's most dangerous play, with Elizabeth herself famously remarking 'Know ye not, I am Richard II?' In the garden scene, the gardeners point out how they prune trees in order to keep them in order: if any grows too high, it will have its head chopped off, the moral being that this is the way the country should be governed in order to pacify its nobility and avert civil war. The nobility think in the same way, but Richard has a not-yet-formulable premonition of some other way of thinking. What appears to be his weakness is really his inkling of another possible role in life, another identity.

The mother-land

Initially the play's 'adventitious poetic gold' (Pater) accrues to the person of Richard himself in a way that reflects the glorious idealisation of the mother-country, expressed in John of Gaunt's famous speech:

> This other Eden, demi-paradise,
> This fortress built by nature for herself
> Against infection and the hand of war,
> This happy breed of men, this little world,
> This precious stone set in the silver sea,
> Which serves it in the office of a wall,
> Or as a moat defensive to a house
> Against the envy of less happier lands;
> This blessed lot, this earth, this realm, this England,
> This nurse, this teeming womb of royal kings . . .
>
> (II.i.42–51)

The fortress island womb, ringing its precious stone, mirrors the crown. But Richard is internally driven to sacrifice his kingship in order to develop as an individual – a progression that is enacted by his social humiliation and death. His story has always moved readers and audiences, yet strangely, it is not generally regarded as a developmental achievement but as 'poetic justice' in the sense of self-directed revenge brought on by a sensitive but deluded and doomed personality.

Gaunt's speech is his emotive swansong, knowing in his heart that the day of that beautiful myth is over. He describes himself as both 'inspired' and 'expiring' and even prophesies the beginnings of modern capitalism:

> This land of such dear souls, this dear dear land,
> Dear for her reputation through the world,
> Is now leased out, I die pronouncing it,
> Like to a tenement or pelting farm . . .
>
> (ll. 57–60)

A new system of government is on the horizon, based on 'inky blots and rotten parchment bonds' and the end of glorious empire (300 years before it happened or had scarcely begun):

> That England, that was wont to conquer others,
> Hath made a shameful conquest of itself.
>
> (ll. 65–66)

He also speaks the only words of truth to Richard, pointing out to him that he is not lord of time:

> *Richard*: Why, uncle, thou hast many years to live.
> *Gaunt*: But not a minute, king, that thou canst give.
>
> (I.iii.225–226)

These are words that come back to Richard for re-digestion in his own final scene. It is Gaunt indeed who first suggests the idea of self-deposition when he prophesies that Richard is 'possess'd to depose himself' – with a pun on possession as both madness and ownership. He will no longer own his mother-country, but Richard has already discovered that that is an illusion. Only on the verge of death can Gaunt say what he means, give voice to the music in his soul, for 'the tongues of dying men / Enforce attention like deep harmony.'

In this way, Gaunt's deathbed exhortations to Richard, though intended as impassioned warning and almost a curse, represent his glimpse of an alternative worldview and have an undercurrent of intelligent truthful vision that in fact awakens Richard's curiosity. Richard's final dismissive comment on Gaunt's demise – 'His time is spent, our pilgrimage must be' – is in a way a perverse

4 The individual and the group: Richard and Julius

and unwilling acceptance of an emotional inheritance. Inspired and expiring, Gaunt breathes a type of poetic responsibility into his nephew, distasteful as Richard finds it. There is a closeness in mindview that is absent in Bolingbroke's relationship with either his father or his uncle York, whom he flatters and smoothly addresses as 'father'.

Speechless death

The process of Richard's relinquishing or deposing his narcissism – in which he is king of the rigid but fragile social organisation – begins with his rebelling against accepted codes of conduct. This occurs when he stops the duel between two of his subjects, Mowbray and Bolingbroke – not from sheer arbitrariness as might appear, but because a feeling-fact is pushing at his consciousness (as Bion would say), demanding to be formulated:

> Let them lay by their helmets and their spears,
> And both return back to their chairs again.
> (I.iii.119–120)

Their blood, he says, would be a waste of an expensive upbringing. Instead of blood he suggests banishment, and the two nobles react in different ways. He who will be the future king (Bolingbroke) says defiantly that he will carry England with him wherever he goes; he is a man of action, and banishment is freedom. The other (Mowbray) feels he has been both humiliated and entombed. What interests Richard (and us) is that Mowbray's sense of imprisonment derives from the feeling that his native language has been taken away from him:

> Within my mouth you have engaol'd my tongue,
> Doubly portcullis'd within my teeth and lips
> And dull, unfeeling, barren ignorance
> Is made my gaoler to attend on me.
> I am too old to fawn upon a nurse,
> Too far in years to be a pupil now:
> What is thy sentence, then, but speechless death,
> Which robs my tongue from breathing native breath?
> (I.iii.166–173)

He goes, he says, to 'endless night': his capacity for self-expression and symbol-formation has been sealed off; both the cutting and the kissing capabilities of his buccal cavity are closed down; his internal mother is incommunicable, guarded by a portcullis of suffocating teeth. Because he will have no-one to speak to in his native tongue, he is overcome by 'barren ignorance'.[1] Knowledge and self-knowledge are lost when facility in language is lost.

During the first two acts Richard has been a man of few words, by contrast with the deluge of insults hurled by the others. But as Stanley Wells has emphasised, this is a play in which 'tongue' is a keyword, often paired with 'heart' in a context of the false and true use of language. It seems to be as a result of Mowbray's heartfelt lament that Richard acquires an interest in language; the idea, and image, of the tongue within the mouth becomes a governing metaphor in the play, undergoing various transformations that echo the images of the 'hollow crown' and the sea-girt isle (from womb to death's head). This, together with Gaunt's prophetic vision, fuels his new adventure.

In Shakespeare's portrayal, Richard's supposed crimes as a king are presented as discontented rationalisations – a casual reference to his alleged homosexuality, and some ruffled talk about 'blanks, benevolences and I wot not what' (II.i.940). What we have seen onstage is not his misgovernment but his disregard of decorum, his exposure of the social lie on which all rely for their sense of security. With a fatalistic inevitability, Richard departs for Ireland while society plots its revenge, and there he undergoes a sea-change. After this point the play enters the realm of dream. When he returns to face his deposition, poetry pours out of him, alongside the evaporation of his political support. Prefiguring the 'tears and smiles' of his final public procession of (Christlike) humiliation, when dust is thrown on his head, he greets his native earth with 'weeping, smiling':

> Mock not my senseless conjuration, lords:
> This earth shall have a feeling . . .
>
> (III.ii.23–24)

Sensuous contact with the earth, the mother-land, is a new source of emotionality, awoken through identification with Mowbray. He appreciates the preciousness of the speaking object – the internal mother – and this will support his own self-imposed banishment from the basic assumptions of society and the court.

Gaunt is uncle to Richard and father to Henry Bolingbroke. The cousins could be seen as split aspects of the same personality, and Richard cannot discover his new identity without foisting onto Bolingbroke those features that he feels imprison him in the social exoskeleton. When on Gaunt's death his tongue becomes a 'stringless instrument', its power is inherited not by his son – whom Richard describes as 'silent king' – but by Richard. It is as though poetic speech and earthly power cannot house together within one skull. The two cousins carry the emotional drama between them in the deposition movement; the other characters are merely time-servers. They are also brothers in 'Necessity', a term very close in this play to the ancient Greek meaning: the force of reality.

6 The individual and the group: Richard and Julius

The hollow crown

Bolingbroke has no difficulty in lopping off the superfluous branches of his political opponents; but the crown he acquires is a death's head, as Richard points out when he hands it over:

> All murthered – for within the hollow crown
> That rounds the mortal temples of a king
> Keeps Death his court, and there the antic sits,
> Scoffing his state and grinning at his pomp,
> Allowing him a little breath, a little scene,
> To monarchise, be fear'd, and kill with looks;
> Infusing him with self and vain conceit,
> As if this flesh which walls about our life
> Were brass impregnable; and humour'd thus,
> Comes at the last, and with a little pin
> Bores through his castle wall, and farewell king!
> (III.ii.160–170)

Remembering Gaunt's phrase 'death's sad tale', Richard begins to 'tell sad stories of the death of kings'. The King Richard who was once infused with vain conceit, identified with the sea-walled fortress-mother, now recognises his vulnerability and with it, his humanity:

> I live with bread like you, feel want,
> Taste grief, need friends – subjected thus,
> How can you say to me, I am a king?
> (ll. 175–177)

His 'subjection' is revelation as well as rhetoric, but the courtly audience does not understand his metaphor, and often, neither does the play's actual audience. Richard is believed by Bolingbroke and the others to be still acting a part (a 'shadow' grief) rather than genuinely trying to shed his actor's robes ('monarchising') and inhabit his own head. By means of what Pater called 'inverted coronation rites', Richard undoes his previous kingly performance by means of an exact gestural reversal, but this time the performance is not just for show.[2] He ignores Northumberland's attempt to make him confess to his crimes against the state; the politics are irrelevant. His intention is to unravel the mystique of divine kingship in such a way as to demonstrate its hollowness and futility. It is an unconscious intention and thereby the more dreamlike: he is demonstrating to himself, not just the group.

Richard is often seen as wallowing in self-pity rather than ridding himself of a poisoned chalice, the 'brittle glory' that 'shines in the face' of a pseudo-divinity. Bolingbroke alone is hypnotised by Richard's performance, and all his movements are a response to Richard's invitation, and insistence, that he 'seize the crown'. Richard demands, in effect, that his enemy acquire the 'face' that had once appeared to have a beauty as potent as that of Helen of Troy:

> Was this face the face
> That every day under his household roof
> Did keep ten thousand men? Was this the face
> That like the sun did make beholders wink?
>
> (IV.i.281–284)

Cracking the mirror that enclosed his surface-face demonstrates his personal triumph over narcissism. He presses the 'sport', the superficial game, upon his alter-ego Bolingbroke, who he says has 'outfaced' him:

> Mark, silent king, the moral of this sport –
> How soon my sorrow hath destroy'd my face.
>
> (ll. 292–293)

He demonstrates the destroyed face by means of the smashed mirror, but Bolingbroke pertinently retorts, 'The shadow of your sorrow has destroyed the shadow of your face'. By the end of the scene they have become intolerably close, by contrast with the impatient onlookers who feel this is a time-wasting charade interfering with state business – the business of the adolescent gang, in Meltzer's picture. Richard has in a sense split his identity and discarded that part of himself (or in the group context, his most intimate friend) that wishes to push ruthlessly towards success; and Bolingbroke hates him for placing him in that position, whilst at the same time exposing the hypocrisies that would soften the group's guilt. Bolingbroke ever afterwards feels he is sin-ridden.

The tension is only released when they can express mutual hatred and separate:

> *Richard*: Then give me leave to go.
> *Bolingbroke*: Whither?
> *Richard*: Whither you will, so I were from your sights.
> *Bolingbroke*: Go some of you, convey him to the Tower.
>
> (ll. 313–316)

The caterpillars of the commonwealth

It has been said that the spiritual regeneration of Richard in the Tower is too sudden a transition (Nuttall) – we don't know how it has happened that he has suddenly become a true poet and a thinker. However, signs have been growing, located in particular in the imagery associated with his queen, Isabel. Her image or influence is taking shape in Richard's mind in direct opposition to the

8   The individual and the group: Richard and Julius

imagery of the hollow crown, in the form of a different model of femininity or female-as-container which is neither fortress nor death's-head. Isabel is seen with mean and lowly characters, not nobles – the gardeners and the despised 'caterpillars of the commonwealth' Bushy, Bagot, and Green, who are like her children. She has an aura of pregnancy, albeit with 'sorrow':

> Some unborn sorrow ripe in Fortune's womb
> Is coming towards me, and my inward soul
> With nothing trembles . . .
>
> (II.ii.10–12)

But 'sorrow' is also what Richard has been moving towards, in the sense of real emotion that contrasts with charade and political manipulation. Richard's response to Bolingbroke's accusation of shadow-sorrow was to agree with his distinction between real and fake and elaborate upon it:

> And these external manners of lament
> Are merely shadows to the unseen grief
> That swells with silence in the tortur'd soul.
> There lies the substance.
>
> (IV.i.303–306)

He sarcastically thanks Bolingbroke for pointing the way to the existence of the soul's substance, as distinct from its shadow. Despite his sarcasm, this is their moment of mutual understanding: now Richard has it, and Bolingbroke does not.

When Richard loses his crown, he regains his wife. In taking the 'heavy weight' from his head, he said 'I must nothing be', 'nothing have', and be 'nothing grieved'.[3] When he finds Isabel again, in the tender scene on his way to imprisonment in the Tower, he begins to understand the substantial nature of this 'nothing'. The meaning of the deposition was his recognition that he was not his own love-object; this paves the way for him to recognise an object outside himself. The obsessional mentality associated with owning the mother-country gives way to a more complex sexuality. The Queen has previously associated herself with a type of mental pregnancy, heavily ripe with 'unborn sorrows' resulting from 'no thought':

> *Isabel*: As, though on thinking on no thought I think,
> Makes me with heavy nothing faint and shrink.
>
> (II.ii.31–32)

As Richard's object or muse, container of thoughts, she laments the end of 'the model where old Troy did stand' – the old Richard whose 'heart' she fears Bolingbroke has 'deposed'. But that deposed Richard is the one who thought he was Helen of Troy, an illusion pinpricked by his own perspicacity. Isabel's fears energise him to reassure her that he has not lost his spirit – rather he has discovered a spirit more true to himself and to her. Speaking as one who has a new faith in words, and who has rediscovered the tongue-soul that Mowbray had lamented, he suggests she convert her 'heavy nothing' into telling his story, using 'the heavy accent of thy moving tongue'. The old type of Troy-king may tumble down, but that was only 'Richard's tomb', his false persona or portcullis, not his inner soul.

Still breeding thoughts

The meeting with Isabel is the transition to Richard's discovery of his own inner world, his thinking mind. She is now his internalised 'tongue'. For the first time, in the last act, we see him alone, yet not alone: soliloquising, and the entire focus is on his dream-world, which the previous acts have constructed by a process of stripping-away the false dream of divine right.[4] It is as though his mind has finally transformed into the container-contained dynamic theatre of symbol-formation (Bion's alpha-function):

> I have been studying how I may compare
> This prison where I live unto the world;
> And, for because the world is populous
> And here is not a creature but myself,
> I cannot do it. Yet I'll hammer it out.
> My brain I'll prove the female to my soul,
> My soul the father, and these two beget
> A generation of still-breeding thoughts,
> And these same thoughts people this little world . . .
> (V.v.1–10)

The deposition of his narcissism is thus the prelude to the rejuvenation of his creativity. Unlike Mowbray, his language is not banished but intensified. He is forced into looking inwards and thinking, discovering the tongue that can speak poetry. His brain is no longer housed in a hollow crown; despite his physical imprisonment, the idea of a male-female internal object is born, with female and fatherly aspects that recall Isabel's own words about the heaviness of thoughts. This is what it means to be a man 'that but man is', not king. He left Bolingbroke a 'well-dress'd actor' with a stifled soul. Now, having abandoned the public stage, Richard's new 'little world' peopled by internally generated thoughts contrasts with the portcullised spiritual prison imagined by Mowbray at the beginning, where the tongue had no outlet and indeed could not act as an organic thought-transmitter. The brain within the skull is now free to create symbols.

Roger Money-Kyrle (1968) has described three innate preconceptions without which cognitive development cannot proceed: the idea of a good breast,

10   The individual and the group: Richard and Julius

the idea of creative parents, and the idea of death – that is, of time, for death-time is the concept that gives shape to experience. At the point when Richard recognises he is 'but a man', he hears music – clumsily played and out of time, but he accepts the awkward numbers as 'a sign of love' and, on another level, as a reminder that he has an obligation not to waste time: 'I wasted time, and now doth time waste me' (V.v.49). He is one of those adolescents who feels he is going backwards as if into childhood: 'my true time broke'. Yet this is how he becomes a working poet, recognising broken rhythms that need repairing. Only through overcoming his narcissism is he able to hear the new music of love. The childlike musician appears (in dreamlike substitution) in the form of his Groom, who comes to wordlessly warn him of his coming death; the 'strange brooch' of love that he embodies replaces the jewelled crown and the sceptred isle. The Groom's message of death is non-verbal, between the lines, imaged in the way Richard's horse or lifeforce – his favourite 'roan Barbary' – has been taken over by Bolingbroke. But this premonition enables Richard to meet his death fighting, with a vitality that seals his new state of mind. Yet Bolingbroke is left with a 'soul full of woe / That blood should sprinkle me to make me grow', the price of his worldly success; his future knowledge is only that 'uneasy lies the head that wears the crown.'

Where Bolingbroke becomes an 'isolated' adolescent, Richard has a new-found capacity to people his mind with thought-characters. His internalised identification with Isabel enables a container where thoughts are no longer stillborn or hollow but 'still-breeding' – with a pun on the word 'still', meaning both not-moving (dead) and then continuously moving (productive). In one sense he is 'nothing' (his old identity is dead), but in another sense he is peopled by internal objects: his crown becomes a speaking mouth, a different type of round container. Richard can hear the female voice in his soul, and his poetic contemplation was echoed by Keats in his 'Ode to Psyche' with its 'wreathed trellis of a working brain' that 'breeding flowers will never breed the same'. The narcissistic mirror is shattered like the basic assumptions of the medieval hierarchic kingdom that strangles truthful speech. It has been replaced by a new world of breeding conceptions, each unique in identity.

Julius Caesar: school life

Henry Bolingbroke becomes isolated from the adolescent group in one sense, the tormented king of the *Henry IV* plays being a natural sequel to the split character established in *Richard II*. Julius Caesar is isolated in another. Julius is destroyed by his own narcissism, something that Richard outgrew. Walter de la Mare's short poem about Napoleon is surely inspired by Shakespeare's portrayal of Julius Caesar:

What is the world O soldiers?
It is I:
I, this incessant snow,

This northern sky;
Soldiers, this solitude
Through which we go
It is I.
(De la Mare, 'Napoleon')

The delusion of being the world, the I-word, was his downfall. Julius is the Napoleon of Rome – his answer to everything being 'for always I am Caesar'. In the world of 'flesh and blood men' he alone is different:

Yet in the number I do know but one
That unassailable holds on his rank,
Unshak'd of motion; and that I am he . . .
(III.i.68–70)

He is also the boy who cannot dream, because he confusedly believes it is beneath him, and who spurns those voices such as Calpurnia's (his female part) that attempt to introduce him to dreams of reality. His internal earthquake of thunder and lightning is somatised into his 'falling sickness' (epilepsy); from 'bestriding the world like a Colossus' he is now falling into a new position in the context of his group. In Cassius' description:

A man no mightier than thyself, or me,
In personal action, yet prodigious grown,
And fearful, as these strange eruptions are.
(I.iii.76–78)

Julius is unable to change course, to adapt to internal pressures of developmental change; his ego-centred persistence removes him from the adolescent ferment of his contemporaries.

Being true to the school: the fight-flight basic assumption

Often in Shakespeare we can take the old Roman world of Plutarch's histories to represent the latency phase and the values of what would later become the English boys' public boarding schools, in which to play the game was to win the war – if done in the right patriotic spirit and according to the comradely code, for the honour of the school, namely ancient Rome. The game of politics is an integral part of school life, and the code begins to break up when individual emotional attachments become more powerful than basic assumptions. The women in the play are really female parts of the personality, embodying emotional intuition. In *Julius Caesar*, written four years after *Richard II*, instead of the 'dependency' basic assumption of the organic mother-country we have the 'fight-flight' modality of the public school system with its implicit Stoic motto

12   The individual and the group: Richard and Julius

and its supposed democracy or republicanism, which really disguises the desire for hierarchy instilled in the plebeians (lower school) upwards.[5] Does being 'true to yourself' mean what it says, or is it a veil for being loyal to the school?

In the play there are various references to school and school-bonds (Casca was 'quick mettle when he went to school'; Brutus and Volumnius were at school together); rivalry is keen and there is a strong sense of age-ranking, with due deference paid to minor differences of perhaps a year or two – Julius and Cassius the eldest, Cassius an 'elder soldier' than Brutus, Antony younger than both, followed by Octavius and finally Lucius, the boy under Brutus' protection. In the plebeians we have the playground hordes, primed with patriotic songs and propaganda – ready to rehearse 'Hearts of Oak' or *Lord of the Flies*, to tease the prefects (tribunes) or lynch the swots for their 'bad verses' (their excuse for attacking Cinna the Poet [III.iii.39]). These demand, above all, entertainment from the 'Roman actors' of the upper school (as Brutus terms them): references are rife to stage play and acting, to earning one's place in the public eye.[6]

The tribunes who would ridicule Caesar's image (pull scarves off his statue) are 'put to silence'. Caesar (like the head boy or cricket captain) is the showpiece of the moment, and it is said that the people would applaud him even if he had 'stabb'd their mothers'; such is the irrelevance of any emotional reality in this context. All they want is a leader, an entertaining politician to wave a banner for them to follow. If not Julius, then 'let [Brutus] be Caesar!' – or Antony! Anyone will do ('knew they not Pompey?'). He is imbued by the messianic basic assumption that has evolved from fight-flight (obsession with winning wars and games). His scarves, medals, and decorations envelop his statuesque self-image and suggest he is already dead inside, ready for toppling. He is upheld essentially by the plebeians, not by those who appear to be close friends, as Antony well knows. The plebeians represent what Bion calls the 'protomental' level of non-thought, the lower reaches of group mentality: en masse the values are those of spectacle and excitement, as against thought or emotion.

The fire of words

Julius Caesar was described by G. Wilson Knight as 'a play of fire and love', and L. C. Knights pointed out 'how often the word "love" appears in this play . . . the effect not only pathos or irony'.[7] There is also a lot about words – as there is throughout Shakespeare – and there are parallel themes especially in *Love's Labour's Lost*, another school-life play. Yet the word 'love' that runs throughout the play has a variety of meanings. When the mind begins to shed its reliance on plebeian values and to enter the sphere of thought and emotion, the idea of love undergoes a change. Emotionality is associated with femininity, or the female principle within the mind as a whole; inevitably suspicion is aroused when it enters the latency setting and disturbs the orderliness of its values.

The thunder-and-lightning scenes flash the message that a head-boy figure such as Julius is no longer required in this new world, albeit he takes a ghostly revenge in the form of the suicides at the end of the play. The time is ripe for him to go (to 'die'), and he senses this but tries to rationalise it away on Stoic lines,[8] death being a 'necessary end' which 'will come when it will come' (II.ii.36). How and by whom will he be succeeded? Brutus is his 'angel' (III.ii.175, the 'noblest Roman' [V.v.73]), but Antony is his 'runner' (he 'touches' his wife, with sexual implications [I.ii.9]). He is not just a 'masker and reveller' but embodies Julius' split-off sexuality, whereas 'young Octavius' remains firmly and frigidly latency-phase to the end. Once upon a time Caesar indeed depended on Cassius, too, to survive the Tiber's flood and stay in power: Cassius was the one who rescued him. These are Caesar's team. But now that he is inflated to a 'god', it seems he is unable to imagine the reality of the other person, and for the older boys this is looming. This means he must be 'dismember'd' (in Brutus' telling phrase – indicating both loss of phallic potency and loss of his team members). A new type of role-model is required that can image the possibility of a love object.

Although the first part of the play recounts dreams, it is not dreamlike in texture. It is when love begins to dynamise the story that Shakespeare switches from social realism to dream mode. The new role-model, someone who is able to get in touch with a genuine capacity for love, is in the first instance Cassius, who not only outswam Julius on sports day but is moreover a 'thinker' – hence Caesar's suspicion of him:

> *Caesar:* Yond Cassius has a lean and hungry look;
>   He thinks too much; such men are dangerous.
> *Antony:* Fear him not, Caesar; he's not dangerous;
>   He is a noble Roman and well given.
> (I.ii.191–192)

Antony has not yet encountered these dangerous forces and believes the 'noble Roman' code still holds sway with Cassius. It is not surprising he misunderstands the undercurrents since Cassius is at the beginning of the play a supreme political manipulator, for whom 'love' means 'ally', and Brutus is just one of his pawns, coveted for his usefulness as an honourable Roman who will be a great asset to the murder conspiracy. He tells Casca he has already persuaded 'three parts' of him and 'the man entire / Upon the next encounter yields him ours' (I.iii.155). It is not Brutus, despite his troubled rationalising soliloquy, who is the intellectual (as Bloom describes him), but Cassius. Brutus is more like Richard than Macbeth in this soliloquy, trying to puzzle it out. He does indeed believe he is a man of reason, and that 'to speak truth of Caesar' he has not known him be swayed by his 'affections / More than his reason'. But this understatement is the very reason why Caesar is toppled from his position as head of the group: he is not a lover but rather has regressed into a cocoon.

14 The individual and the group: Richard and Julius

Meanwhile Brutus, far from being reasonable, undermines Cassius' judgement at every stage with a sort of automatic contradiction, and time and again is proved wrong – a movement which is echoed later in *Antony and Cleopatra* in the relationship between Enobarbus and Antony in a kind of counterpoint. He doesn't want an oath; he vetoes the murder of Antony and then insists he speak at Caesar's funeral; he decides the fateful march to Philippi, etc. Cassius knows these unwise decisions set their enterprise at risk, yet he acquiesces, not from stupidity but owing to the power of the parallel, unconscious dream story in which his love for Brutus overtakes his political ambition. Step by step, failure in the external world becomes a metaphor for dawning achievement in the inner world.

At his height, the 'word of Caesar stood against the world' (III.ii.118). After his fall, we learn a lot about the power of the word in the world – above all how it is dependent on the audience of plebeians for its ability to excite and incite. This is the world that is being gradually abandoned by the new leaders, Cassius and Brutus.

Brutus' great nationalistic speech to the plebeians at Caesar's funeral on the theme of honour is his swansong at the school of Rome: 'Not that I loved Caesar less, but that I loved Rome more. . . . Who is here so rude, that would not be a Roman?' It has been much denigrated owing to the fact that Antony wins the debate with 'Friends, Romans, countrymen', but it is also brilliant in its way and would have won the day in *Henry V*. It isn't Brutus' debating skills that are lacking but his political acumen.[9] A. D. Nuttall (2004) has categorised the two speeches as 'Attic' and 'Asiatic' in their rhetorical styles, of which each is an excellent example. Moreover, Antony speaks second, which gives his oratory the conclusive position, building on the rabble-rousing that Brutus has already instigated. Antony does not negate the work Brutus has already done; rather he cannibalises Brutus' momentum. He stands on Brutus' shoulders and upstages him:

> He was my friend, faithful and just to me;
> But Brutus says he was ambitious,
> And Brutus is an honourable man.
>
> (III.ii.87–89)

It is the rhetoric, more than the content of the argument, that holds sway, with its provocative, crescendoing refrain: 'For Brutus is an honourable man'. Honour is a word that like the Delphic oracle can be read equivocally, and Antony uses it, premeditatedly, to mean 'Cry havoc, and let loose the dogs of war' (III.i.273).

The real meaning of such rhetoric is imaged in the lynching by the mob of Cinna the poet for his 'bad verses' and the burning of Brutus' house ('Go fetch fire'), which will contrast with the fire of love metaphor. The power of the public or political word is by nature destructive, anti-poetic. After Antony has let loose the mob however, we never see the plebeians again. The anti-poetic word has been exorcised by exposure, on the lines of Orwell's 'war is peace – freedom is slavery' in *1984*.

The fire of love

The emotional heat of the play is at its most intense, therefore, not at the death of Caesar (which is still the realm of excitement and entertainment, superstition, and sentimentality) but during the famous quarrel between Brutus and Cassius in Brutus' tent at Sardis. They are haunted by the 'dismembered spirit' of Julius: whom does it still govern, and in what sense? The intimate confrontation is needed to clarify their relationship before they can move on to the military defeat at Philippi, which now takes on an emotional inevitability, and whose meaning needs to be worked out on a dreamlike level.

It is a lovers' quarrel – dreamlike, not rational. Through it, the play approaches the idea of 'catastrophic change', the forging of new values in the fire of love. The superficial pretexts for the quarrel consist in misunderstandings that could easily have been clarified had it not been for the emotional heat underlying them that demands confrontation and resolution. It begins with Brutus' fear, muttered to another soldier, that Cassius is behaving like 'a hot friend cooling' (IV.ii.19), and it continues in private with bitter mutual accusations of feeling slighted by each other, until the point at which Cassius expresses his own heartfelt fear that Brutus finds him unworthy – and the ghost of Julius has won:

> I, that denied thee gold, will give my heart:
> Strike, as thou didst at Caesar; for I know,
> When thou didst hate him worst, thou lov'dst him better
> Than ever thou lov'dst Cassius.
>
> (IV.iii.103–106)

This is the crux of the matter: jealousy of the superseded lover. Instantly Brutus understands and responds with 'Sheathe your dagger';[10] he embraces the 'fiery temper' that characterises the Cassius he knows, now that he realises this dagger of jealousy is a proof of love, and even admits his own 'ill temper':

> *Cassius*: Do you confess so much? Give me your hand.
> *Brutus*: And my heart too.
>
> (ll. 116–117)

Emphasising the dreamlike quality, at this point comes the strange intervention of the so-called poet who bursts in with his 'vile rhymes', declaring his intention to make the two generals friends again. The comical episode relaxes the tension and exorcises the false use of words for persuasion and control, worthless by comparison with the pledge of commitment.

16 The individual and the group: Richard and Julius

Immediately afterwards comes the news of Portia's death from swallowing fire. This too is a strange, dreamlike passage, and there is a puzzle about how it gets into words. I am among those who believe that Shakespeare intended to erase a first version (the message brought from outside by Messala) and substitute it with Brutus' own words beginning 'O Cassius I am sick of many griefs' (IV.iii.143). Brutus' dream of her death at this precise point at the finale of the quarrel images the new fiery spirit which infuses the deepened bond between Brutus and Cassius, sealed in the pledge of wine: 'I cannot drink too much of Brutus' love' (l. 161).

Having a wife, a feminine side to their nature, is one of the traits which Brutus and Julius would seem to have in common, just as they might appear similar in their sanctimony and obstinacy. But these similarities are really ground for contrast, as shown for example by the twin domestic scenes: Caesar with his nervous, despised wife and false friends contrasts with Brutus who will 'never find any man but was true to him' and whose wife is 'dear as the ruddy drops that visit my sad heart' (II.i.290). The tomboy Portia with her self-wounding is Brutus' link with the Stoic tradition in the sense of the ability to bear meaningful pain. The ruddy drops then fill the wine-cup of the pledge with Cassius. Brutus' feminine identification is also shown by his tender care of the boy Lucius who plays him music, helping him metabolise his 'evil spirit' (Caesar's ghost) and the ghost of his own ambition that still haunts him but, with Lucius' help, he manages to conquer.

As later in *Antony and Cleopatra*, where it is intensified on a heterosexual level, commitment to love is thrown into relief and therefore partly described via the contrast with worldly success. In key scenes we observe how the followers of Julius, in the face of anxiety, are suspicious and quarrelsome, at first sight like Cassius and Brutus. But it is in a cold and cynical way. Octavius contradicts Antony over political and military strategy in the same impulsive, pointless way that Brutus contradicts Cassius:

> *Antony*: Octavius, lead your battle softly on
>   Upon the left hand of the even field.
> *Octavius*: Upon the right hand I. Keep thou the left.
> *Antony*: Why do you cross me in this exigent?
> *Octavius*: I do not cross you, but I will do so.
>   (V.i.16–20)

Octavius in 'crossing' Antony is staking out his future Caesar-ship by practising the voice of command; Brutus, on similar occasions, is unconsciously testing Cassius' love and its capacity for hazard. The blood of Julius has no warmth, no fire: his body is a 'dismembered spirit' and bleeds like the scarves on his statue or the blood-bath of Calpurnia's dream, and as such drives the avenging principle of his followers – the road to becoming Napoleon.

The individual and the group: Richard and Julius 17

It is love that leads to the political 'suicide' of Brutus and Cassius imaged in the consummation of Philippi – a new slant on the traditional Roman style of honourable death. Bad productions of the play focus on the political blood, not the schoolboy (alchemical?) blood-sealing of an intimate relationship. The two protagonists succeed in emerging from the protection of the group's basic assumption values but their internal progress appears from the outside to be political suicide. Shakespeare emphasises, in the way he tells the story, that in each case their suicide does not come from a failure of fighting spirit, nor even from straightforward military defeat, but rather from the power of an inner vision, almost with a sense of absurdity. Cassius, declaring it is his birthday, is convinced that his life has 'run his compass' and therefore misconstrues a skirmish on a neighbouring hill, saying 'My sight was ever thick'. His vision is changing so appears blurred. Brutus too knows his 'hour is come', and in a sense wants it to come. Both attribute their death to the avenging ghost of Julius, the power of the Roman basic assumption group and its idolisation of tyranny, in response to which they turn their swords inwards to their 'proper entrails' – now a dream metaphor for looking inwards to the source of real emotion. Hence Brutus' moving elegy over Cassius' body:

> The last of all the Romans, fare thee well!
> It is impossible that ever Rome
> Should breed thy fellow. Friends, I owe more tears
> To this dead man than you shall see me pay.
> I shall find time, Cassius, I shall find time.
> (V.iii.99–103)

The repetition of 'find time' and the idea of private tears opens up a sense of internal space and contrasts with the concreteness of Antony's pact with Caesar's body – the 'bleeding piece of earth' – which has the spurious heat of paranoia and revenge. The body politic has become separated from the inner fire and the 'noblest Roman of them all' laments, or celebrates, the end of the Romans as they were once known: 'The sun of Rome is set' (V.iii.62).

Notes

1　Stanley Wells (1969) observed the key symbolism gravitating around the word 'tongue', which highlights the problem of the 'disjunction between what men mean and what they say' (p. 43). The play dramatises the evolution of a different type of speech.

2　M. M. Mahood in *Shakespeare's Wordplay* (1957) defined this reversal in terms of 'the words of a poet against the words of a politician' (p. 73). Richard exchanges one role for the incompatible other.

3　It is the beginning of Shakespeare's well-known preoccupation with the meaning of 'nothing' in many subsequent plays (see Willbern, 1980).

4　This point of change is seen by Harold Bloom (1999) as Richard acquiring an 'aesthetic dignity' but not a 'human' one; in terms of internal catastrophic (developmental) change, they are the same. A. D. Nuttall (1988) thinks Richard's genuine maturation happens

18 The individual and the group: Richard and Julius

too suddenly and inexplicably, but does not mention the relationship with Isabel which precipitates the turning-point. It appears to be a different kind of play: the world of 'symbol rather than reality', according to Wells; it is a creative dream.

5 Bion classifies the three main 'basic assumptions' of protomental life as fight-flight (aggression), dependency (parasitism), and messianic or pairing (the illusion of an ideology that will save the world, relieving everyone else of responsibility).

6 Anne Righter (Barton) (1962) describes the explicit parallels between the show at the Capitol and the audience at the theatre. The glorified idea of the play belongs to, and illustrates, a particular phase in life, soon to be outgrown.

7 G. Wilson Knight, 'The Torch of Life' (1931, p. 60); L. C. Knights, 'Personality and Politics in *Julius Caesar*' (1979, p. 87).

8 On stoicism in the play, see Anson (1969), 'Caesar's Stoic Pride'; Nuttall (2004), Berry (1999).

9 Harold Bloom (1999) finds Brutus' oration 'inept', but Ernst Schanzer (1969) analyses convincingly the skilful way in which Brutus' series of rhetorical questions 'ingeniously forestall any objections from his audience' (p. 185).

10 Wes Folkerth (2002) notes the changing relation of 'words like daggers' in this play and in *Hamlet*, in the context of the early modern view of sound and the ear as a site where problems of identity focus and fluctuate.

Chapter 2

The reason of love objects: *A Midsummer Night's Dream**

Bion humorously says in one of his late talks that it is not enough to consider the patient as 'bringing a dream'. The real or interesting question is, 'Where *were* you last night?' (Bion, 2018, p. 158). The sleep-world is a real place, and our task is to divert the organ of attention (consciousness) inwards rather than outwards as in waking life. In traditional myths, fables, and romances, the Unknown is a green world, a wood or forest where nature rules, not man; and the omnipotence of 'proud man dressed in a little brief authority' (as Shakespeare put it in *Measure for Measure*) is confined to the illusory protection of castle, court, or city (Bion's 'exoskeleton'). The venturing knight falls asleep under a tree and dreams the meaning of his quest.

The traditional comedic pattern followed in *A Midsummer Night's Dream*, Shakespeare's funniest and most optimistic play, from city to green world and back again, is generally and truly seen in terms of the interaction of conscious daytime rationality and unconscious night-time dream.[1] As in the old romances, the lovers and mechanicals who have escaped from the rigid restrictions of Athenian decorum circle around the 'Duke's oak' at the heart of the wood while their vision is altered by the fairies. In addition to this, the 'story of the night told o'er' can be seen in Bionian terms as an expansion of proto-mental 'basic assumption' restrictions by means of true unconscious thinking (alpha-function or symbol-formation). In the transformation of Theseus' mind through dreaming, on the threshold of the 'catastrophic change' of his wedding night, we see the birth of a philosopher-ruler, or creative playwright.[2] When negative capability is engaged, the mind's creative work is done not by some authoritarian superego controlling a chaotic unconscious but by a 'thinking breast', an internal 'combined object' in the form of the primal-scene dream-image of Bottom and Titania embowered in the moonlit wood. Bottom is Oberon's alter-ego, teaching the humility required in becoming a reasonable lover. The complementary identities of fairy and mechanical combine into a

---

* This chapter enlarges on a shorter analysis in *The Chamber of Maiden Thought* (Williams & Waddell, 1992).

complex internal superego-ideal that guides Theseus' unconscious mind. The ordinary ruler, initially bound by society's basic assumptions, shows he is capable of learning from his unconscious dream-life. The play charts the movement out of the protomental city, learning to look with the mind in a new key.

The protomental city

So where is Duke Theseus the night before his wedding to Hippolyta? It has often been observed that the opening of the play has all the classic ingredients of a potential tragedy, which then mysteriously and almost accidentally turns into a comedy (while *Romeo and Juliet* does the opposite). The opening scenes of the *Dream* suggest a confused and ill-starred nuptial is forthcoming, not so much a celebration as a submission to a rigid superego-authority. We are reminded of the well-known history of their courtship, of Theseus' sexual philandering and Hippolyta's tomboy taunting at the head of her group of man-hating Amazon schoolgirls. Theseus 'won her with his sword' and claims to wed her 'in another key', but the new music is not at all convincing as yet, as is evidenced by his management of the four young lovers. His internal understanding of 'reason' leads him to conformity with a rigid and punitive old-fashioned 'law' of Athens, represented by Hermia's father Egeus (really Theseus' own father in classical mythology), a law which can end only in death or in perpetual virginity, but not in a happily consummated marriage of equals. In this old-fashioned system – alien to any 'new key' – the feminine principle is thus constrained or subjugated, as indicated by the parallel picture of aesthetics in which the work of art (the 'child' or the marriage) is compared to a 'form in wax', 'imprinted' on the woman by the dominant man. As Theseus formulates the standard or prevailing view:

> To you your father should be as a god
> One that composed your beauties, yea,
> To whom you are but as a form in wax,
> By him imprinted and within his power
> To leave the figure or disfigure it.
> (I.i.47–51)

The basic assumption behind this false or outdated aesthetic is insisted on by Egeus, and Theseus has no answer to it; he is convinced it represents reason, law, and order, and if it is not maintained there will be social chaos. In emotional terms however he is uncomfortable about it, as indicated in his rather feeble 'What cheer, my love?' to Hippolyta as she walks out of the room in disgust at his judgement upon Hermia. The young lovers, who are just emerging from their own schooldays (referred to in vivid vignettes in the course of the play), will resort to the dream-world outside Athens to enact (or 'dream') unresolved aspects of the love relationship that also disturb the primary, older pair of lovers.

The inspired moment at which Theseus, echoing Hippolyta, turns his back on the situation and leaves the room presents to the play's audience the turning-inward of consciousness. Leaving the room of state, and leaving the lovers to themselves to plot their escape, shows that he is not a genuine tyrant. Theseus, not just Hermia, needs time to think, to 'dream away the time' under the aegis of the moon. He is intuitively aware that conscious reason has failed to deliver a true verdict, and that other mental forces are required to sort out the confusion. Another perspective is required, but from his position of authority he cannot imagine what that may be; it is left to the young lovers (adolescent aspects) to set revolution in motion, for as Helena says more truly than she yet knows:

> Love looks not with the eyes but with the mind
> And therefore is winged Cupid painted blind.
> (I.i.234–235)

The play now investigates what it means to 'look with the mind', beyond the sway of Egean protomental laws.

Looking with the mind

As soon as the young lovers have decided to take themselves to the wood, where these laws do not apply, we are introduced to the 'mechanicals', the mind's workmen or craftsmen. They too realise they need to get out of the city in order to function as a work group. Their method is to 'play' or rehearse the idea of marriage: 'This green plot shall be our stage, this hawthorn-brake our tiring-house; and we will do it in action, as we will do it before the Duke' (III.i.2–5). As in Freud's definition of thought as experimental action, 'doing it in action' means that they are exploring the symbolic possibilities of the view-point to be promoted by the Duke. Their rehearsal will be the unconscious means by which they can work out a new key for the aristocratic marriage and enable it to be blessed by the fairies (the mind's internal objects). Is it indeed possible for reason and love, those classical antipathies, to transcend their division and become 'friends'?

It is only in the wood of the unconscious however that we see the full extent of the mortals' problem, which is mirrored in the fairy world of the mind's internal objects. The quarrel between Oberon and Titania over the 'changeling child' portrays the 'distemperature' of the fragile mental planet; in essence, who owns the creative, semi-immortal idea?

> Therefore the moon, the governess of floods,
> Pale in her anger, washes all the air,
> That rheumatic diseases do abound.
> And through this distemperature we see
> The seasons alter: hoary-headed frosts

Fall in the fresh lap of the crimson rose;
And on old Hiems' thin and icy crown,
An odorous chaplet of sweet summer buds
Is, as in mockery, set; the spring, the summer,
The chiding autumn, angry winter, change
Their wonted liveries; and the mazed world,
By their increase, now knows not which is which.

(II.i.103–114)

Here is a genuine loss of 'reason', diagnosed by the loss of the capacity to distinguish between properties (seasons). Titania's description of the 'mazed world' has classical roots and prefigures the modern results of global warming – man's arrogance in his control of natural forces, just as the manmade laws of Athens attempt to rule the forces of love. The 'progeny of evils' resulting in this disruption of nature, insofar as it is human nature, is caused by the 'dissension' between the Fairy King and Queen: 'we are their parents and original'. This is the one point on which they are of accord. For these fairy gods, unlike those of any official religion, are neither perfect nor omnipotent but are subject to forces which mirror those of the mortal or infant-self, just on a slightly higher (more knowledgeable/powerful) plane, for this kind of soul-nourishing knowledge is represented as belonging to immortal powers and distributed through them. These internal objects represent the parts of the mind which are 'most advanced' (Meltzer, Money-Kyrle) and most influential for creativity. The mind cannot 'learn from experience' (in Bion's loaded sense) without cooperation between these two spheres of self and objects. Yet the dream-wood of Athens serves to reveal the non-cooperation that governs the mind's internal objects in the real world of unconscious phantasy.[3] Although the Fairy King and Queen have come to the wood outside Athens in order to bless the wedding of Theseus and Hippolyta, their own disturbance shows that they too have learning to do before they can perform their functions harmoniously.

If anyone can find the answer to the discordance of internal objects, it is the indomitable Bottom the weaver (traditionally a metaphor for a storyteller). He is in a sense an unknown part of Theseus' mentality, an internal object relegated to the lower orders of his internal society. Despite (or because of) his limited education, he is willing to learn a new language, and is selected for sexual initiation owing to his openness to the new role of becoming an actor – that is, identifying with others. In his artistic fervour for playing as many parts as possible, he is neither modest nor narcissistic but takes an innocent delight in the opportunities for expanding his identity: behind all this 'I am but a man, as other men are' (III.i.42). He is Richard, discovering the many parts that can be played within his own mind. He is the playwright-analyst before he has become tired and jaundiced. He is a genuine natural philosopher who is not fazed by any apparent contradictions but finds a way to transcend them by weaving contraries together: 'I will roar that I will do any man's heart good

The reason of love objects: A Midsummer Night 23

to hear me . . . I will aggravate my voice so, that I will roar you as gently as any sucking dove; I will roar you and 'twere any nightingale' (I.ii.66–78). He is a 'very paramour for a sweet voice', a 'lion among ladies' – an acoustic orientation that (as Folkerth, 2002 has suggested) signifies openness to receiving sounds and being penetrated by them, rather than merely wishing to dominate.

This antiphonal music is the beginning of the 'new key' to the Duke's marriage. In order for unmusical law to be transcended and rewritten, the mind needs to renew contact with the preverbal sources of words, the sounds and fluid half-sense not yet confined to fixed signification. When he declares he has a 'reasonable good ear in music; let us have the tongs and the bones' (IV.i.17–18), his apparently primitive lower-class taste is underlain by a deeper truth. For Bottom has a sensitivity to both feminine and childlike parts of the mind (excluded by Athenian rationality) that prepares him for his sojourn with Titania and her childlike entourage of fairies – Peaseblossom, Cobweb, Moth, and Mustardseed, with whom he establishes an instant rapport, entering into their world and dimensionality: 'Monsieur Cobweb, good monsieur, get you your weapons in your hand, and kill me a red-hipped bumble-bee on the top of a thistle . . . have a care the honey-bag break not' (IV.i.10–15).

Titania instructs the fairies to leave her in privacy when she goes to sleep, and this is when she has her own dream about the gentlemanly husband whom she would prefer – a vision which goes beyond Oberon's intention and understanding, even though he was implicated in its engendering. 'Thou art as wise as thou art beautiful', she tells Bottom. 'Not so neither', demurs Bottom, without vanity but also without abasement: he believes she has 'little reason' to love him, but at the same time, he thinks it is not such a bad idea to expand the boundaries of reason in a 'friendly' way, and he is willing to be an agent in this traditional philosophical experiment, for 'reason and love keep little company together nowadays. The more's the pity that some honest neighbours will not make them friends' (III.i.137–140).

Bottom is not hampered by insecurities, suspicions, and masochistic impulses like the young lovers; he is level-headed, reasonable. He is motivated above all by a wish to be of service; he is the traditional lover-as-servant – an attitude foreign to Oberon. Titania's preference for Bottom, with his ass-head of humility, is the core dream of the play:

> Sleep thou, and I will wind thee in my arms.
> Fairies, be gone, and be all ways away.
> So doth the woodbine the sweet honeysuckle
> Gently entwist; the female ivy so
> Enrings the barky fingers of the elm.
> (IV.i.39–43)

Titania (daughter of the Titans) fell asleep in the midst of the mortal adolescent lovers' quarrels in the wood, and she lies at the centre of the stage while these are presented to her as part of *her* dream. Her response to their plight is to exchange her role as the chaste huntress Diana for that of Venus and to momentarily unite with mortality, becoming their unconscious guide even though none save Bottom actually see her. The Duke's oak is transformed into the male-and-female entwisting of ivy and bark – a lesson for Amazon Hippolyta also. It is a version of Beauty and the Beast, and the idea of aesthetic conflict is central, with its illumination of the drama between the inside and the outside of the object, 'gross' (external) sensuousness which is as ugly as it is beautiful, and (internal) spirituality – the hidden truth which no play can enact directly but which has to be evoked by the playwright and imagined beyond the action, as reinforced by Theseus' famous speech in Act V. To this end Titania instructs her fairies to 'tie my love's tongue, bring him silently' – words being a feature of mortal grossness that interferes with seeing with the mind.

The mechanicals are astonished by Bottom's elevation from their latency group: 'O monstrous . . . Bless thee, Bottom, bless thee! Thou art translated' (III.i.114). Although they flee from the wood, they do in a dream-sense remain but transformed into the fairies – another group of childlike parts of the self, seen from a different vertex, as Bottom's entourage. Bottom's solidity and imperturbability contains their panic, and ultimately he re-gathers them around him. The fairies are also instructed to carry Bottom around – another visual absurdity which has its emotional truth; his own artisanship has to be disabled to be reformed, touched with the fairy wand. The idea of children or childlike characters surrounds and supports the central tableau of the fairy-mortal lovers (the Oedipal primal scene).

Bottom in his 'translation' (his new incarnation) finds himself enwrapped in a dedicated acting role in which he is willing to suspend disbelief that he is loved by the muse, the Fairy Queen – like Keats' Belle Dame but with a different awakening. It is only superficially absurd, as is any acting role, but by its means we can see through to a deeper, bottomless truth:

> Man is but an ass if he go about to expound this dream . . . The eye of man hath not heard, the ear of man hath not seen, man's hand is not able to taste, his tongue to conceive, nor his heart to report, what my dream was. I will get Peter Quince to write a ballad of this dream: it shall be called 'Bottom's Dream', because it hath no bottom; and I will sing it in the latter end of a play, before the Duke.
>
> (IV.i.210–216)

The mechanicals, led by Bottom, have paved the way for a translation or transformation of the Duke's mental state, something beyond the reach of didactic exposition ('expounding') and which can only happen through a series of dream-identifications. He is in a sense the analyst counter-dreaming the lovers' confusions by receiving them in his own ass-man person and transforming them through reverie. He is the burlesque prophet who jumbles up the senses

The reason of love objects: *A Midsummer Night*   25

with a holy fool-ishness which will seem mad to the sophisticated courtiers of Athens yet expresses something uncannily close to their dream-experience.[4] He is also Mercutio, but instead of riding away with Queen Mab and coming back to earth with a bump (or a sword thrust under the arm), he is able to absorb the catastrophic change and get on with the playwrighting work, rewriting the story of *Romeo and Juliet* in tragicomic form as *Pyramus and Thisbe*.[5]

In this way the mechanicals' play is adapted to Theseus' emotional needs – provided he is prepared to receive it. For he too has to learn to see darkly, and this will constitute the serious drama underlying the comedy of the final act. And it is not only the fairies who serve an object function for the mortals but also the workmen who change the vision of the Fairy King and Queen. Despite the best-laid plans of Oberon, he is not omnipotent, and the new harmony is due to unconscious 'mistakes' or links made unintentionally by Puck – his agent of consciousness, watching with him in the shadows.

The new key

Puck has been weaving in the dark some fateful pattern of necessity unknown to all until it reveals itself, beyond the control of any single character. The union of Bottom and Titania is enacted alongside the violent misapprehensions of the young lovers, unconsciously receiving and containing them. The wild fantasies that lie unacknowledged beneath their idealisation of falling in love are delineated and almost simultaneously exorcised. They are the 'apotrype of the violent mythologies they draw on', writes Nuttall: Pasiphae, the Minotaur, and others (Nuttall, 2007, p. 119). In addition to all the scratching and muddying they undergo, Helena has been snake-like, Hermia on the point of scratching out her eyes, Lysander and Demetrius go 'cheek by jowl' to duel with swords. In the quarrel scene they attack one another verbally with their confusions. But it is this violence and confusion that finally brings their love to life, where previously it had been a mixture of idealisation and self-idealisation, of irrational fusion or splitting combined with academic, textbook rationalisation; hence its inherent instability. For the first time the young lovers become real characters instead of cardboard cut-outs, especially the two girls: Hermia with her fierceness ('a vixen when she went to school'), Helena with her languorous masochistic tendencies which she sadistically exploits to the full once she is the object of both men's attention.

They become real when their emotions are made real through life in the dream-world. Hence they 'wake up' to find love, really for the first time: 'Begin these wood-birds but to couple now?' asks Theseus (IV.i.138) when they are all revealed by the huntsmen, lying on the ground according to the fairies' arrangement, not yet awake after the night's adventures and not yet cognisant of their new pairings. The hunt is a metaphor indicating that the organ of attention has switched from internal to external again; consciousness hunts out the answer to the emotional dilemma entrusted to unconscious action. The dream of irrationality, having been

26 The reason of love objects: *A Midsummer Night*

worked through by all in their unconscious linkages, transforms into the educational 'higher dream' or divine madness of the Platonists (Garber, 1974).

It is the precious moment of awakening from the dream, on the borders of consciousness, that affirms the new state of mind; in Demetrius' words:

> These things seem small and undistinguishable,
> Like far-off mountains turned into clouds . . .
> $\qquad\qquad$ (IV.i.186–187)

Demetrius, who didn't know whether it was Helena, Hermia, or her father (a version of himself) that he loved, has exchanged confusion for vaporous cloudy insight, disturbed 'mazedness' for amazement: it is the effect of the moon-and-water perspective, a distant landscape recalling the seascapes of Titania and Oberon that stretch beyond the green space of the wood. It is the same for all of them. The lack of clarity, the sense of merging, hints at the greatest profundity; the dream cannot be wholly remembered, just a residual sensation of its message: as Dante put it, the oracle written on leaves is lost, but the imprint of the passion remains.

Theseus has no difficulty now in dismissing Egean law; his reiterated complaint is simply ignored. Out with his harmonious Spartan hounds and their 'musical discord', he has found a 'new key' to his confusion on the threshold of marriage. But he still has to unlock the door, to assimilate the symbolic work done unconsciously by the inhabitants of his mental dukedom. He needs to reciprocate Bottom's faith in the beneficial effects of the dream he is going to 'sing before the Duke'. The difficulty lies in tolerating the aesthetic conflict of the new order of things in relation to the loved object – the hated or humiliating aspect that is inseparable from the admired aspect. This presents an emotional crux that is investigated in the final act by means of the lessons imparted by the mechanicals' play. The return to the court is like the return to Plato's cave, after being dazzled by moonlight rather than sunlight. The dream still has to be digested, as it is when it becomes art (*ekphrasis*).[6]

It is of course not the play of *Pyramus and Thisbe* alone but the entire context of the play-within-a-play that models the lesson to be learned by everyone: this is 'Bottom's Dream', his personal demonstration. Preparation is made by Theseus' speech marvelling at the powers of imagination (though its surface intention is to conventionally disparage it):

> And as imagination bodies forth
> The forms of things unknown, the poet's pen
> Turns them to shapes, and gives to airy nothing
> A local habitation and a name.
> $\qquad\qquad$ (V.i.15–18)

In accepting the play he implies his readiness to acknowledge Bottom's dream as his own, however much of an 'airy nothing' it appears. Hippolyta points out that however subjective imagination may be, its truth may be corroborated by diverse instances; the Aristotelian method of building-up evidence supports the Platonic one of direct intuition:

> But all the story of the night told over,
> And all their minds transfigur'd so together,
> More witnesseth than fancy's images,
> And grows to something of great constancy;
> But howsoever, strange and admirable.
>
> (ll. 23–27)

Although Theseus and Hippolyta appear to be disputing, they each learn from the other's response. Her contradiction is really a confirmation of the poetic meaning behind his hymn to imagination. Ideas are born, 'bodied forth', by linking minds; and these embodied ideas are differentiated from 'fancy's images', mere illusion (this is the basis of Coleridge's distinction between fancy and imagination). It is a new aesthetic for symbol-formation, catching elusive 'shapes' through imagination and watching them grow (Bion's psyche-lodgement), replacing the 'form in wax' of the opening formulation.

So when Hippolyta next disagrees with Theseus, over the matter of whether they will hear the mechanicals' play or not (having been told 'It is not for you', since the workmen are incapable of 'labouring in their minds'), he is fortified sufficiently to trust his instinct and to be able to explain his decision:

> Trust me, sweet,
> Out of this silence yet I pick'd a welcome . . .
> Love, therefore, and tongue-tied simplicity
> In least speak most, to my capacity.
>
> (ll. 99–105)

He remembers unconsciously when Bottom (his hierophant) was 'tongue tied' by the Fairy Queen, learning the value of silence in the mysteries of love – the poetry beyond words – and on this basis he has faith that the workmen's play may be a fitting epithalamion for marriage in a new key.

The play-within-a-play is the funniest scene Shakespeare ever wrote, and in some ways the most daring; he burlesques his own art of play-presentation in a way which, instead of making it look ridiculous, elevates it to a neoPlatonic sphere. We don't think how much better Shakespeare writes and directs than these foolish jobbing actors or shadows; we think he does essentially the same kind of thing, and it is both delighting and teaching us. Indeed it was a reluctance to be forced to laugh at incompetence – what we might call cheap laughs – that lay behind Hippolyta initially desiring not to see the play, fearing it would create a bad atmosphere. But Theseus understands that the craftsmen's 'welcome' is the first rung on the ladder that leads upward to divine love, if we look at the intention or spirit behind the performance, and this is itself a blessing. The workers who are endeavouring earnestly to elevate their manual dexterity to a more abstract level are modelling the performance of the lovers on their wedding night, and also mirroring the night in the wood. The lovers, though they do not admit it, are laughing at themselves and at this mirroring of tragicomic features they unconsciously recognise; and they are all relying on the fairies to bless their forthcoming efforts at putting love into practice – the next night's dream.

The height of the comedy is the appearance of Starveling the undersized tailor as Moonshine, representing the Man in the Moon; he is childlike in his size and they joke he is not 'crescent' (growing – a phallic pun). There are echoes of Titania's description of the 'full-bellied' Indian votaress, but smaller and more pathetic, and the lovers' comments revolve around who is inside who – the inside and the outside (is the actor inside his object, or vice versa?). Yet Starveling, despite his initial hesitancy and his habitual state of nervousness, insists on the validity of his performance: 'All that I have to say is, to tell you that the lantern is the moon; I the Man i'th'Moon; this thorn-bush my thorn-bush; and this dog my dog.' Theseus reminds them they must, 'in courtesy', 'stay the time' and not turn their eyes away from the kind of 'mistake' that is revelation. They understand now, from the players' example, that it is necessary to work at love, and that 'first sight' is the beginning, not the end of a story. In love, humiliation can be distinguished from humility with its godlike ass's head. The aristocratic lovers, like the mechanicals, can learn to 'labour in the mind', and this is the meaning of love seeing not with the eyes but with the mind. It is a new kind of thinking, a new key.

'The best in this kind are but shadows', says Theseus, 'and the worst are no worse, if imagination amend them' (V.i.208). 'It must be your imagination then, and not theirs', retorts Hippolyta, and this is indeed the point: the players/artists cannot do all the work – the audience also has to work to identify and empathise, and make the playwright's dream their own. In the dreamworld of psychic reality, the truth is lit by the moon and told by shadows. 'All for your delight we are not here.' The novitiate interpreter of shadows has to learn to 'pick a welcome', if one is there to be found, through aesthetic reciprocity. A dream can only be received through a dream, involving a series of translations or transferences on many levels.

The play-within-a-play ends with the mechanicals' bergomasque dance, which echoes the dance of the fairies 'beating the ground' whilst they were at the edge of the wood and consciousness. The visual parallel in the two dances reinforces both similarities and differences between these two levels of the mind – the self and its objects – replacing the older dichotomy between body and soul. Despite themselves, the aristocratic lovers have courteously watched the Man in the Moon, using their imagination, and have earned the visitation of the fairies who flood the 'hallowed house' of the mind like moonlight:[7]

Through the house give glimmering light
By the dead and drowsy fire . . .
(V.i.377–378)

They will bless the mortals' union with 'fortunate issue'. The ruler has become a learner and therein finds happiness and the promise of creative conception. In this way Shakespeare demonstrates how a dream constitutes work by the mind's fairies and workmen, its 'objects' and their various functions and avatars. Watching a play, too, constitutes work insofar as it is an emotional experience made real through a 'local habitation' in the audience's own dream-world; the moment of separation from the theatre's hallowed house of shadows marks the transference point between dream and illusion:

> *Puck*: If we shadows have offended,
> Think but this, and all is mended,
> That you have but slumber'd here
> While these visions did appear.
> And this weak and idle theme,
> No more yielding but a dream . . .
> (V.i.409–414)

It prefigures the movement described by Garber (1974) as 'from metaphor to metamorphosis' in the late plays: the illusion (analogy) stresses the present reality (a vision in the mind of the audience), moving over a transient shadowy threshold from mind to mind.

Notes

1 See for example Frye (1965), or Garber (1974), who relates the dream-landscape to classical journeys to the land of the dead and to neoPlatonic dream theories popular from medieval times.
2 In *Love's Labour's Lost* (the prototype for *A Midsummer Night's Dream*, with its play-within-a-play and its 'low' actors embodying the greatest reality), Shakespeare was forced to artificially end the play's academic word-games with the announcement of a death. But the death itself has no emotional impact; it merely signifies that the game has come to an end.
3 In this book I use the Kleinian spelling 'phantasy' where the emphasis is on the underlying state of mind as expressed in either action or fantasy. However there is no significant difference between conscious fantasy and unconscious phantasy; both indicate a real state of mind.
4 It is not 'burlesque' of neoPlatonism (Wells, 2005) but Shakespeare's characteristic mode of allotting the natural expression of profounder philosophical truths to the superficially naïve, thus emphasising their authenticity and reality. Garber (1974) sees it as a serious dream condensation, the basis for *ekphrasis* (transformation into art). Folkerth (2002) relates the dream to Bottom's social fluidity, at ease on all levels; 'it is his dream not because he created it but because it contains him' (p. 94). Frye sees it as portraying the 'paradox' of the privacy of a dream together with its connection with 'the creative faculties, which are powers of communication' (1965, p. 108).
5 Nuttall (2004) sees it as a 'parody' of *Romeo and Juliet*. One's impression, again, is that Shakespeare is reacting against elements in his earlier plays by injecting realism where he felt it was lacking.
6 Garber points out that from the medieval romances on, it is typical that 'the dreamer never fully understands, just feels the change' (1974, p. 743).
7 The implication, often noticed, of how superseded religious or folk ghosts seep into the sleeping consciousness gains validity from Milton's echo in the *Nativity Ode* of the pagan gods infiltrating the Christian to mingle their colours and motifs.

Chapter 3

Dreamlife and adolescent identity in Hamlet and Ophelia*

Hamlet is Shakespeare's classic exploration of the multiple different worlds of adolescence, with their confusion between thought and action, intrusiveness and intimacy – the drama between the inside and outside of the object, and how the adolescent rocks back and forth in constant instability, in and out of the adult world.

In *Julius Caesar* Shakespeare was still looking for a 'noble' hero, possessing admirable qualities such as loyalty, endurance, integrity, constancy, stoicism. He endowed Brutus – 'noblest of them all' – with such qualities, but was instinctively drawn rather to the faulty, hot-blooded Cassius and, perhaps even in that play, the hidden potential of the opportunistic Antony. His implicit definition of a hero was coming to be a person capable of development, and increasingly that meant a person who could dream creatively rather than just be assaulted by ghosts. *Hamlet* begins where *Julius Caesar* ends, with a paternal ghost of the traditional persecutory kind, a relic of the monitory dream (Garber). But when the creative dreams begin to flow, Shakespeare allows himself to follow their power to take over the entire narrative, to the extent of expanding out of the realistic boundaries of a stage play (*Hamlet* in its entirety plays for five hours and is almost always cut). In this sense, as a dream-play, it is a new genre.

The analytic relationship

There are other plays that end with a suggestion that their story needs re-telling, or at least re-viewing; but in *Hamlet* it is structurally important that the story is ultimately handed over to the figure of Horatio who serves a function analogous to a helpless psychoanalyst (or playwright), able only partially to 'contain' the dreams in the sense of helping Hamlet to think them through.[1] He says little, yet maintains a presence at all the significant points. Hamlet describes him as the ideal observer – as 'one who in suffering all, suffers nothing' (III.ii.60).

---

* Previous versions of this analysis of *Hamlet* are in *The Apprehension of Beauty* (1988) and in *Hamlet in Analysis: A Trial of Faith* (1997 [2014]).

He allows the characters to dream and notes down what he sees. Like the playwright himself, he is intimately identified with, and yet distanced from, their emotional trials. His job is to weave them together into a meaningful symbol, and this, as Hamlet sees, is a type of 'suffering' also.

Hamlet declares he could be 'bounded in a nutshell' were it not for his 'bad dreams', and complains that Horatio does not capture those unreachable thoughts that are not contained in his 'philosophy' (that is, his interpretive theory):

> There are more things in heaven and earth, Horatio,
> Than are dreamt of in your philosophy.
> (I.v.167–168)

Hamlet, too, has studied academic psychology at Wittenberg – 'your philosophy' is his as well – but that is not the same as feeling it on the pulses in the context of becoming himself. His internal father has 'burst the cerements' of his sanctified imago and brought the possibility of 'thoughts beyond the reaches of our souls'.

If, as Martha Harris has phrased it, 'The struggle to find an identity is the central task of adolescence' (Meltzer & Harris, 2011, p. 1), this is indeed Hamlet's burning desire in the first half of the play. He wants to find the 'undiscover'd country' of his future self, to penetrate the difference between 'is and 'seems', 'For I have that within which passes show / These but the trappings and the suits of woe' (I.ii.85–86). He wants not to act (as in 'actions that a man might play') but to *be* (as in, becoming himself). He wants to know the 'heart of [his] mystery' (III.ii.330), and is overwhelmed by the aesthetic conflict this entails in his attitude to 'the world', its beauty and ugliness. As he phrases it:

> What a piece of work is a man, how noble in reason, how infinite in faculties, in form and moving how express and admirable, in action how like an angel, in apprehension how like a god! The beauty of the world, the paragon of animals – and yet, to me, what is this quintessence of dust?
> (II.ii.303–312)

By contrast, his statement near the end of the play that 'to know a man well were to know himself' (V.ii.140) is delivered offhandedly, like a language game, devoid of emotionality. By then he has given up trying to find meaning in the 'quintessence of dust'.

In the context of this structural dialogue, the play can be seen as a sequence of dreams told by Hamlet to Horatio. Yet ultimately, Horatio in his role as a type of paternal counsellor, although more trustworthy than any of the other father-figures, does not fulfil Hamlet's plea to 'Let me not burst in ignorance' (I.iv.46). Perhaps the playwright has too strong an investment in his hero; in no other play does the audience have the same intensive adhesive identification with a character: as Hazlitt said, 'It is *we* who are Hamlet.' This might be considered one of its problems – a problem that would be understood psychoanalytically in terms of countertransference interference, as not achieving a sufficiently objective viewpoint, but overloading the analysand with expectations. Denmark is described as 'sick'. As the great hope of the state to which he is heir – soldier, scholar, statesman, 'Th' expectancy and rose of the fair state' (III.i.152) – this prince, a mere adolescent, is expected to reform everybody else's murky emotional problems and disappointments. Marriage with Ophelia would fulfil what Bion denotes the 'messianic' basic assumption of the surrounding group, and create a 'new heaven, new earth' – the Biblical phrase which finally attains credence not here but in *Antony and Cleopatra*. Horatio as analyst is unable to relinquish what Bion calls the 'chains of memory and desire', his vision of Hamlet's identity. During the second half of the play we feel that Hamlet, now older, ensconces himself in the exoskeleton of words and philosophical quibbles that as a teenager he used to despise, while Shakespeare switches the vitality of the adolescent mind over to Ophelia, to question what lies behind her apparent passivity.

The Ghost dream

The encounter with the Ghost that constitutes Hamlet's first powerful dream brings to light the complexity of his emotional ambivalence, dredged up from the deep unconscious that is symbolised by the space underneath the stage (the 'cellarage') where the Ghost resides, like a mole burrowing 'in the earth' (I.v.165).[2] This is the context in which Hamlet calls on Horatio's help, and indeed Horatio was the first to see the Ghost and to bring it to Hamlet's attention.

To other characters, the Ghost is invisible; and indeed will only speak to Hamlet, even though Horatio is termed a 'scholar' – someone who knows about how to speak to ghosts – about which there were definite opinions in Shakespeare's day, just as there are today amongst psychoanalysts, and speaking to ghosts was considered quite a science. Hamlet's plea to the Ghost is 'Let me not burst in ignorance' (I.iv.50). He means not solely ignorance of the Ghost's story but ignorance of his inner self, which is his essential or core anguish. The Ghost is an internal figure projecting into his son a dream of his own, in which milk was turned into poison by his mother–wife and poured through his ears:[3]

> Sleeping within my orchard,
> My custom always of the afternoon,
> Upon my secure hour thy uncle stole
> With juice of cursed hebenon in a vial,
> And in the porches of my ears did pour
> The leperous distilment, whose effect
> Holds such an enmity with blood of man
> That swift as quicksilver it courses through

The natural gates and alleys of the body,
And with a sudden vigour it doth posset
And curd, like eager droppings into milk,
The thin and wholesome blood. So did it mine.

(I.v.59–70)

The dream of the Ghost makes clear Hamlet's claustrophobic state and near-schizophrenic delusion that his father is his uncle. This dream of his father-uncle (rather than his 'uncle-father', as he calls Claudius) who is lost in a kind of hellish limbo demonstrates his ambivalence to his internal father. A childhood idealisation of a godlike and heroic figure who could defend his country by means of single-handed duels has switched to his current disillusion with Claudius' middle-aged decay, depression, and over-indulgence in sensual pleasures. The two images compare as 'Hyperion to a satyr' in his mind. It becomes clear that this ambivalence is rooted in his distrust of hidden, invisible feminine treachery and false 'beautified' appearances in his mother and Ophelia. The Ghost claims the milky food of his mind has been poisoned by treachery and passes this feeling on to Hamlet, inciting him to revenge, whilst at the same time warning him not to 'taint his mind or harm his mother' (I.v.85).

These are contradictory demands of his internal object, and Hamlet reacts ambiguously: he is prompted to act out his vengeance and at the same time to seek a receiver for his dreams, as is suggested by wanting to 'write down' his feelings. As Meltzer has said of the adolescent, he is stimulated to go forwards and backwards at the same time. The encounter with the Ghost ends with Hamlet trying to find a container for his emotional disturbance and implying that Horatio will not be able to do it because it goes beyond his 'philosophy'. The 'antic disposition' which he adopts – his 'madness' – becomes both a cover for the verbal acting-out that follows and his aesthetic self-expression. Polonius points this out when later he admiringly says that madness is often nearer the truth than sanity.

This artificial madness is not, however, a true symbol of Hamlet's inner 'mystery'; it has the sense of a temporary refuge whilst awaiting further developments. And Horatio, too, in his countertransference role, needs to deepen his philosophy in order to match or receive Hamlet's communications, which take the form of both communicative and evacuative projections. His status and age is ambiguous: is he a fellow-student, a 'good lad' like Rosencrantz and Guildenstern (he too knows Hamlet from Wittenberg), or one of the older generation (he remembers old Hamlet)? There is an implication of almost imperceptibly lower social status ('Why should the poor be flatter'd?' [III.ii.59]), yet he is seen by the royal family as a measure of disinterested sanity. Our glimpses of Horatio's perspective are few but telling, and it is not Hamlet alone but his entire family with whom he feels involved. When we consider Horatio's role, therefore, we may see an analogy not only with that of the dramatist and his multiple identifications but also with the psychoanalyst and his state of mind – the 'psychoanalytic attitude' as described by Meltzer in *The Psychoanalytical Process*:

'We must turn our attention to the fundamental unit of the setting, the state of mind of the analyst, and explore the various aspects that are embodied in the concept, the *psychoanalytic attitude*' (Meltzer, [1967] 2018, p. 79).

The maintenance of the analyst's state of mind, his 'attitude', in 'race-horse condition', depends on the interaction of two factors: 'scientific curiosity and devotion to method'. The challenge for Horatio is not to load Hamlet with his own expectations, making a hero of him through moral improvement (therapeutic zeal); correct interpretation in itself is ineffectual, as Hamlet's impervious reactions to his ironic interjections demonstrate.[4]

The madman dream

Hamlet feels the Ghost-as-internal-father has projected its madness into him, and this stimulates an intrusive attitude towards Ophelia. Hence his next dream conveys his appearance in her 'closet' or private room, half undressed like a traditional caricature of a madman, looking as if, like the Ghost, he had just been released from hell 'to speak of horrors'.

> *Ophelia*: My lord, as I was sewing in my closet,
> Lord Hamlet, with his doublet all unbrac'd,
> No hat upon his head, his stockings foul'd,
> Ungarter'd and down-gyved to his ankle,
> Pale as his shirt, his knees knocking each other,
> And with a look so piteous in purport
> As if he had been loosed out of hell
> To speak of horrors, he comes before me.
> *Polonius*: Mad for thy love?
> *Ophelia*: My lord, I do not know,
> But truly I do fear it.
>
> (II.i.77–86)

Ophelia says Hamlet gazes on her face, unspeaking, 'as if he would draw it'. This is in response to Polonius' interference with their relationship, Polonius having told Ophelia to deny Hamlet access to her because his motivation was bound to be dishonourable. Then her obedience is taken by Hamlet as a masochistic passivity; this is how he 'draws her face' in his mind, his non-verbal interpretation. It is a kind of 'dumbshow' that is repeated later with the play-within-a-play, when the actors mime a nonspeaking prelude to the violent drama to come. The 'closet' may represent literally her body, or her mental ambience, her mind. The spirit of vengeance is inextricable from a false aesthetics, introduced into the space by Hamlet himself. This episode is a prelude to the later similar scene in which Hamlet tells Ophelia to go to a nunnery to conceal the falseness of her beauty.

Polonius, to whom this episode is related, is excited by his half-understanding of the problem: 'Mad for thy love?' He then uses Ophelia as a tool to investigate Hamlet's mystery, so the paternal transference becomes mixed up with fixed assumptions about how girls should think and behave. Polonius is a great admirer of Hamlet and in a sense yet another father – the one who has nurtured his intellect and interests such as philosophy and theatre. He is not merely a senile old fool who talks too much. He is the court counsellor but, as with Horatio, Hamlet's state of mind goes beyond the reach of existing philosophy; as we saw in *Julius Caesar*, it is not so easy to put into practice the Stoic doctrine of being true to yourself so that 'Thou canst not then be false to any man' (I.iii.80). His advice is good and the content of his interpretations is correct, but it has inflammatory results owing to his own lack of self-knowledge regarding the intrusive, controlling nature of his curiosity.

Polonius' unaesthetic methods of investigation – finding 'directions by indirections' – stimulate action rather than contemplation; he cannot place thought between impulse and action (in Freud's formulation). His actions inevitably lead in the direction of Bion's 'minus K', as in the case of a bad psychoanalyst. He tries to 'spy out where truth is hid', treating Hamlet's inner mystery as if it were a riddle to be solved:

> I will find
> Where truth is hid, though it were hid indeed
> Within the centre.
> (II.ii.149–151)

He wants to ferret out the quarry rather than receive symbolically its meaning. Consequently Hamlet complains justly that all the court – the adult world – want to 'pluck out the heart of my mystery', his internal Ghost. Polonius is oblivious to the fact that the means are essential to the end, and as Bion points out in another context (1985, p. 52), those who disregard the means are following the path to the Sirens and will end up with nothing but a pile of old bones.

At the same time, and by a further analogy, Shakespeare uses Polonius as a way of criticising certain temptations which the playwright is subject to: the dramatist who is seduced by his own virtuosity and who takes a directorial role, determined that everything shall fall out as planned. These inhibiting and omnipotent attitudes become clear during the fiasco of the Mousetrap, the play-within-a-play. In later plays this type of character appears as the Prospero-wizard in *The Tempest* or the Duke of *Measure for Measure*. The dominating, controlling mentality does not help the adolescent who is concerned with the difference between 'being' and 'playing'. As he says to his mother, it is not his outward appearance and gestures (the 'forms, moods, shapes of grief') that can 'denote me truly':

> I have that within which passes show
> These but the trappings and the suits of woe.
> (I.ii.85–86)

His clothes and body echo his mental state, as with the typical adolescent, but they are not the same thing as his inner 'grief', which neither he nor they

36 Adolescent identity in Hamlet and Ophelia

understand. The result of the Madman Dream is not just to confirm Hamlet's disturbance but to demonstrate how this is increased by the adult world's messianic expectations of the young couple. The adults are as much responsible as Hamlet for creating an anti-aesthetic container for emotional trouble that strangles personality development. They hope Hamlet will rescue them from their middle-aged sloppiness, drinking, and so on, but allow him no space to do so. He says truly that Denmark is a 'prison', represented by the way he feels confined within the Lobby, a corridor with windows from which the sky is just visible, and where he paces up and down reading 'words, words, words', full of emptiness yet in search of dreams (II.ii.184).

The Mousetrap dream

Although *Hamlet* is traditionally a play in which the hero thinks too much and cannot act, in fact the opposite is the case. Hamlet's danger is in thinking too little and acting too precipitously; it just happens that because of his verbal virtuosity, his actions often take the form of words, speeches, and cutting remarks. Acting-out can be verbal or visual; it is not the medium that makes the difference but the way it is used – for exploration or for evacuation of the emotional conflict, K or minus K.

This is the drama of the Mousetrap – which again may be seen as an extended, enacted symbol of Hamlet's contempt for the nature of his ageing parents' sexuality and the 'sick soul' which he has truly glimpsed in both Gertrude and Claudius. It is at the centre of the play and knots together its various contradictory, conflictual strands of meaning, trying to define the adolescent condition that has become 'trapped' by its own dreams.

The performance of the Mousetrap itself is preceded by the long investigation into the nature of acting as an artform, conducted by Hamlet, Polonius, and the Players; and by the 'nunnery' scene with Ophelia. The sequences about acting might appear to be a digression, but if we remember that the nature of aesthetic conflict lies at the heart of the play, then acting as an art form becomes central to how plays are conducted and to the question of whether they are truth-revealing or truth-obscuring, for both the viewers and the participants. It is Hamlet who gives the play-within-a-play its title 'Mousetrap', indicating that he is well aware it is not produced for truthful purposes but in order to impose a meaning which he has preconceived – namely, a lie. It is not necessarily a lie about external facts or events but a lie about their meaning in the soul. In fact we are no longer interested in the original question posed by the plot, namely did Claudius kill old Hamlet or not, and was Gertrude an accomplice. Once we understand the dreamlike structure of the entire play, it is clear that these are subjective matters of the adolescent's changing attitude to his parents and their puzzled but guilty reactions to his state of mind – far more interesting than literal matters of plot.

The scenes with the Players are significant not just for their investigation of the theme of truthful symbol-formation based on aesthetic reciprocity (as can happen between actors and audience); they are also significant for their presentation of Hamlet's schooldays and his former relationship with Polonius, which was clearly based on a mutual infatuation with acting as an art form – with words, their presentation, their effect on a listener. In this situation the play is itself the aesthetic object. What is the actor doing inside it: is his position intrusive or demonstrative? What sort of transference goes on when the actor becomes vehicle for an idea? 'What's he to Hecuba, or Hecuba to him, / That he should weep for her? (II.ii.518–519) asks Hamlet, questioning the authenticity of the actor's emotion, and hence his own, in directing the Mousetrap. 'Suit the action to the word, the word to the action', he instructs the player, in the identical manner to Polonius (III.ii.16). The actor is a vehicle for feelings which are distinct from his own person. When do they tell the truth about a situation, and when are they a lie?

Obsessed by these distinctions and unable to find a truthful answer to his inner confusion, Hamlet as before projects them onto Ophelia in the nunnery scene. Ophelia enters at a critical moment after Hamlet has been trying to authentically contain his emotional anxieties by shaping the 'To be or not to be' soliloquy:

> To die – to sleep,
> No more; and by a sleep to say we end
> The heart-ache and the thousand natural shocks
> That flesh is heir to: 'tis a consummation
> Devoutly to be wish'd. To die, to sleep;
> To sleep, perchance to dream – ay, there's the rub;
> For in that sleep of death what dreams may come,
> When we have shuffled off this mortal coil,
> Must give us pause . . .
>
> (III.i.60–68)

In this speech he considers the possibility of replacing action ('resolution') by the pale and sickly colouring of thought; it is the 'pause' in his manic rush towards revenge:

> And thus the native hue of resolution
> Is sicklied o'er with the pale cast of thought,
> And enterprises of great pitch and moment
> With this regard their currents turn awry
> And lose the name of action. Soft you now,
> The fair Ophelia! Nymph, in thy orisons
> Be all my sins remember'd.
>
> (ll. 84–90)

38 Adolescent identity in Hamlet and Ophelia

Ophelia's entry at this point brings him back to earth, to the kind of dream that undermines abstract philosophical speculation and anchors him back in the messy emotionality of his 'madness', which has become further complicated by Polonius and his directorial manoeuvres designed to expose the root of Hamlet's madness.

In this false kind of play, Ophelia – like Rosencrantz and Guildenstern – is a tool, as Hamlet very soon suspects: 'Where's your father?' he demands, sensing his presence hidden behind a pillar in the Lobby. Polonius is an intruder in his dream-space, his internal mother, an intrusion which Hamlet will re-project when he hides behind the arras in Gertrude's closet, making it a claustral compartment in Meltzer's (1992) sense.

The consequence of Hamlet's misinterpretation of Ophelia's own life-space means that, in his view, she becomes a traitor to aesthetic values: 'Get thee to a nunnery. . . . I have heard of your paintings well enough. God hath given you one face and you make yourselves another. . . . it hath made me mad. I say we will have no more marriage' (III.i.137–149). She becomes in his eyes a puppet manipulated from within by the domineering aspect of Polonius to which he is allergic, all the more since it is also an aspect of himself. Obedient to Polonius' instructions, she returns the various gifts and poems Hamlet has given her. This offends Hamlet not just because she is Polonius' agent rather than acting of her own volition, but because he (like Polonius) believes his poems are no good, and this is a critical but objective judgement on his own literary failure. All these pile up together in the way he experiences Ophelia's rejection. After this Hamlet gives up the apparently impossible business of thinking through his emotional ambivalence to all his friends and family, but particularly his mother and Ophelia. He gives over the struggle to nurture the embryonic, fragile 'pale cast of thought' and abandons himself to revenge, destroying the very possibility of any authentic emotional link: 'no more marriage'.

Hence while the Mousetrap is playing in front of the assembled court, Hamlet provides a commentary of pornographic wordplay while he lies with his head on Ophelia's lap. This stance, at the front of the stage, colours the Players' performance as seen by the rest of the court. He is deliberately converting the story into a symbol of sexual perversion. The actors, like Ophelia, are manipulated to suit his fantasy of a tainted beauty ('face') which disguises an ulcerated secret, a false coition. So after the dumbshow, which enacts a poisoning, Ophelia asks Hamlet what this 'show' meant; and he answers, 'Be not you ashamed to show, he'll not shame to tell you what it means' (III.ii.140).

> *Hamlet*: It would cost you a groaning to take off my edge.
> *Ophelia*: Still better, and worse.
> *Hamlet*: So you mis-take your husbands. – Begin, murderer. Leave thy damnable faces and begin. Come, the croaking raven doth bellow for revenge.
>
> (III.ii.244–249)

The pun on 'taking' (sexually, and semantically) indicates that husbands and wives are a 'mis-take'; what is desired is revenge on the whole idea of marriage.

The only exception to this anti-aesthetic or manic mode occurs in the brief private conversations with Horatio, just before and just after the Mousetrap itself. Beforehand, Hamlet takes Horatio aside and tells him that for him, he has been

> As one in suff'ring all, that suffers nothing . . .
>   Give me that man
> That is not passion's slave, and I will wear him
> In my heart's core, ay in my heart of heart,
> As I do thee.
>
> (III.ii.66–74)

The idea of a type of suffering that is felt on the pulses but is not personally generated is an apt description of the countertransference of either psychoanalyst or playwright: intensely involved and yet objective. Bion (1970) distinguishes between 'pain', which is just a sensation not much different from pleasure, and 'suffering', which entails an attempt to think through the meaning of feelings and is characterised by turbulence and contradictory emotions, not by simple sensation.

After the Mousetrap, Horatio with gentle sarcasm tries to defuse Hamlet's triumph at the chaos he has let loose (like Antony in *Julius Caesar* with 'cry havoc'). But these moments of near communication do not have any impact, because Hamlet has in a sense seduced Horatio through a kind of princely tolerance; Horatio in his psychoanalytic capacity is de-skilled and cannot penetrate Hamlet's mania. This is a further triumph for the manic side of Hamlet and leads directly to the scene with his mother in her closet, echoing that earlier with Ophelia. When he kills Polonius by blindly stabbing him as he hides behind the arras, it doesn't make much difference whether it is the king (as he first thinks) or Polonius. It is a phallic intruder – a 'rat', confused with a baby – the intruding male who is also an aspect of himself, stage-managing the inner spaces of his mother: 'Thou wretched, rash, intruding fool, farewell' (III.iv.31).

The interview then becomes dominated by another intruding fool – by Hamlet's 'wagging tongue', as Gertrude calls it:

> What have I done, that thou dar'st wag thy tongue
> In noise so rude against me?
>
> (III.iv.39)

When the Ghost reappears, she cannot see it; her incomprehension of what is inside Hamlet reinforces his isolation. The Ghost almost inspired a change of heart in Hamlet, talking of 'tears' instead of 'blood', but the Queen's blindness means that no such emotional link is achieved. This scene is the culmination of

40 Adolescent identity in Hamlet and Ophelia

the vengeful action that has been coming to a crescendo throughout the first half of the play, with Horatio helplessly looking on, but failing in any way to contain Hamlet's mania, owing to the seductive force of this particular adolescent's qualities – the potential 'soldier, scholar, statesman', actor, philosopher, and lover that everybody can see in him, and that never comes to fruition. It all ends in the disaster imaged by the stage strewn with corpses – the 'accidental judgements, casual slaughters' of the final scene.

But meanwhile the second half of the play is given to Ophelia and the female voice, while Hamlet is away on his sea-voyage, dreaming about pirates and conspiracies.

The dream of Ophelia's madness

During the second part of the play (Acts IV and V) Shakespeare seems to put his interest in Hamlet aside, as if he needs him out of the way in order to concentrate properly on the feminine aspects of this adolescent disturbance.

The dream of Ophelia's madness is really a dream that Horatio has on behalf of Hamlet. The King appoints him to 'watch' Ophelia – to become her special observer. In literal terms of the plot, Horatio makes a very bad guard, since Ophelia then goes and drowns herself – and not only this, but she appears to have done it in full view of the Queen. At least, this is what the vividness of the Queen's narrative of the drowning appears to evoke. The drowning is thus Horatio's dream of Gertrude's dream of Ophelia's internal preoccupations. All this goes to emphasise the extent to which *Hamlet* has become a dream-play, not an ordinary revenge tragedy. In this section the women come to the fore and express their feelings in a different kind of symbolic language.

Shakespeare's most recent heroines, Viola and Rosalind, escape the conventional confines of their sex by dressing as men. In the case of Ophelia, Shakespeare tries another method, using dream instead of disguise as a means of self-expression. Ophelia brings in the idea of a different type of symbol-seeking, one in which words – in the sense of explanations – have little use. In the Mousetrap scene she said to Hamlet, 'I think nothing', meaning she did not want to collude in his dirty thoughts, contain his 'sins'. Nonetheless she has taken them in and digested them in an idiosyncratic way. She seems retiring and over-obedient at first, as though still stuck in latency. Yet when pushed to the point she shows she has more resilience in a sexual relationship than either Hamlet or Laertes. Earlier, when Laertes tried to lecture her on how to behave with Hamlet, she made a spirited if quiet response, reminding him to concentrate on managing himself (I.iii.45). Possibly because she is not encumbered with the same career expectations as the boys, she can quietly develop more of a private mental space. The world of her mind and imagination only becomes evident through her 'madness'. This is itself an introjection of Hamlet's madness, which Polonius had admired for its 'pregnant' verbal vehicle and which

Ophelia now reshapes. It is not however a masochistically received projection but a reforming mirror.

By this point in the play, 'words, words, words' have got a bad name for emptiness, trickiness and game-playing – for manipulation rather than communication. The aesthetic potential of words for emotional communication has been lost. Hamlet's sanctimonious 'reforming' of the players' speeches showed how easily art may be turned into pornography under the guise of cleaning up its message.

Ophelia's madness presents an alternative possibility. At first the Queen does not wish to speak to Ophelia, knowing she would find it too painful. The messenger describes the quality of her speech:

> Her speech is nothing,
> Yet the unshaped use of it doth move
> The hearers to collection. They aim at it,
> And botch the words up fit to their own thoughts,
> Which, as her winks and nods and gestures yield them,
> Indeed would make one think there might be thought,
> Though nothing sure, yet much unhappily.
>
> (IV.v.4–13)

Her speech is 'nothing' and 'unshaped', yet it has aesthetic potential, by contrast with Hamlet's view of the glory of the world as a 'quintessence of dust'; it moves the listeners to emotional contact and imaginative response. Ultimately it is the Queen who, despite her reluctance, receives Ophelia's communications most intuitively, thereby strengthening the feminine parts of the adolescent self and their capacity for thinking and symbol-formation. 'Lord we know what we are, but know not what we may be' (IV.v.44), philosophises Ophelia, echoing Hamlet's many queries about adolescent identity. She then sings a 'Valentine' song about the loss of virginity:

> And I a maid at your window,
> To be your Valentine.
> Then up he rose, and donn'd his clothes,
> And dupp'd the chamber door,
> Let in the maid that out a maid
> Never departed more.
>
> (ll. 50–55)

With Ophelia's mad songs, music enters in to the play, having been notably absent (for Shakespeare) till that point. There is a sense in which all poetry seems nonsense, yet it speaks through its music. It is the beginning of a search for a symbolic mode, and a form of restitution for the way the actors and their art were abused in the Mousetrap.

42 Adolescent identity in Hamlet and Ophelia

Ophelia's pregnancy is implied by the poetic imagery of flowers and water. It is the Queen who picks this up and empathises with it in the form of her dream of Ophelia's drowning:

> Her clothes spread wide,
> And mermaid-like awhile they bore her up,
> Which time she chanted snatches of old lauds
> As one incapable of her own distress,
> Or like a creature native and indued
> Unto that element.
>
> (IV.vii.174–179)

The drowning represents her flowering as an individual in a kind of quiet rebellion that distances her from the rotting values of the adult world, the court. Realistically, the Queen cannot have been an eyewitness of Ophelia drowning, nor can Horatio. What Horatio notices through his countertransference dream is not an external reality but an internal one, through identification – in this case with the feminine vertex or dimension. The structure of the play is becoming dream-within-dream.

The Grave dream

The last major dream in *Hamlet* is the Grave dream, the prelude to the final catastrophe when, in effect, Hamlet's personal development is abandoned by the playwright and Horatio is given the task of re-writing his entire story. This dream comprises the enforced ending of Hamlet's story, and has three successive movements: the first reawakening a nostalgic longing for his childhood relation with a combined male-female object; the second marking the loss of Ophelia as a feasible relationship; and the third acknowledging the resulting mess made of his life, with the death of all these hopes and potentialities.

Throughout the play Hamlet as a character has been set in a context not just of the adult world – the court – but the world of his own contemporaries, in particular the male adolescent group represented by Rosencrantz and Guildenstern, Laertes, and Fortinbras. The first two he came to regard as traitors in the sense of acting as spies for the king, creatures of the establishment; Laertes he has antagonised owing to his effect on both Polonius and Ophelia (even if we see their 'deaths' metaphorically); Fortinbras remains as a possible route for the adolescent to follow, even though up to this point Hamlet has found him absurd and unthinking, as when he wondered why the Norwegian prince bothered to lead a huge army to conquer a worthless patch of ground, just to make his name sacrificing life 'even for an eggshell':

> Witness this delicate and tender prince,
> Whose spirit with divine ambition puffed

Makes mouths at the invisible event,
Exposing what is mortal and unsure
To all that fortune, death, and danger dare,
Even for an eggshell.

(IV.iv.48–53)

Fortinbras ('strong arm'), the ambitious military adventurer, illustrates the defensive 'thrust for success' described by Meltzer as some adolescents' reaction against the 'dreaminess' of this developmental phase when it becomes too painful (Meltzer & Harris, 2011, p. 27). This route to success is what Richard passed to Bolingbroke and Brutus to Octavius. It is really (Meltzer explains) an extended latency, with symptoms that appear only later from about age thirty when they become 'neurotic'. Yet this seems to be the lesson that Hamlet is trying to learn from Fortinbras, against his better judgement, and against the better nature of the inner child-self that was truly a 'sweet prince'. His conclusion, in defiance of his thinking capacity, is that he, like Fortinbras, needs to have 'bloody thoughts' or they are 'worth nothing' (Bion's minus K). Hamlet, as many readers have noticed, seems to switch from being around age eighteen to being age thirty in the second part of the play. It is at precisely this point that Shakespeare abandons Hamlet and turns to Ophelia and her madness.

Fortinbras passes on his way with his army, but his example hovers at the back of Hamlet's mind. Hamlet, after Ophelia's death, is sent away from the court, supposedly to England where 'everyone is as mad as he is' (V.i.150). In terms of the plot, of course, Hamlet never reaches England, since he returns by jumping onto a 'pirate ship' – another dream, in which he turns his ex-friends Rosencrantz and Guildenstern over to the establishment to be 'killed' (that is, absorbed into some type of reformatory or respectable career) in his stead. Earlier, when they questioned him about the nature of his disturbance, he told them sarcastically: 'I lack advancement' (III.ii.331). The question of what is advancement, for the adolescent, lies at the heart of the entire play. Hamlet means he cannot advance his mental progress; they understand him to mean he is not sure he will inherit the kingship.

The separation or split with Ophelia however – the death of their relationship – results in Hamlet giving up the struggle for advancement in the complex psychological sense. He feels he has to pursue some simpler, more predetermined role or identity. When he reappears on Danish soil with the taunting announcement to the King that 'High and mighty, you shall know I am set naked on your kingdom' (IV.vii.41), he is implying that he is not really naked but on his way to be king. Ultimately his name will be Fortinbras.

The following scenes, with the Gravedigger, Ophelia's burial, and the duel with Laertes, are a series of dream-sequences during which he proceeds to transfer his identity to that of Fortinbras the Norwegian. Hamlet is cured of his original form of 'madness' by the time he meets the Gravedigger, who he encounters with Horatio at his side. Indeed he is no match for the Gravedigger's

44 Adolescent identity in Hamlet and Ophelia

verbal 'equivocation'; it is as though the Gravedigger demonstrates the futility of Hamlet's own earlier wordplay and highlights the fact that it has the effect of disguising the truth. At the same time the (partial) truth is turned up, during the conversation, by digging with the spade (an analytic metaphor). The results of this digging shake his equanimity by showing him the ruin of his childlike and his feminine side. He remembers what it was to be a child playing and riding on the back of Yorick the jester or actor (the father of his early childhood); now all that remains is an empty skull, like an empty stage, where once there was a face and lips: 'Here hung those lips that I have kissed I know not how oft.' The skull turns into 'my lady's chamber' – the feminine space – and revolts him: 'how abhorred it is'. We remember the nunnery scene when he accused Ophelia of a 'painted' beauty whose face disguised a deep ugliness: 'You jig and amble, and you lisp, you nickname God's creatures' (III.i.145). In each situation the nature of the ugliness recalls the specific art of acting and the true or false faces of its movements, its language, its scene-painting.

Horatio tries to stop Hamlet's phantasy going entirely down the anal route – to Alexander's 'bunghole':

> *Hamlet*: Why, may not imagination trace the noble dust of Alexander till a find it stopping a bung-hole?
> *Horatio*: 'Twere to consider too curiously to consider so.
>
> (V.i.195–197)

But his efforts are aborted by the next dream, the one of Ophelia's burial, which is in a sense also the grave of Hamlet's hopes of revitalising the 'sweet prince' that he was in his childhood. When he leaps into the grave with the words 'This is I, Hamlet the Dane' (V.i.233), it is the status of princeliness that is dominant, even though there is also a hint of authenticity in his declaration that he loved Ophelia. The predominant emotion is that he cannot endure being 'outfaced' by Laertes (implying that his is a less important form of love):

> Dost come here to whine,
> To outface me with leaping in her grave?
> Be buried quick with her? – and so will I.
> And if thou prate of mountains let them throw
> Millions of acres on us, till our ground,
> Singeing his pate against the burning zone,
> Make Ossa like a wart! Nay, an thou'lt mouth,
> I'll rant as well as thou.
>
> (V.i.272–279)

His feminine side is buried under 'mountains' and his Fortinbras side takes over the kingdom of his mind, as is represented by his own death and the sudden arrival of Fortinbras to take over the Danish court which has obliterated itself.

Throughout the play there have been two Hamlets: the one who dreams and feels thought-sick, and the other who acts. For the Hamlet who is acting-out his emotional disturbance, words are weapons or evasions, not symbolic containers of meaning. His tragedy is not that he thinks too much but on the contrary, that he cannot think through his dreams, and evacuates his confusion into action – the action of words. At the very end, when he has given up the struggle, he recovers a vision of his lost inner poetry when he hands his story over to Horatio:

> O God, Horatio, what a wounded name
> Things standing thus unknown, shall I leave behind me.
> If thou didst ever hold me in thy heart,
> Absent thee from felicity awhile,
> And in this harsh world draw thy breath in pain
> To tell my story.
>
> (V.ii.349–354)

Only Horatio is left to try to make sense of Hamlet's story. Hamlet still has a vestigial desire for this to happen and therefore prevents Horatio from drinking from the poisoned cup of melancholic futility. That vital part of himself is in the custody of Horatio as storyteller, playwright, or analyst – but in another play.

After Horatio's failure to contain Hamlet, however much he held him in his heart, Shakespeare gives up the attempt to construct a personal hero on the pattern of his own desires; as a playwright he had perhaps loaded too many expectations onto his character. Instead in future he stands back with evenly suspended attention in order to dramatise the dreams evoked by the play as a whole, in the way later advocated in the use of the psychoanalytic method. It is the play, not the hero, that is the heart of the mystery, just as it is the analysis – not the analyst or the analysand – that is the aesthetic object.

Notes

1 Marjorie Garber (1974) sees Horatio as the Freudian dream censor of Hamlet's 'individual mythmaking' focusing on his 'conscience'.
2 The Ghost is often imagined to dramatise something of Shakespeare's relationship with his own Catholic father (Wilson, 2003; Greenblatt, 2013). There are other indications also (mentioned by various scholars) of a personal family story, not least the name of Shakespeare's dead son Hamnet.
3 See Folkerth (2002) on the significance of the ear as a 'liminal site' where body and mind (identity) are negotiated. Philippa Berry (1999) describes dense associations of sexual identity that lie behind the ear and hearing, 'timbre' according with the Renaissance idea of (female) unformed matter and of the tonality that precedes formed utterance.
4 Shakespeare almost seems to invest too much in Hamlet; after this he ceases actively searching for a hero; heroes grow from the basic conflicts of the play. Horatio himself is drawn excessively to action, in Bion's (1970) sense of morality: he writes of 'the close relationship between moral attitudes and action, as contrasted with thought or meditation' (1970, p. 8). Horatio's attitude mirrors that of Hamlet in the attempt to impose morality rather than to take inner responsibility through contemplation.

Chapter 4

Dreams of dark corners: legalism at play in *The Merchant of Venice* and *Troilus and Cressida*

Although it is Vincentio in *Measure for Measure* who is dubbed the 'Duke of Dark Corners', the idea of sexual hypocrisy generated by the 'problem plays' of Shakespeare's mid-career is investigated in a dreamlike way in other ways that likewise include the idea of the playwright himself as observer and the problematic nature of his relation to the play as well as to the audience. This chapter considers two of Shakespeare's so-called problem plays in terms of disturbed dream narratives.

Anne Righter (Barton) (1962) noted the disillusion with the idea of the play and acting that surfaces in Shakespeare's middle period and attains a savage intensity in *Hamlet*. None of Shakespeare's straight comedies really recover the revelatory optimism of *A Midsummer Night's Dream* or the same conviction that the audience will 'take hands' with the playwright and be 'friends' with the audience. The poison of serpents, darts, and monsters of the mind is exorcised: a bear becomes a bush. The play – the dream incarnate – can save the world. But philosopher-rulers like Theseus who can learn from their imaginations, and have benevolent internal objects who can also learn, are few and far between. In subsequent plays Shakespeare becomes more interested in non-integration within the comedic setting; as Northrop Frye pointed out, 'Some of the most haunting speeches in Shakespeare are connected with these shifts of perspective provided by alienated characters' – the fool as *idiotes* rather than as clown (1965, p. 101). There is an underlying pattern of melancholic alienation (the person of the playwright) in the context of egotistical self-indulgence or wish-fulfilment by bright young things (aristocratic patrons) who have somehow hijacked the life of the play and turned it to their own ends, even if not as blatantly as Hamlet with the Mousetrap. Society marginalises or excludes figures such as Yorick, Shylock, and Malvolio from the benefits of their own play-work, ridiculed owing to class or religion and yet parasitised. And at the end, there is no integration because society itself takes no responsibility for its sadism: 'I'll be revenged on the whole pack of you.' The happy couplings are essentially paranoid-schizoid in their value systems, with internal objects imprisoned and denigrated.

The Merchant of Venice: a sober house

The Merchant of Venice, written some years before *Hamlet*, is Shakespeare's first dark comedy, with its anti-heroines Portia and Jessica between them squeezing the life out of the despised Jew with his despised 'thrifty' ethics. The entire play is Shylock's dream of his role in society: a 'dog' to be spat upon, subhuman, an 'alien' in the commercial world of Venice which nonetheless depends on him for the stability of its capitalist enterprises. The hazardous argosies of Antonio the Christian merchant don't reliably bring in the revenue unless they are underpinned by Jewish usury to plug the gaps when his ships may or may not have foundered. Working Venice is a society of efficient mutual exploitation. It makes the murky money that supports the pleasure palace on the hill of bright Belmont where Portia abides with the vast wealth inherited from her father. The Christian community projects its sanctimony into the Jew who is the only one honestly to own the emotion of hatred, just as he is the only one to believe in the rule of law as a moderator of unruly emotions ('Is it the law? . . . I am content.'). As Lyn Stephens writes: 'For all his envy and hatred he attempts to find an ethical way of being' (1993, p. 124).

The tyrannical nature of the ruling hierarchy is shown in the unwritten bonds within society that Shylock brings to the surface:

> *Shylock*: Say this:
> 'Fair sir, you spet on me on Wednesday last,
> You spurn'd me such a day, another time
> You call'd me dog; and for these courtesies
> I'll lend you thus much moneys'?
> *Antonio*: I am as like to call thee so again,
> To spet on thee again, to spurn thee too.
>   (I.iii.123–126)*

Only when the contractual basis of the relationship has been fully aired and agreed does Shylock say, 'Go with me to a notary, seal me there / Your single bond.'[1] His hidden bondage is rewritten as Antonio's (projected back). For the Christian community we can perhaps read Protestant or aristocratic patronage; for the Jewish, any other ethnicity or religion, including perhaps underground Catholic. They all have their own superstitions and basic assumptions, but Shylock is the only one who insists on exposing the hypocrisy: 'I hate him for he is a Christian' (I.iii.37).

---

* Quotations are from *The Merchant of Venice*, ed. J. R. Brown (1955). London: Methuen.

48 Dreams of dark corners: Shylock and Troilus

The Christian values are embodied *in absurdum* by Antonio, who is a caricature of Christ, motivated not by generosity but by masochism in his 'love' of Bassanio his egocentric parasite:[2]

> I am a tainted wether of the flock,
> Meetest for death, – the weakest kind of fruit
> Drops earliest to the ground and so let me;
> You cannot better be employ'd Bassanio
> Than to live still and write mine epitaph.
> (IV.i.114–118)

Bassanio in writing his epitaph is pictured as a caricatural poet, as is Lorenzo in his famous paean to Orpheus, delivered whilst he is seated with Jessica on the heights of Belmont hill:

> The man that hath no music in himself
> Nor is not moved with concord of sweet sounds,
> Is fit for treasons, stratagems, and spoils,
> The motions of his spirit are dull as night,
> And his affections dark as Erebus:
> Let no such man be trusted: – mark the music.
> (V.i.83–88)

The trouble with Lorenzo is that he has 'insufficient harmony in *his* soul' (Fernie, 2005, p. 6).[3] This is not the music of psychic change as it was with Richard II; it is aristocratic entertainment by servant-musicians, only audible to those who have nothing else to do but sit on moonlit banks and wait for pleasurable sounds to drift in on the breeze. It's what Jessica calls 'table-talk', and it is underpinned by Portia's equally hypocritical speech about mercy, which is being spoken at that very moment far below, down in the courtrooms of Venice. They are two versions of Christian entertainment: throwing a Jew to the lions and converting 'savage beasts' to a 'modest gaze' – complementary movements but equally satisfying. Anyone who is not eligible for this kind of music (not a member of the Belmont club) is 'dark as Erebus', or perhaps Jewish, or at least has not had their 'manners' converted as has Jessica (II.iii.19), becoming thereby elevated in the social hierarchy. Shakespeare here, as on other occasions, gives a very quotable passage to someone who doesn't deserve it, and it has to be seen in context, as highlighting the hypocrisy through pretty wordplaying.

Using money and talent wisely have been connected since the parable of the talents. The connection is the sense of obligation to internal gods. Shakespeare, like Shylock, has to manage his accounts within the basic assumptions of a society ignorant of its sadism and ingratitude. But it is neither the dumb Bassanio nor the sacrificial Antonio who are the prime target for anti-poetry or minus K: it is the two daughters, Portia and Jessica (Nerissa being just an adjunct to Portia). Initially they both feel constrained or depressed by their fathers, but they each find a way to acquire their wealth and direct it to their self-satisfaction. Bassanio is one of several 'Jasons' in search of Portia's golden fleece, and she instructs him how to choose the right casket lest she should find herself tied up with the Moor. But he needs Antonio's money to make his application in this lottery, having wasted his own.

Portia, having first played her father's game of three caskets in order to ensnare a husband, seems to adopt projectively her father's identity when she dresses up as a man in order to pretend to be a real judge presiding in the courtroom. It is another game. She makes up the law as she goes along, with impunity, hounding her naïve prey with a serious of rhetorical questions. Her cross-examination, conducted in pompous paternal robes, contrasts with the dispensations of Rosalind in the forest of Arden, whose femininity always shines through her tunic.

Jessica's is a more complex betrayal. Like many teenagers she feels 'Our house is hell', but she acts out her rebellion in a way destructive of her internal objects. Shylock naively but trustingly asks her to lock the window against external follies so that his house is protected from within:

> Let not the sound of shallow fopp'ry enter
> My sober house.
>
> (II.v.35–36)

Instead she takes a perverse pleasure in penetrating the house's boundaries as she casts down her 'casket' to Lorenzo in the street below: she is 'asham'd' only of her appearance in boy's clothes but makes up for this by 'gilding' herself with her father's money:

> *Jessica*: I will make fast the doors and gild myself
>   With some more ducats, and be with you straight.
> *Gratiano*: Now (by my hood) a gentle, and no Jew.
> *Lorenzo*: Beshrew me but I love her heartily,
>   For she is wise, if I can judge of her,
>   And fair she is, if that mine eyes be true
>   And true she is, as she hath prov'd herself.
>
> (II.vii.49–55)

She is clothed in a false identity, the means by which she gets a 'gentle' husband – a leg-up to Belmont – silly and worthless though he is. Her betrayal is not only of her father but of her internal parents, when she takes her mother Leah's turquoise ring and later sells it in the market for a monkey (like the casket, with implications of sexual impulsiveness; certainly not 'wise and true'). Again, this contrasts with Rosalind later, who confesses to 'desires giddy as a monkey'; it is the negative version of the monkey-sexuality metaphor. Shylock's equation of

50 Dreams of dark corners: Shylock and Troilus

his daughter, his ducats, and his precious stones is black tragicomedy as, taken together, they are the nearest he comes to an aesthetic internal object. He can survive his external denigration in a Christian city but not the vulnerability of his containing 'house' so treacherously rifled from within.

It is Jessica therefore who has filled Shylock with the pain and vengefulness he can barely express: 'Thou stick'st a dagger in me . . . I'll plague him, I'll torture him . . . thou torturest me Tubal – it was my turquoise, I had it of Leah when I was a bachelor: I would not have given it for a wilderness of monkeys' (III.i.100–113).[4] His real pain contrasts with Antonio's masochistic sighs and moans. As Leonard Tennenhouse observes, Shakespeare positions Jessica's defection in relation to Antonio's failed argosies in such a way that Shylock's revenge on Antonio becomes really 'retaliation for the loss of his daughter' (1980, p. 58). He indeed says it is 'dearly bought' (IV.i.100), meaning in exchange for his daughter; and this is the way it is seen by both Bassanio's and Shylock's friends: Antonio will 'pay for this', says Solanio (II.viii.36); 'Antonio is certainly undone', concludes Tubal (III.ii.114). Shylock is driven like a dog into a kennel – namely the kangaroo court of an abstract justice which he would like to believe overarches hierarchical social divisions. Did Shakespeare feel like that before a court performance?

The pathos lies in his confidence in Portia and his belief that she is a 'well-deserving pillar' of the law (IV.i.235), not a sadistic tease and equivocator who makes up the rules as she goes along. This belief, essentially in an old-style analogy between legal and religious institutions (Raffield, 2011), is his undoing. Portia has had a modern education in the technical skills of inquisition. Step by step she undermines Shylock's position, under the rhetorical banner of 'mercy' and the guise of fair play for all, until the point at which he can be deprived of both identity (forced to become a Christian) and means to live. He has become a non-person at last. We are left to ask ourselves, what is the significance for the playwright of this so-called comedy: what is the 'dream' behind the plot? What is the relation between the desecration of Shylock's internal world and the playwright's sense of being used, the 'house' of his mind and stage ransacked by its sybaritic patrons rather than experienced as a mirror to nature, its female jewels perversely appropriated?

Ultimately, the test for the play's actual audience – that is, the audience that has been shown the cruelty stirred up by the fight-flight basic assumption on the Inns of Court benches – lies in asking ourselves, which is the more devastating of those two key speeches: 'The quality of mercy is not strain'd', or 'Hath not a Jew eyes?' It is the merciless taunting of Solanio and Salerio, playing on the idea of Shylock's 'flesh and blood', that brings forth his famous definition, not of a Jew or Christian, but of a human being:[5]

> Hath not a Jew eyes? Hath not a Jew hands, organs, dimensions, senses, affections, passions; fed with the same food, hurt with the same weapons, subject to the same diseases, heal'd by the same means, warm'd and cool'd

by the same winter and summer, as a Christian is? If you prick us, do we not bleed? If you tickle us, do we not laugh? If you poison us, do we not die? And if you wrong us, do we not revenge? If we are like you in the rest, we will resemble you in that.

(III.i.52–66)

Jessica, his flesh and blood, has not only deserted but made a hole in his heart, for which, in response to their taunts, he now seeks a 'matching' revenge:

Shylock: I say my daughter is my flesh and blood.
Salerio: There is more difference between thy flesh and hers than between jet and ivory . . . but tell us, do you hear whether Antonio have had any loss at sea or no?
Shylock: There I have another bad match . . .

(III.i.33–39)

The Christians do not understand what it is to have a hole in the heart. Shylock is the only one with real feelings and he makes a futile attempt to get them across, in the delusion that there is a court of fair play even in Venice.

Portia's apparent humility in her 'mercy' speech is based on the rhetorical plea of being God's agent, dropping words of wisdom from the heights of Belmont:

The quality of mercy is not strained.
It droppeth as the gentle rain from heaven
Upon the place beneath. It is twice blessed:
It blesseth him that gives and him that takes.
'Tis mightiest in the mightiest . . .
(IV.i.180–184)

It is a pretty speech in decorous blank verse (unlike Shylock's passionate prose), but anti-poetic insofar as it is made without insight into her own sadism and high-handedness. With casual Christian brutality she addresses Shylock, as they all do, as sub-human:

Therefore, Jew,
Though justice be thy plea, consider this –
That in the course of justice none of us
Should see salvation. We do pray for mercy . . .
(IV.i.193–196)

The standard Christian attitude is what makes Shylock insist on Antonio being treated as a piece of meat. Words are a means of subjugation in this court. Their purpose is not to deliver meaning but to assert control.[6] Portia can play-act in

52   Dreams of dark corners: Shylock and Troilus

the surety that she holds all the cards and can therefore whiten the sepulchre of her judicial robes. The jokey asides between Portia and Nerissa when their husbands offer to sacrifice them for Antonio reinforce the meaninglessness of Bassanio's protestations: 'I would lose all, ay sacrifice them all / here to this devil, to deliver you' (IV.i.281–283). Nobody believes it – it is not intended to be taken as sincere; the purpose of the words is to demonstrate that he is one of the gang, the 'Christian' establishment with its hypocritical basic assumptions of mercy and self-sacrifice. Shylock is the only one to be shocked, even though he likewise knows the words are empty boasting: 'These be Christian husbands!' And at this point he re-owns his daughter, in the present tense: 'I have a daughter' (IV.i.291). It is not of course reciprocated, since thanks to his money she has become an honorary Christian. Although 'damn'd both by father and mother', as Lorenzo puts it with Belmont drollery, she replies in the spirit of repartee: 'I shall be sav'd by my husband – he hath made me a Christian!' (III.v.17).

Troilus and Cressida: the woman as the play[†]

The legalistic mentality, the controlling and voyeuristic observer, destroys the body of the play and its capacity to genuinely educate the audience. It is the playwright's enemy, a special form of the ubiquitous suspicion of 'words, words, words' that is to be found in both Shakespeare and his contemporaries, with their formal rhetorical education. The danger (often presented as a male-female tension) lies in the playwright's own temptation to tyrannically control the aesthetic object that is the play, directing it towards propaganda or moralism rather than allowing it to organically evolve from within, as in Coleridge's distinction between mechanic and organic, or fancy *versus* imagination; or as in Bion's distinction between exoskeletal and endoskeletal personality development. The play-as-container has to evolve in an analogous way to the analysis-as-container; and in this process the playwright, like the analyst, is not the omnipotent inventor of dreams but an observer of dreamlife and a learner.

Portia with her legalistic trickery is a type of anti-playwright, an abuser of power and rhetoric – the privileges endowed by wealth and upbringing. Her aim is to destroy the aesthetic potential of the ugly alien ethic and to substitute it with the courtly piped music of Belmont – but only for the select few who repose far above the city's dirty streets and canals. Hamlet tried to pick up Richard's realisation of his mind as a theatre full of players; he was well aware of the dangers of intrusive curiosity but was hijacked from within by his failure to work through aesthetic conflicts in relation to Ophelia and his mother, ultimately leaving his story to be told by another. The analyst-playwright has

---

† An earlier version of this section was published in *The Chamber of Maiden Thought* (1991). Quotations are from *Troilus and Cressida*, ed. K. Palmer (1982). London: Methuen.

Dreams of dark corners: Shylock and Troilus   53

ultimately to rediscover its potential through other plays. Before that happens, in *Measure for Measure* the Duke of Dark Corners splits his unacknowledged possessive desire for unsullied Isabella into his 'deputy' (Angelo-Lucifer), whilst covertly observing from behind his friar's hood how his designs are progressing. The hypocritical pair are made for one another, engendering between them a convoluted bed-trickery that masquerades as a play; only the 'low' characters are allowed to have humanity. It is 'a melancholist's dream', as Keats would say. Later, Shakespeare has to revise the dark-cornered playwright – the one who prefers omnipotence to dreaming – when he comes to Prospero.

Meanwhile, his most brilliant and satiric dissection of the legalistic mentality is given in *Troilus and Cressida*, which was probably written shortly after *Hamlet* for an Inns of Court audience. Here the anti-playwright is vividly embodied in the twin roles of Pandarus and Thersites, one acting and the other observing the going-between or false links made by the players, neatly summed as 'war and lechery'. It is a sharp-edged dream of the theatre-world's attempts to victimise the play in the form of the woman as aesthetic object: to demean, possess, abuse, idealise as fashion, etc. The woman at the heart of the play – not Helen with her ideal beauty but Cressida with her real beauty – represents the play that is trapped in the midst of grotesque voyeurs and clever clipper-clappers.

But Cressida is no masochist; she is a survivor. As has often been observed, she is a different kind of character from the others; John Bayley thought she really belongs in the world of the novel but does not have time or space to develop.[7] Perhaps owing to Chaucer's influence, Shakespeare's Cressida is not just a realist but real. Angela Sheppard asks, 'What happens if a woman starts to take responsibility for herself? Does she become Cressida, rather than Juliet?'[8] Her position is supremely vulnerable as the daughter of a traitor, and not even a widow as in Chaucer. Love is a luxury, but she is the only character in the play who gives the impression of being capable of it, in different circumstances. The only choice she is offered is that of belonging to a particular man, on whatever side, or to be 'whore in general'.[9] She and her pandering uncle have a down-to-earth homely language distinct from that of anybody else, although Pandarus seasons his with bawdy innuendo, titillated by his duty to get her suitably allocated, which he does in as well-meaning a manner as he is capable of, and with genuine dismay at his failure.

Other characters don't speak, they make speeches out of textbooks – full of 'vices of style' notable even in their Renaissance rhetorical context.[10] The pervading linguistic texture of the play is one in which flocks of metaphysical abstractions are generated like flatus by a seething mass of indigestible cookery and bodily malfunctions. The 'stewed phrases' of pornography's language-games revolve in the 'hot digestion of this cormorant war' (II.ii.6); love is a 'generation of vipers' (III.ii.129) and the pageant of pride 'bastes' itself in the cooking-pot (II.iii.186). In this context, Greeks and Trojans are not heroic contraries but blind basic-assumption groupings, in which a sense of status is substituted for a sense of identity. Each camp has their mascot: the 'elephant

54   Dreams of dark corners: Shylock and Troilus

Ajax' for the Greeks, the 'ransack'd queen' Helen for the Trojans. The background atmosphere is a farcical mixture of soap opera, sports match (the 'sport' of bed or battle), and election campaign. And Cressida, as she well knows, is expected by everyone to follow the example of Helen, the willing passive monument to the play's equation of woman, the city, and art as fields to be 'toppled', conquered, and degraded.[11]

The buzzwords of the Greek camp are distinction, degree, policy, wisdom, dignity, and import. The specialised function of Ulysses (the master-contriver) is to rearrange 'degree' within its disturbed ranks so that mutual subservience can be achieved and the army become an effective fighting machine again:

> Take but degree away, untune that string,
> And hark what discord follows. Each thing melts
> In mere oppugnancy; the bounded waters
> Should lift their bosoms higher than the shores,
> And make a sop of all this solid globe . . .
>
> (I.iii.109–113)

To admire this Renaissance soapbox cant as 'Shakespearean' is to fall into the trap of being the type of audience Shakespeare is attacking. The underlying assumption of the play is that the intransigent (female) world whose 'saucy boat . . . co-rivals greatness' (in Nestor's words) or lifts its bosom higher than the shore, must be brought to heel: 'distinction . . . winnows the light away', as Agamemnon says (I.iii.28). They voice the perennial anxiety of the fascist or totalitarian mind, that without 'distinction' and 'degree' there must be 'chaos' (I.iii.125).

The present problem of the Greek council is that Achilles, who is their prize tool for maintaining order, has gone 'womanish' and spends his time with his 'masculine whore' Patroclus, making a 'pageant' of the Greek hierarchy and ridiculing it. A. D. Nuttall has described how Shakespeare intuits the 'Greek mindset' behind his Latin sources, characterised by both 'a reductive intellectualism and a gross (oddly abstract) physicality'.[12] On the burlesque side are Ajax and Achilles, whose physical weight, undirected, undermines Ulysses' position as the ruling intellect:

> They call this bed-work, mapp'ry, closet-war
> So that the ram that batters down the wall,
> For the great swing and rudeness of his poise,
> They place before his hand that made the engine,
> Or those that with the fineness of their souls
> By reason guide his execution.
>
> (I.iii.205–210)

Ulysses, an extension of the Egeus-mentality, represents the false artist who believes his own 'fineness' or 'reason' manipulates his tools (the 'ram') in a type of sordid 'bed-work' which will batter down the wall of the city of art. The battering-ram Achilles has rebelled, but Ulysses contrives to seduce him by appealing to his sense of fashionability: presuming (correctly) that this is the 'touch of nature' which makes him 'kin' with everybody else in the play. If Achilles is not admired in the eyes of others, there is little point in his rebellion against Ulysses and the principle of order. Ulysses reminds him that

> to have done is to hang
> Quite out of fashion, like a rusty nail
> In monumental mockery. . . .
> One touch of nature makes the whole world kin –
> That all with one consent praise new-born gauds . . .
> (III.iii.151–176)

He undermines Achilles by insinuating that, through his police-state information service, he is somehow inside his head, in the place where 'thoughts unveil in their dumb cradles':

> There is a mystery, with whom relation
> Durst never meddle, in the soul of state,
> Which hath an operation more divine
> Than breath or pen can give expressure to.
> (ll. 200–203)

The tyranny of the omniscient 'watchful state' is the archetypal anti-artistic stance, subverting the individual's thinking processes and the artist's 'breath or pen' and hijacking the language of creativity – mystery, birth, divinity. Ulysses uses words, as Frye said, 'like a human Aeolus, controlling his bag of wind'.[13] In the event however all his tyrannical psychical manipulations are themselves subverted when the basic-assumption mentality which he has been relying on gets beyond his control; and Ajax (the Achilles substitute), instead of fighting Hector in a duel, is overcome by the pseudo-revelation of their kinship, in the ludicrous episode of 'my sacred aunt' (IV.v.133).

Shakespeare's point is that tyrannical structures based on the enforcement of codes rather than the growth of true value-systems are ultimately not even effective, resulting in the football-hooliganism quality of the last battle, in which the two sides start 'clapper-clawing' and eventually 'swallow' one another (in Thersites' words [V.iv.1, 34]).

In this play, Shakespeare shows how the hooligan gangster mentality is by no means the prerogative of the lower classes but is generated by the highly educated. It is important that codes have words to put in their boxes, otherwise nobody knows where or what they are. Thus the Trojan court embodies a sophisticated sub-mentality precisely equivalent to that of the Greek camp, with its own set of buzzwords: value, honour, worth, truth, merit, taste, estimation, right. The irrelevance to real life is indicated by Hector's not even bothering to vote for his own well-presented argument to let Helen go – contriving the argument is an end in itself.[14] Their academic debate ('What's aught but as 'tis valued?') focuses on Troilus' narcissistic excitement at his approaching union with Cressida (though this is of course not overtly confessed, since it is a union both clandestine and public). He argues:

> How may I avoid,
> Although my will distaste what it elected,
> The wife I choose? There can be no evasion
> To blench from this and to stand firm by honour.
> We turn not back the silks upon the merchant
> When we have soil'd them, nor the remainder viands
> We do not throw in unrespective sieve
> Because we now are full.
>
> (II.ii.66–73)

He has not yet met Cressida, but this speech foreshadows the inevitable history of their abortive love, since it expresses a mentality in which the very idea of love presupposes a 'soiled' object, modelled on the 'ransack'd' Helen. It is a pervading assumption which Cressida has already recognised, despite her cloistered existence observing the world from a 'watch tower'; anticipating Ulysses' words to Achilles, she tells Pandarus, 'Things won are done' (I.ii.292). According to the Trojan code, here perfectly expressed by Troilus in his institutional maiden speech, the woman is inevitably violated in accepting the man and therefore will inevitably become 'false as Cressida' (as in their strange marriage pact). But this in itself is an excellent opportunity for narcissistic gratification, since it reinforces his own worthiness, that of an 'eternal and fixed soul' which will never betray its code.

Troilus' elder brothers are indulgently impressed by his grasp of what it takes to be officer material. Cressida, however, is less easily reassured. During the few minute scraps of dialogue which she has alone with him, she attempts to inject some fear, respect, and realism into the concept of love between them. Troilus indeed has expressed to Pandarus his fear of losing 'distinction':

> I fear it much; and I do fear besides
> That I shall lose distinction in my joys . . .
>
> (III.ii.24–25)

He has some sense of the power of love to dissolve his system of codes but is frightened and repelled by Cressida's voicing the same feeling: her 'fears have eyes', she says, but it is better to acknowledge fear and be led by reason than to deny its existence: 'Blind fear, that seeing reason leads, finds safer footing than blind reason stumbling without fear. To fear the worst oft cures the worse' (III.ii.69–71). Troilus is filled with anxiety because she is speaking to a level of deep emotional reality which he recognises but would prefer to deny, and which suggests that she knows more about love than he supposed, immediately prompting the suspicion: are all women whores, even when they are virgins?

Immediately Troilus takes shelter in his code, and praises his own virtue: 'Few words to fair faith: Troilus shall be such to Cressida as what envy can say worse shall be a mock for his truth, and what truth can speak truest, not truer than Troilus' (III.ii.94–97). In this way he avoids the exploration of uncomfortable feelings – including why he should imagine he is soiling her in the first place, or guilt about taking advantage of her social position as the daughter of a traitor, or any self-questioning later in the Greek camp, where she is given the choice of being 'whore' either to Diomed or to the Greeks 'in general', as Ulysses puts it (IV.v.21). Although he insists he is a man of chivalry and of 'few words', this is another facet of his identity-shielding code; in fact, like Ulysses, he is obsessed with his own rhetoric, and is displeased when Cressida interrupts him before he has finished his 'protestations'. In flight from all emotional reality, Troilus concentrates on writing his posthumous reputation, when 'fame [will] canonize us' (II.iii.203) and

> 'As true as Troilus' shall crown up the verse
> And sanctify the numbers.
>
> (III.ii.180–181)

Again this is a caricatural poetic role; Troilus has read Shakespeare's sonnets and thinks he can do a passable imitation. Cressida isn't a feature of his poetic renown, but she gamely enters into the spirit of his extravagant declaration and matches it with a reversed piece of hyperbole that ends 'As false as Cressid' (meaning the opposite).

Thus the story of Troilus and Cressida, though it takes up little space in the play as a whole, is at the core of its presentation of false art and of relationships based on status-shuffling and emotional unreality. The tenuous abortive link between the lovers is mirrored in that between play and audience. The putative audience here is not 'thought-sick' like Hamlet but sick for lack of thought. Pandarus includes the audience in his epilogue as fellow panders, 'good traders in the flesh', 'brethren and sisters of the hold-door trade'. Through his pander, Shakespeare is intimating that insofar as his audience go to the play as if to a brothel, prompted by an addiction to pornography and ideological wordplay, concerned only with winning and losing cases, they are bawds to their own minds and the play will appear to be soiled goods. Indeed at the beginning, the armed Prologue warned that he did not come 'in confidence / Of author's pen or actor's voice'; he was not expecting any genuine meeting of minds. Beneath the 'painted cloths' of legalistic rhetoric lie the 'aching bones' of psychic venereal disease. Behind the figure of Cressida lies the reality of the play itself, the

Notes

1 Richard Wilson (2003) notes the 'all-pervading contractarianism of the age'. There is a pathos in Shylock's clinging to the sanctity of the bond as some guarantee of an equal status in society in that respect if not in others.

2 A. D. Nuttall (2004) notes the hypocrisy of Venetian economics, yet he considers Antonio a selfless example of Christian goodness, while Shylock 'remains a figure of darkness' by contrast to Portia who is 'one of light'. Their deceptive appearances are in fact features of the consistent hypocrisy underlying the play. Lyn Stephens observes how the 'dying fall in the half-line presents [Antonio] as an implacable victim, match for an implacable enemy' (1993, p. 93).

3 Yet often Lorenzo's passage is taken at face value; Robin Headlam Wells, for example, writes of Shakespeare's 'symbolic defence of his own art' against Shylock's Puritanism (2005, p. 18).

4 It has been noted that in that era of state terrorism, the language of torture and the rack is a constant feature of Shakespeare's writing (Wilson, 2003, p. 28). Perhaps Shylock the Jew is nearer to the racked Catholic than to the elevated Puritan.

5 Northrop Frye differentiates clown from *idiotes* and observes that 'some of the most haunting speeches in Shakespeare are connected with these shifts of perspective provided by alienated characters' (1965, p. 101).

6 Paul Raffield (2011) describes a tension in Shakespeare's day between 'saleable rhetorical skills' in the hands of 'legal technocrats' and the Inns of Court attempt to redress the ethical deficit by importing tenets of neoPlatonism and theology. Portia's performance could be considered a cynical exploitation of this process of trying to inject ethics into wordplay.

7 John Bayley, *Shakespeare and Tragedy* (1981).

8 Angela Sheppard, 'Soiled Mother or Soul of Woman?' (1993), p. 138.

9 Kay Stockholder (1987) points out that the machinery of Cressida's exchange is set in motion the night Troilus sleeps with her – a dream-image of his inability, as an individual, to sustain the relationship.

10 T. McAlindon, 'Language, Style and Meaning' (1976), p. 209. The texture of the entire play.

11 John Kerrigan (1991) sees Cressida in the context of the medieval tradition of the poem as a female space, a 'concave womb' full of echoes in which the androgynised poet figure becomes the mouth and emblem of female 'complaint' or self-expression. This helps to account for the different type of characterisation allotted to Cressida and our sense that she is the play-poem in dialogue with the playwright.

12 A. D. Nuttall, 'Action at a Distance: Shakespeare and the Greeks' (2004), p. 215.

13 Northrop Frye (1965, p. 42).

14 Nuttall finds Hector's sudden collapse after a good argument inexplicable (2007, p. 217). I think Shakespeare is demonstrating that he doesn't really *mean it*; it is just a piece of rhetoric, like all the other language games.

Chapter 5

Explorations in minus K: *Macbeth* and *Othello*

Macbeth and *Othello* are dramas about the boundary between protomental and mental life, dramatised in the form of the transition from a wartime or basic assumption group mentality and a domestic mentality which potentially could encompass a work group but is in fact perverted or diverted into a situation of torment, the 'rack'. Macbeth is 'racked as homeward he did come'; Othello is set 'on the rack' by Iago's ministrations. In both cases, but in different ways, dream is replaced by nightmare. This chapter differentiates the anti-symbolic content from the poet's dream about it. Shakespeare explores how the destruction of dreaming can occur and then invites us to analyse the distinction between the ambiguities of poetic investigation and the equivocations of the devil within that destroy the protagonist. Meltzer's concept of the psychic 'claustrum' is used to identify the prison from which Macbeth can be released only when he dies and becomes Macduff, an alternative, split-off good part of himself. Bion's concept of 'minus K', the negative or absence of a quest for self-knowledge, is used to illuminate the susceptibility of Othello to Iago. Unlike Macduff and Macbeth, they are not split aspects of a single identity but embody antithetical responses to beauty and its connection with truth, as in Meltzer's definition of 'sincerity' as a personality dynamic.

Macbeth in the claustrum*

In *Macbeth* Shakespeare pursues his investigations into anti-thought or 'minus K' (in Bion's formulation) to the ultimate degree. Minus K is the reverse of curiosity, in particular curiosity about the inner world and its objects, linkages, and germination of thoughts. It leads to 'reversal of alpha-function' and the inability to think with the help of internal objects. It is possible to kill an idea, says Bion, 'and that is not a metaphor *only*';[1] it is a metaphor that houses

---

* A version of this section appeared as 'Macbeth's Equivocation, Shakespeare's Ambiguity', as an appendix to Meltzer's *The Claustrum* (1992). Quotations are from *Macbeth*, ed. K. Muir (1962). London: Methuen.

60 Explorations in minus K: *Macbeth* and *Othello*

a truth: there really is a correspondence between the growth of ideas and the growth of personality, and insofar as it is a live process of 'becoming' it can also be stopped, stagnated, or perverted. Essentially, in Bion's description, it derives from 'envy of the growth-promoting objects', which disables the 'language of achievement' founded on love.[2]

As seen in previous plays, anti-thinking often takes the form of the abuse of language, even or particularly when words are used as a dazzlingly effective form of action, to confuse and manipulate others. Such action is generally unconsciously designed to kill or pervert the nascent struggle of the developing mind to find an appropriate shape or form, a 'local habitation and a name'. In *Macbeth* the abuse of language is presented more simply and obviously in the form of equivocation: the play's hallmark of 'Fair is foul, and foul is fair' can hardly be misunderstood by even the most naïve of readers; and it is in a sense a fairytale carrying the obvious moral that crime does not pay – at least internally. Where poetic ambiguity is an imaginative exploration of the penumbra of meanings around a phrase, equivocation is a means of self-deception, of which Macbeth is the prime example.

The story begins and ends with a battle, and in a sense the entire play is the playwright's dream of Macbeth's state of mind during battle; as in Golding's *Pincher Martin*, a dream that may only have taken a few minutes is spun out to novel-length. It is a dream about a man who cannot dream, who is increasingly divorced from those parts of himself in touch with the emotionality necessary for dreaming and thinking, and in desperation sinks deeper into the mire of self-destruction in the delusion of staying afloat, as if (as Bradley put it) compelled to carry out some 'appalling duty'.[3]

The witch-mind

The idea of what it is to 'be a man' is a response to the governing idea of woman or femininity; and from the opening of the play this is a perverse femininity in the form of the witches. Their cauldron (a bloody faecal container) concocts equivocations and lies, spreading a smog of confusion, in the form of the traditional iconography of hell – dismembered and poisonous ingredients generating a blood-smoked haze; 'Double double toil and trouble.' This smog is the opposite of uncertainty or openness to new knowledge; it is an illusion of omniscience, of seeing and thereby controlling the future, and is derived from the witch mentality associated with the killing fields and the underlying (fight-flight) basic assumption of 'success', namely, disposing of the other, the enemy. Like all basic assumptions, this belongs to society as a whole, and Macbeth is lauded for his wounds and words alike: 'so well thy wounds become thee as thy words – they smack of honour both'.

Macbeth is 'Bellona's bridegroom', married to the idea of war and creator of 'strange images of death' that then reappear as gory pieces in the witches' cauldron, a stew of wounds. The witches hail him according to a progressive pattern in marchlike promotion: Glamis – Cawdor – King; and each time Macbeth is subsequently hailed by his new titles, he seems further bound to the witch-mind as the source of what are equivocally known as 'truths':

> Two truths are told,
> As happy prologues to the swelling act
> Of the imperial theme. . . .
> This supernatural soliciting
> Cannot be ill; cannot be good:
> If ill, why has it given me earnest of success,
> Commencing in a truth? I am Thane of Cawdor:
> If good, why do I yield to that suggestion
> Whose horrid image doth unfix my hair. . . .
> My thought, whose murther yet is but fantastical,
> Shakes so my single state of man,
> That function is smother'd in surmise,
> And nothing is, but what is not.
>
> (I.iii.127–142)

These truths are of course lies, in the Bionian sense of anti-truths. The predicted events may occur, but their meaning is antithetical to their appearance: thought is smothered not enabled by this kind of success. The language of pregnancy and birth, the 'swelling act', is used to disguise the 'horrid image' of murder, presented ambiguously as murdering in thought and the murder of thought itself. The progression of these equivocal 'truths' (a rhythmic balance between 'ill' and 'good') mounts to an automatic culmination in murder. It is a goal which Macbeth prefers to find 'fantastical' and allows to be 'smothered' over again by reverting to cryptic equivocation, again based on the idea of pregnancy: 'And nothing is but what is not'.

Macbeth then dreams up his image of his wife (or mother), making her into a real-life witch though still hoping to evade responsibility. 'They met me in the day of success', he writes in his letter to her, projecting his expectations of murderous success. Witchlike stirrings are evoked in the female receptacle. Her body is identified with the castle, appearing 'fair' on the outside, a 'cradle' for 'temple-haunting martlets' to nest, but once inside the male is fatally trapped, the container turned into a claustrum (in Meltzer's sense of the internal mother's rectum):

> The raven himself is hoarse
> That croaks the fatal entrance of Duncan
> Under my battlements.
>
> (I.v.38–40)

The answer to L. C. Knights' famous question, 'How many children had Lady Macbeth?' is probably, two:[4] the elder being the angelic Duncan, the younger

62 Explorations in minus K: *Macbeth* and *Othello*

born violently by caesarean section and known alternately as Macbeth and Macduff. The mother's role is explicitly perverted, through violent projective reversal, as in the 'unsex me here' speech:

> Come to my woman's breasts,
> And take my milk for gall, you murth'ring ministers . . .
> Come, thick Night
> And pall thee in the dunnest smoke of Hell,
> That my keen knife see not the wound it makes,
> Nor Heaven peep through the blanket of the dark,
> To cry, 'Hold, hold!'
>
> (I.v.47–54)

The focus is on not seeing the wound, not taking responsibility, and on using Macbeth as a dehumanised 'knife'.

Meanwhile Duncan is described as if he were a satisfied infant laid to sleep, 'shut up / In measureless content', surrounded by other images of childhood, including his young sons; even his bodyguards are mere children. His murder takes on the meaning of infanticide, and on another level, the murder of infant thoughts that cannot develop to fruition within the witch-mind's deadly cauldron. Duncan is associated with 'Pity like a naked new-born babe', guarded by cherubim (angels of spiritual knowledge), and the 'sightless couriers of the air' that ineffectively surround him contrast with Lady Macbeth's 'sightless ministers' who inhabit the witchlike fog of equivocation that enshrouds the brazen image of infanticide:

> I have given suck, and know
> How tender 'tis to love the babe that milks me:
> I would, while it was smiling in my face,
> Have pluck'd my nipple from his boneless gums
> And dashed the brains out.
>
> (I.vii.54–58)

Perhaps Lady Macbeth is herself a ghost, like Hamlet's internal father, returned from the infernal realms to haunt her son with witchlike nightmares.[5] In the grip of this false feminine blanket, Macbeth is as helpless as Duncan, despite his one attempt to release himself by asserting his manliness: 'I dare do all that may become a man / Who dares do more, is none.' He too is Lady Macbeth's baby, once filled with 'the milk of human kindness' (as she put it) but then, owing to the false link created between them by witchlike ambition, his capacity for reverie is aborted and alpha-function reversed, the brains 'dashed out'.

From this point Macbeth allows his 'hand' to become her 'dagger', a negative phallic part-object, violently intruding into the hallowed mother-baby space. He is no longer himself, 'a man', but a mere agent or vehicle of the witch-mind created by this false container-contained relationship. He carries out the murder in a hallucinated state, as though drugged, led by the dagger in mid-air: 'I go, and it is done'. The 'eye wink[s] at the hand' as if not knowing or seeing what he was doing:

> No, this my hand will
> The multitudinous seas incarnadine,
> Making the green one red.
> (II.ii.60–62)

The 'multitudinous' variety of life is permeated in every aspect by the matching 'incarnadine'; while the monosyllabic 'this my hand' is confirmed with deadly emphasis in 'green one red' (recalling the word 'done' that is echoed throughout the play). In the play's starkly reduced language, hand and deed are substituted for sight and thought. The space between impulse and action (Freud's definition of thought) is eliminated.

The murder of sleep

Sleep is the state in which dreams are possible and nascent thoughts can germinate. Internal voices cry that 'Macbeth hath murdered Sleep – the innocent sleep', the source of fruitful dreaming. Thereafter, in the classical pattern of the Furies, he is hounded by psychotic symptoms. Instead of dreams he has hallucinations, fuelled by 'nameless dread' (Bion), and envy of the dead who are 'safe' from such nightmares. These are features of the claustrophobic state of mind described by Meltzer as resulting from intrusive projection into the internal object, in this case the rectum of the primal mother:

> Those who have lived in the rectum are posed a severe depressive problem, for they may have done real damage in the world by enacting this state of mind. . . . The claustrophobic quality of mind generates both restlessness . . . and/or ambition to climb some existent or non-existent social ladder, to imagined safety at the top.[6]

Macbeth, having murdered the state of mind in which he can sleep and dream, is now obsessed with safety, escape from the mind's revenge:

> To be thus is nothing, but to be safely thus:
> Our fears in Banquo
> Stick deep, and in his royalty of nature
> Reigns that which would be fear'd . . .
> (III.i.47–50)

The pursuit of 'safety' takes on the characteristics of political ideology, false art, and anal obsessionality. It is necessary to his ideology that the agents of

64 Explorations in minus K: *Macbeth* and *Othello*

murder (his masturbatory hands, personified in the hired murderers) should pretend they are doing it for the good of the state, not just for the money. When they insist they are just 'men', Macbeth savagely replies they go 'by the name of dogs', taking no responsibility for his abuse.

Macbeth wants his crown – his position in the hierarchy – to be safe, clean, perfect. He demands 'a clearness' in the murder of Banquo, leaving 'no rubs or botches in the work'; and on hearing that Fleance has escaped, he feels trapped by this flaw in the perfection of his sculptural self-image:

> Then comes my fit again: I had else been perfect;
> Whole as the marble, founded as the rock,
> As broad and general as the casing air;
> But now, I am cabin'd, cribb'd, confin'd, bound in
> To saucy doubts and fears. – But Banquo's safe?
>
> (III.iv.19–24)

His goal of sculptural perfection is a kind of deadness in which he believed he could remain safe, but it is pierced by his 'fit', his terror. Only now does he become obsessed with his lack of heirs – the 'barren sceptre in [his] gripe' – but less as regret for his lost creativity than for his fear of Banquo's issue which makes his kingship unsafe. Macbeth is persecuted not by remorse, or even guilt (at this stage), but by the consumerist suspicion that he has been tricked into a false kingship; he has paid the asking price and delivered his 'eternal jewel' to 'the common Enemy of man' but has been returned faulty goods, with defective safety features and no guarantee. His reign of terror therefore begins under the banner of a massive clean-up operation, designed to rectify his position which is 'unsafe the while'. And this time there will be no defilement, no paying over the odds; it will be a clean job, for the ideals of safety and of cleanliness are concurrent, and are both euphemisms for murder.

Banquo's ghost returns in the form of a vengeful hallucination, threatening not the easy revenge of death (a type of safety) but the nightmare terror of dispossession: squeezing Macbeth from his place at the table, so that (he believes) there is nowhere for him to sit. Banquo is 'safe' in the sense of dead, but not in the sense of his image having been 'taken off' or erased. Instead of Banquo's removal, it is Macbeth who is first squeezed ('cabin'd, cribb'd, confin'd') and then evacuated into non-existence. Macbeth is prey to his own equivocation as the ghost comes and goes several times, responding to his invitation to 'our dear friend Banquo – would he were present'. Whenever it appears, Macbeth finds that his seat (the place of his own crown) is blocked by the gory faecal 'crown' of Banquo's mutilated corpse – the 'twenty mortal murthers on his crown' caused by 'twenty trenched gashes in his head'. The bloody gashes or faeces of the hallucination are what Bion calls 'beta-elements' in the sense of 'reversal of alpha-function' – not just unthinking, but the murder of a nascent thought that is trying to form.

The solidity of this apparition literally 'pushes' Macbeth 'from his stool'. It is poetic justice with a vengeance. Shakespeare clarifies the link between the 'doing' (of murder – in this play's euphemistic shorthand) and defaecation, through Lady Macbeth's rebuke: 'When all's done, you look but on a stool.'[7] For a short while, in fact, Macbeth rises above his fear, wondering at the metaphysical aspect of the situation:

> The time has been
> That, when the brains were out, the man would die,
> And there an end. But now they rise again
> With twenty mortal murders on their crowns
> And push us from our stools. This is more strange
> Than such a murder is.
> (III.iv.77–82)

The 'strangeness' of this false intimacy with the dead Banquo is Shakespeare's poetic correlative to his false intimacy with the dead Duncan; it presents the true character of his usurpation and 'success', and as such represents a momentary approach to Bion's K vertex. For a moment Macbeth is perplexed, since he had not (any more than his wife-mother) imagined the nature of 'even-handed justice' (retribution) as something arising out of his own consciousness. They knew there was such a thing as 'remorse', which could be 'stopped up', but not that this very constipation would conjure up a world of delusion. Lady Macbeth is the first to see the approach of madness, but her only defence is to stop 'thinking', for 'it will make us mad' (II.ii.33); in fact it is not simply her action but its meaning of killing her own thoughts that is what precipitates her madness. Her 'thoughts' have indeed 'died / With them they think on' (III.ii.10).

Macbeth's 'wonder' at this strangeness is transient, 'like a summer's cloud', since he has no means of investigating its meaning, with his internal communication blocked. He is driven to the witches, like a heroin addict to the needle, for further injections of what he knows is bad for him ('damned all those that trust them'), in search of the pseudo-knowledge which will give him a delusory protection from the future: 'for now I am bent to know / By the worst means, the worst.' He pretends to be stoically facing up to unpleasant facts, but 'strange things' in his head prevent him from knowing or thinking anything:

> Strange things I have in head, that will to hand,
> Which must be acted, ere they may be scann'd.
> (III.iv.133–139)

The 'strange things' in his head (like the 'strange images of death' from the battlefield) are masqueraded as ideas which insist upon realisation. Until those uncomfortable 'things' have been 'acted' (evacuated), he cannot 'scan' the information contained in them and get an overview for the state's efficient functioning – reliable predictions of the course things will and must take in the future. Through this pseudo-logicality, Macbeth perpetrates the lie-in-the-soul that he is prepared to sacrifice his personal comfort in the interests of political necessity.

Bion cites Coleridge's 'frightful fiend' (another version of the Furies) as an example of the nameless dread that pursues the mind blocked from contact with its internal objects:

> Like one that on a lonesome road
> Doth walk in fear and tread
> And having once turned round walks on,
> And turns no more his head;
> Because he knows, a frightful fiend
> Doth close behind him tread.
>
> ('The Ancient Mariner',
> cited in Bion, 1970, p. 46)

Macbeth hopes that speed will pre-empt the nightmare catching up with him, so actions must take place *before* they are 'scanned', not just at the same time, through psychic evacuation – 'be it thought and done'. The significance is, again, of thought-murder, taking the form this time of the murder of the Macduff family and the real children:

> From this moment
> The very firstlings of my heart shall be
> The firstlings of my hand. And even now,
> To crown my thoughts with acts, be it thought and done:
> The castle of Macduff I will surprise;
> Seize upon Fife; give to th'edge o'th'sword
> His wife, his babes, and all unfortunates
> That trace him in his line. No boasting like a fool;
> This deed I'll do, before this purpose cool.
> But no more sights!
>
> (IV.i.146–155)

The hand-firstlings are substitute or faecal babies, like those comprising the crown of hallucinosis, the negative of dream. The murder of the Macduff child on stage in front of its mother parallels Lady Macbeth's phantasy of infanticide, yet on a raised level of news-style realism (French *actualité*), and through this break with classical decorum Shakespeare manages to render the idea still shocking – to show that the murder of thoughts is a real thing, not just a metaphor, and that the poetry of the play has relevance to the audience who exist outside the play.

Macduff's castle-mind is an alienated aspect of Macbeth's castle-mind, fertile with the milk of human kindness and yet vulnerable, exposed to the political hitmen of his own employment. 'I'll do, I'll do and I'll do' is the witches' refrain as they stir the cauldron of mutilated alpha-elements (anal masturbation). All 'sights' are now witch-generated hallucinations, not images of dream or imagination. And dreams are not cleaned-up nightmares but a different genre of mental activity.

Restoring the mind diseased

Can the reversal of alpha-elements ever itself be reversed? Macbeth only begins to understand this when he steps back to observe his wife, or that part of himself that is projected into her, his femininity. He is no longer alone but has the assistance of a 'doctor', albeit one who is nervous about speaking his mind and insists that in these delicate respects the patient must 'minister to himself' – this psychoanalyst has to maintain some care for his own survival.

Macbeth's own 'diseased mind' is mirrored in that of his 'partner in greatness', his wife-mother, as in her hallucinated sleepwalking she obsessively relives the original murder. Unable to dream, her repressed emotions haunt her in the form of poisonous, undigested elements or 'spots', in the same way that Macbeth was confronted by the bloody 'crown' of Banquo's ghost:

> Out, damned spot! . . . Hell is murky. Fie, my Lord, Fie! A soldier, and afeard? – What need we fear who knows it, when none can call our power to accompt? – Yet who would have thought the old man to have had so much blood in him? . . . Here's the smell of the blood still: all the perfumes of Arabia will not sweeten this little hand. . . . To bed, to bed: there's knocking at the gate. Come, come, come, come, give me your hand. What's done cannot be undone. To bed, to bed, to bed.
>
> (V.i.34–65)

Lady Macbeth never appreciated that hell was an internal condition rather than a picture-book catechism; her courage was the spurious type resulting from a lack of imagination. She could not imagine the consequences of inviting mental 'illness' to fill her, replacing milk with gall – the witches' brew. When she chastised Macbeth with 'a little water clears us of this deed . . . wash this filthy water from your hand', she had no conception of the literalness with which lies as murdered truths could poison the mind; the 'old man' full of blood now takes revenge on her 'hand' in the form of another filthy witness. All her false assumptions and points of thoughtlessness recoil upon her in the form of the 'damned spots' – murdered feelings which she hoped to expel or evacuate but cannot mentally metabolise. Her simplistic belief in 'power' crumbled when she lost her hold over her husband and she saw 'madness' coming upon her, its severity equivalent to her own loss of omnipotence. Yet in her total isolation she nevertheless shows a greater need for communication than hitherto: the 'little hand' seems part of her body not merely a machine for holding a knife;

68 Explorations in minus K: *Macbeth* and *Othello*

'give me your hand' echoes Duncan's words to her when he originally entered her castle; and her invitation 'to bed' suggests following the summons of the 'knocking at the gate' to a final place of rest.

Macbeth understands full well that ministry of a 'divine' or religious character would be required to 'minister to a mind diseas'd', and that this could not be applied like a drug or a dose of witches' spirit. He watches her progress intently, recognising the symptoms of his own diseased inner world. Her sleepwalking images the 'walking shadow' of his inner state of non-existence, the antithesis of the actor-shadow as conveyor of meaning in plays like *A Midsummer Night's Dream*. At last he is learning to observe the shadows on the wall of his mind and to dream meaningfully. Shakespeare gives him an inspired speech at last, a recognition of the meaning of meaninglessness:

> Tomorrow, and tomorrow, and tomorrow
> Creeps in this petty pace from day to day,
> To the last syllable of recorded time;
> And all our yesterdays have lighted fools
> The way to dusty death. Out, out, brief candle!
> Life's but a walking shadow; a poor player,
> That struts and frets his hour upon the stage,
> And then is heard no more: it is a tale
> Told by an idiot, full of sound and fury,
> Signifying nothing.
>
> (V.v.19–28)

His life is a play which means nothing, by contrast with other plays and other nothings in Shakespeare – the reverse of Richard's recognition of time or Theseus' recognition of imagination.[8] Macbeth's shadows are empty wordsters, his idiocy sterile foolery; through his story we understand the mental paralysis that lies behind minus K. But at last he has learned there is such a thing as a mind diseased, whereas all Lady Macbeth could see was a body discoloured. She commits suicide, but he fights to the end.

Ultimately there is only one way back for Macbeth: he has to cease being Macbeth and to become Macduff, as indeed he probably was before he went into battle and started unseaming traitors from the nave to the chops. Macduff was never actually trapped inside the claustrum – the castle, or its banqueting hall, or the coronation ceremony at Scone, or indeed his own sitting-room; he has always been a figure who hovers on the edges, never there when 'it' happens, the moment of murderous success. After abandoning his family he committed himself to the enlightened psychiatric hospital of the English court, whose atmosphere is one of cool, pious circumspection and whose methods are those of religious catechism. While Macbeth is hopelessly incapacitated in Scotland, in the grip of the witchlike pressure to be 'more than a man', Macduff is learning to 'feel it as a man' (IV.iii.225) and to face up to his cowardice.

The first premonitions that the condition of Macduff may be returning to the disturbed mind of Scotland take the form of the young servant who brings Macbeth news of the approaching English army. Macbeth rounds on him contemptuously as a 'cream-fac'd loon', 'lily-liver'd' and 'whey-fac'd', using adjectives for whiteness which remind us of his lost 'milk' of human kindness and of the white-haired Duncan. He orders the boy to 'take his face away', disturbed by potential contact with his own child-self cowering within him, unrecognised. Then the 'cry of women' which heralds the announcement of Lady Macbeth's suicide seems to waken him further from his apathy. He had 'almost forgot the taste of fears', but this taste of reality brings a new hope that death may be possible after all, though it had seemed as unlikely as Birnam Wood uprooting itself. For unlike Lady Macbeth's total incomprehension of her symptoms, Macbeth's 'death' is in essence a religious reversal through the person of his alter-ego Macduff, equivocally described as 'not born of woman', that is, born by the knife. The bloody birth is echoed in the bloody death in a sort of purging of the witch-mother of vengeance. Macbeth's spiritual revival is imaged in the way he fights valiantly, for he is the stronger fighter and is winning until Macduff identifies himself in a way which allows Macbeth to be slain by the image or the idea rather than by simple physical force.

Through this switch or 'death', the mind of Macbeth-Macduff emerges from the claustrum in an atmosphere of avenging piety. Truth has in a sense been achieved, but in a negative way, by recognising its opposite and capturing it in the form of a dream-play about the negation of dreaming and the sterile condition in which this leaves the mind. At the same time it has become clear that the patient cannot truly 'minister to himself'. A temporary solution may be achieved by the use of splitting, such that the weak or destructive part of the self relinquishes dominance to a more ethical part of the self. But the indication is that this is unlikely to last: what will happen at the next battle? For at a deeper level, the sick or traumatised mind needs the help of internal objects as 'doctor', something which Shakespeare explores in his late plays.

Othello: honesty versus sincerity

The other play in which Shakespeare explores in a dreamlike way the ultimate limits of the 'minus K' mentality is *Othello*, whereas in *Macbeth* it is associated with a shift from a military mindset to a domestic one – something that is then worked through most sublimely in *Antony and Cleopatra*. Whereas Macbeth's murder of thought through equivocation was a mental disease, the operation of Iago in relation to the mind of Othello is a different portrayal of minus K, in the form of nihilistic cynicism. Iago does not give the impression of being a split-off part of Othello. He embodies a type of mentality that is incapable of any links with another, even in the sense of splitting, yet one to which in certain circumstances a noble or beautiful mind is vulnerable.[9] And as always, the negative mentality is associated with the abuse of language and the perversion

70 Explorations in minus K: *Macbeth* and *Othello*

of poetry. Othello is innocent of such destructiveness, but not in the sense of self-idealisation, rather in the sense of disorientation owing to having entered a brave new world, previously imagined or dreamed but newly realised. On his marriage to Desdemona and the sea journey from Venice to Cyprus, with which the play begins, he finds himself on the verge between pre-conception and conception. This is where Iago steps in – the action that interrupts the passage from impulse to thought.

The nobility of Othello lies in his poetry and poetic qualities, associated with his blackness (ugliness, strangeness, unknowability), as with Caliban later, a metaphor for a primal richness, the fountainhead of poetry itself. He confesses to being 'rude in [his] speech', in contrast to the courtly 'smooth Venetians' or the verbose Iago. The storytelling with which he won Desdemona is sneered at by Iago as 'bragging and fantastical lies' (II.i.222); yet Desdemona was drawn not to the literal picture of Anthropophagi and men with heads below their shoulders but to the 'mind' beneath the superficial rhetoric of his outlandish adventures: 'I saw Othello's visage in his mind' (I.iii.252).[†] Essentially she can read the stories of his inner life, and he responds to this empathy or 'pity' ('I loved her that she did pity them'). His 'blackness' and fascinating alienness within the Venetian context symbolise the poetic veil that demands a dreamlike inner vision to penetrate its mystery.[10] Desdemona, in the earlier part of the play, displays a spirited social poise, able to engage in banter with Iago, and she is direct about her sexual attraction ('those rites for which I love him') just as Othello is direct about his blackness, and therefore not vulnerable to humiliation on that count: 'She had eyes, and chose me' (III.iii.193). His vulnerability instead derives from the inner beauty that derives from a capacity to see beauty beyond himself. This sense of beauty has been in a sense asleep and is newly awoken by Desdemona's courtship of him, resulting in a switch in identity from being a soldier to being a lover, something even stranger than the Anthropophagi.[11]

Othello has two 'lieutenants' in his life: Iago, who has served his purpose in the wars, and Cassio, who has served as go-between in the courtship. To Iago, Othello's infatuation with Desdemona is a temporary aberration of the appetite; to Cassio it is the culmination of Othello's role as saviour of the state, an extension of his heroism as a soldier. Cassio, Othello, and Desdemona are especially receptive to beauty; but none of them are armed against its enemies. Cassio's weakness is expressed through his drinking, Desdemona's through her innocence, and Othello's through his susceptibility to Iago's 'honesty'. William Empson, in his famously clever essay on the wordplay on the word 'honest' in *Othello* (1951), still does not penetrate the psychological condition. This is

---

† Quotations are from *Othello*, ed. M. R. Ridley (1965). London: Methuen.

something which is only picturable in the context of its antithesis, beauty. G. Wilson Knight in 'The Othello Music' wrote:

> [Iago] hates the romance of Othello and the loveliness of Desdemona because he is by nature the enemy of these things. Cassio, he says, 'hath a daily beauty in his life / That makes me ugly.' This is his 'motive' throughout: other suggestions are surface deep only. He is cynicism loathing beauty, refusing to allow its existence. . . . Iago is cynicism incarnate and projected into action.[12]

Iago's recognition of his ugliness by contrast with Cassio's 'daily beauty' is his only sincere statement, the equivalent of Macbeth's 'Tomorrow and tomorrow' speech. Yet the words probably do not belong to him as a character (where they would suggest a moment of insight) but to Shakespeare. The analyst-observer is not some internal feature of Iago as a character but the playwright confirming his diagnosis of the true nature of Iago's state of mind, to make it clear to himself and the audience. Macbeth's death images his change of mind when his good part takes over; Iago's death is an ugly confirmation of his cynicism incarnate.

The puzzle of Iago's 'motiveless malignity' (as Coleridge called it) has always interested readers. For it is certain that he has no motives in the usual sense; plenty of plausible motives are suggested in the play, by himself and others (ambition, rebuff, envy, etc.), but neither he nor we believe in their authenticity. The closest to a motive in the conventional sense of the word is Hazlitt's ennui (describing him as 'a philosopher who stabs men in the dark to prevent *ennui*'), namely boredom: he abhors the vacuum which results from the absence of exciting and violent action; hence his fire-raising and stabbing in the dark.

Much admiration has been expressed for Iago's psychological acuteness, his cleverness in plotting and playing on the Achilles' heel – the weak spots – of his victims.[13] Yet his many opportunistic lies and manipulations merely follow on from his state of mind or being; they are not artefacts in the service of a specific desire or intention. Meltzer writes that in the Kleinian 'hagiography of the internal world' there exists a satanic part of the personality that often presents itself as highly intelligent, but this is not borne out on closer examination:

> Examination of the techniques of the pamphleteer and pornographer, the demagogue and the propagandist, suggests that what looks like high intelligence is in fact a compound of speed and negativism that 'dazzles' the mind and interferes with rational honest thought.[14]

The stated aims of Iago change casually as the plot goes along – first merely to make Othello 'an ass'. He simply takes advantage of Cassio's self-confessed inability to hold his drink; no detective work of psychological penetration is required. His intellect expresses itself in imitative aphorisms and epithets which give the illusion of profundity and integrity: 'I am not what I am' (I.i.65); ''tis in ourselves that we are thus, or thus' (I.iii.319); 'no, let me know, / And knowing what I am, I know what she shall be' (IV.i.72–73). He employs a bullying alternation of 'soft' and 'hard' stabs at his victim, a mixture of suggestion and brutally driving his point home:

> *Iago*: Faith, that he did . . . I know not what he did.
> *Othello*: But what?
> *Othello*: Lie.
> *Othello*: With her?
> *Iago*: With her, on her, what you will.
>
> (IV.i.32–34)

Such is the crude nature of his artistry. Its vulgar imitative quality evokes from the other characters in the play the illusion that Iago personifies some myth of the common man's earthy wisdom, unable from sheer 'honesty' to wrap itself in language more tactful or sensitive. Like many who appear to have dazzling talents, he is simply an opportunist.

The basic assumption of 'honesty' which is the justification for these methods is a delusion left over from the war, where the appearance of comradeship found violent expression that was legitimised by the context. Iago says he has seen the cannon 'like the devil from his very arm puff his own brother, and can he be angry?' Macbeth's underlying phantasy in his battledress is anal masturbation; Iago's is of a type of homosexual intimacy that revels in the excitement of destructiveness, stirred by his fake dream about Cassio seducing him in the night: he 'laid his leg / Over my thigh, and sigh'd, and kiss'd' (III.iii.430–431); it is no accident that it is Cassio's leg that is injured, so he is brought into the final scene in a wheelchair. It is a fantasy in which he assumes Othello must collude:

> *Othello*: Now art thou my lieutenant.
> *Iago*: I am your own for ever.
>
> (III.iii.486–487)

'O thou art wise, 'tis certain', says Othello (IV.i.74). Just as Macbeth seeks 'safety', Othello seeks 'satisfaction' ('You would be satisfied' [III.iii.399]), that is, confirmation of his delusion. Iago's projection of common-sense wisdom is the equivalent of the witches' projection of foreknowledge – both types of false knowledge, anti-thought. Iago teasingly implies that he is full of knowledge but naturally wishes to protect his integrity from any intrusive curiosity – even a slave has the right to hide his thoughts (III.iii.138), leading Othello finally to demand 'By heaven, I'll know thy thought' (166). The hidden 'thought', this pearl of wisdom, is a veritable 'monster' of honesty:

> *Iago*: Honest, my lord?
> *Othello*: Honest? ay, honest.

Iago: My lord, for aught I know.
Othello: What dost thou think?
Iago: Think, my lord?
Othello: Think, my lord? By heaven, he echoes me,
   As if there were some monster in his thought,
   Too hideous to be shown: thou didst mean something . . .
Iago: It were not for your quiet, nor your good
   Nor for my manhood, honesty, or wisdom,
   To let you know my thoughts.
(III.iii.105–158)

The pseudo-thoughts that are the product of 'honesty' are by nature exhibitionist and inciting to action. At the nadir of the play, the word 'honest' falls thick and fast, applied equally to Iago's honesty and Desdemona's dishonesty:

Iago: O wretched fool,
   That livest to make thine honesty a vice! . . .
Othello: Nay, stay, thou shouldst be honest.
Iago: I should be wise, for honesty's a fool,
   And loses that it works for.
Othello: By the world,
   I think my wife be honest, and think she is not,
   I think that thou art just, and think thou art not;
   I'll have some proof . . .
(III.iii.381–392)

Shakespeare distinguishes honesty from sincerity. Desdemona may not tell the literal truth about the handkerchief to Othello ('it is not lost, but what an if it were?'), but her state of mind is sincere. Iago, in contrast, makes various statements which might appear to be true, such as how his 'free and honest' advice is indeed to way for Cassio to 'win the Moor again' (II.iii.328), yet he is fundamentally insincere.

Donald Meltzer's definition of 'sincerity' links it to Wittgenstein's category of 'meaning it', which is in turn integral to the capacity to experience beauty:

> There is a qualitative aspect of sincerity that has to do with richness of emotion. Clinical work strongly suggests that this aspect of the adult character is bound up with the richness of emotion characterizing the internal objects. It can be distinguished from other qualities such as their strength or goodness. It is different from their state of integration. It seems perhaps most coextensive with their beauty, which in turn seems related to capacity for compassion.[15]

74 Explorations in minus K: *Macbeth* and *Othello*

It also, he suggests, has an 'aspirational quality'. In this description of richness, without (necessarily) corresponding strength or integration, we begin to see the possibility of characters such as Othello and Cassio, in touch with and daily governed by an inner ideal of beauty which may not have been tried and tested but which encompasses all their potential for 'meaning it', for being themselves – expressed by Othello as the place 'where I have garnered up my heart, Where either I must live or bear no life' (IV.ii.58–59). Even Cassio's casual treatment of Bianca is a type of boyish self-deprecation that separates his own sexual games from his ideal of Desdemona-and-Othello as combined object; it is very different from Iago's contempt for his wife's sexual desires ('a common thing'). Again the contrasting tales of the sex-lives of Othello's lieutenants are told in parallel, focusing on their each (for different motives) coveting the prize handkerchief which has 'magic in the web' (III.iv.67).

The clouds of superstition

Othello's vulnerability, on his wedding night, is presented in the context of a vestigial superstition that is brought to light in Othello's mind by Iago's honesty. Othello says he is 'not easily jealous', and indeed it is not jealousy in the usual sense but something more primitive, imaged in the 'magic in the web' of the handkerchief. The handkerchief becomes a concrete symbol:[16] that is, not a true container of meaning but a fetish that claims to embody spiritual values but is in effect a form of tyranny over whoever 'believes' in it. It is a pseudo-object whose superficial beauty may be 'copied'. This primitive corner of his mind is the point at which Iago's destructiveness can intrude. It was Othello's 'first gift' to Desdemona, associated with his mother and ancestral magic, like Sycorax later in *The Tempest*. The handkerchief spotted with strawberries is a miniature equivalent of the wedding-sheet spotted with blood, traditionally in many societies exposed to public view as proof of the bride's virginity. It thus marks a private genital pact which gets mixed up with public display. Emilia, Iago, and Cassio all desire the handkerchief for their own ends, though only Iago intends to steal it – both Emilia and Cassio intend to have it copied (as if in admiration of Desdemona), which arouses the jealousy of Bianca.

At the beginning of the play, Othello had been convinced that passion could not shake him, that sensual 'disports' would never 'corrupt and taint my business' (I.iii.271). But his jealousy has never been tested. The 'noble nature, / Whom passion could not shake' (IV.i.261–262) has as yet no idea of the perturbation of love. Desdemona is his 'fair warrior', the only trade he knows. When Othello and Desdemona are reunited on Cyprus (the island of Venus' birth), his words accompanying their embrace are:

> If it were now to die,
> 'Twere now to be most happy, for I fear
> My soul hath her content so absolute . . .
> (II.i.189–191)

This is in effect the poetic expression of the marriage consummation. It is often thought that Othello's vulnerability to Iago's insinuations is owing to a failure to consummate his marriage – mainly since he doesn't seem to have had time.[17] But on the poetic rather than the plot level, it seems to derive from the complications of emotion which are aroused in him by consummation itself and which have no time or space in which to resolve (Desdemona's 'cold chastity' at the end of the play is not virginity). There is no ebb and flow process of getting to know another sexually. The 'double time' in *Othello* is part of the confusion generated by the story: the wildness of the marriage-night is set in the social context of drunkenness and mindless violence in the streets of Cyprus, including Cassio's degradation. The wild uproar enacts the basic assumptions of protomental expectations – the 'rout that made the hideous roar', as Milton put it in *Lycidas*. The translocated soldiers are also driven by the 'messianic basic assumption' of a divine birth which the couple appear to fulfil.

After consummation, however, Othello's speech loses the calmness of 'Keep up your bright swords for the dew will rust them' and becomes full of the sensual imagery of aesthetic conflict – the ambivalence of love and hate in the face of the mystery of the aesthetic object: 'O thou black weed, why art so lovely fair?' (IV.ii.69).

This is the context in which the handkerchief is lost, and Othello confusedly believes that it is the marriage itself that is lost or tainted, not just a social symbol. It is not Desdemona but Othello himself who loses it. When she tries to soothe him by placing the handkerchief over the pain in his forehead (in his fantasy, his cuckold's horn), he throws it off. This for him is evidence that she has betrayed him for the Venetian boy (like Antony's 'Roman boy') and is now trying to appease him. Already his inner turbulence is seeking the relief of 'oracular proof': it is easier to feel that she is unfaithful than it is to tolerate the emotional tensions aroused by aesthetic experience – the uncertainty of the woman's intentions. So 'my relief must be to loathe her' (III.iii.272). It requires no especial cleverness for Iago to turn him into a fool at this specific moment and in these particular circumstances.

Thus Othello, disoriented by his inability to think through this aesthetic conflict, is prey to the substitute thinking of Iago owing to his investment in the 'oracular proof' of the handkerchief with its role as a pseudo-symbol for honesty or honour (a word with the same root and more or less interchangeable in the play). It concretely represents the female genital whose 'essence is not seen':

> *Iago*: But if I give my wife a handkerchief –
> *Othello*: What then?
> *Iago*: Why then 'tis hers, my lord, and being hers,
>   She may, I think, bestow't on any man.
> *Othello*: She is protectress of her honour too,
>   May she give that?
> *Iago*: Her honour is an essence that's not seen,

76 Explorations in minus K: *Macbeth* and *Othello*

> They have it very oft that have it not:
> But for the handkerchief –
>
> (IV.i.10–18)

After Othello's complete disintegration into unconsciousness, Iago presses home the idea of seeing the unseeable:

> *Othello*: O Iago!
> *Iago*: And did you see the handkerchief?
> *Othello*: Was that mine?
> *Iago*: Yours, by this hand.
>
> (V.i.168–171)

The oracular proof of the pseudo-symbol is sealed by the pseudo-genital of his hand, with a similar concreteness to the idea of the murdering hand in *Macbeth*. It is the opposite of a dream. It is this concreteness that leads Othello ultimately to look down for the cloven hoof of this 'demi-devil' (V.ii.302), recognising at last that 'that's a fable'. Just as 'magic in the web' is a fable and never contained the mystery of womanhood – it was just a handkerchief. 'O fool, fool, fool!' It was his own hand that threw away the pearl, just as he loaded false significance onto the handkerchief in order to unconsciously throw it off his cuckold's horn:

> Then must you speak
> Of one that lov'd not wisely, but too well:
> Of one not easily jealous, but being wrought,
> Perplex'd in the extreme; of one whose hand,
> Like the base Indian, threw a pearl away,
> Richer than all his tribe: of one whose subdued eyes,
> Albeit unused to the melting mood,
> Drops tears as fast as the Arabian trees
> Their medicinal gum . . .
>
> (V.ii.344–352)

Only when honesty is jettisoned, along with its false artistry and tissue of lies, can Othello's 'subdued eyes' recover their medicinal truth – and their poetic language.

Notes

1 W. R. Bion, *A Memoir of the Future* (1994), p. 418.
2 W. R. Bion, *Attention and Interpretation* (1970), pp. 127–128.
3 A. C. Bradley, *Shakespearean Tragedy* (1905), p. 358.
4 L. C. Knights, 'How Many Children Had Lady Macbeth?' (1979), pp. 270–288.
5 Marjorie Garber (1974) points out that after *Macbeth* Shakespeare has no more ghosts. It is as though the ghost-theme has worked itself through to the hallucinatory end of the dream spectrum and exposed its delusions.

Explorations in minus K: *Macbeth* and *Othello*   77

6 Meltzer, *The Claustrum* ([1992] 2018), pp. 103 and 115.
7 The term 'stool' had the same faecal connotations in Shakespeare's day as in our own (OED).
8 David Willbern (1980) describes Macbeth's speech as the 'reciprocal negative' to Theseus'. The candle, says Garber, 'reverses Banquo's "husbandry in heaven"'. The play is based on a negative grid (to borrow Bion's formulation): the lie as a truth-covering.
9 Othello is often denigrated for the folly of which he accuses himself at the end, but this is to misunderstand the essential beauty of his nature – a difficult notion for the sophisticated modern mind to tolerate, but understood by Coleridge and Bradley. Bloom too sees him as 'a tower among men' (1999, p. 447).
10 Philippa Berry (1999) writes of the origins of creative blackness as distinct from the traditional Western association of blackness with evil; Desdemona too is 'thou black weed', and in arriving on Cyprus like Venus from the sea there are hints of the dark Venus Libitina and love's emergence from chaos.
11 Evelyn Gajowski (1992) stresses Othello's vulnerability in heterosexual relations by contrast with his life as a soldier but sees his 'generosity as limited' and in a sense small-minded. I think his confusion ('perplexity' as he calls it) is the passionate and great-hearted one associated with Shakespeare's portrayal of aesthetic conflict – the 'black weed' in the 'lovely fair'.
12 G. Wilson Knight, 'The Othello Music', in *The Wheel of Fire* ([1930] 1989), p. 129.
13 Harold Bloom, for example, considers Othello 'a great soul hopelessly outclassed in intellect and drive by Iago' (p. 438).
14 Meltzer, *Studies in Extended Metapsychology* ([1986] 2018), p. 113.
15 Meltzer, *Sincerity: Collected Papers of Donald Meltzer* (1994), p. 205.
16 In Hanna Segal's sense of 'symbolic equation' (1957), really something which blocks out true symbol-formation (Bion's 'alpha-function') which is an abstracting, analogising process.
17 See for example Bloom (1999), Folkerth (2002).

Chapter 6

The turbulence of aesthetic conflict: *King Lear**

In the two 'tragedies of synthesis' considered in this chapter and the next, Shakespeare goes to the heart of 'aesthetic conflict' (Meltzer): the turbulent tension between the contrary emotions of love and hate that drives the personality onwards towards knowledge of the object (LHK in Bion's formulation). Illustrating the classical meaning of tragedy as a 'serious play', the protagonists work towards metaphorical 'deaths' which have the significance of transcending one state of existence and entering another – Bion's 'catastrophic change' or 'death to the existing state of mind'. Hence the cosmic scale and imagery, the sense of a world undergoing elemental transition, and the realignment of all the characters around the protagonists as features or directions of their mentality in its volcanic restructuring. The emotional process is one of 'suffering' in Bion's sense of tolerating turbulence as distinct from simple pain: not only the turbulence of a spectrum of emotions ranging between love and hate but also the disorientation of oscillating between paranoid and depressive value systems, which he formulates as Ps↔D with a double arrow. On a microscopic level, the developing mind never progresses in a straight line but is always assailed by distrust and anxiety regarding the meaning of any new idea that tries to enter its existing confines.

The same emotional turbulence that is being explored by the poet is experienced by readers and audience at one remove, often resulting in very contradictory interpretations of the plays. Even now people continue to ask, are they about achievement or disaster, progression or regression?[1]

Throughout his career Shakespeare has been assailed by the devil Wordplay, his own mastery of words. Early on in *Love's Labour's Lost*, the only way he could deal with it was to bring in the accidental and arbitrary fact of 'death' as an abstract notion to try to inject some seriousness into Love's Academy: Jack

---

* A version of this chapter was published as 'The True Voice of Feeling: Lear's Pilgrimage' in *Psychodynamic Practice* (2011), 17 (2), 141–158. Quotations are from *King Lear*, ed. K. Muir (1963). London: Methuen.

does not get Jill after all. The play had to be brought to an end somehow, but death has nothing to do with the language games that have entertained us up to that point, and there is no organic integration in terms of the marriage of contrary emotions and from there, the development of thought. Shakespeare knew very well that the alternative was to pursue the language of dreams with its mysterious subterranean thinking processes, but especially in the middle comedies, the spectre of Wordplay kept rearing its ugly head and was only relieved by shadowy melancholic figures such as Shylock and Malvolio, increasingly alienated in themselves even when they had a constructive role in the action: the meaning of their existence remained a mysterious disturbance.

Lear is often considered in the light of tragic mistake and regression rather than a developmental psychic achievement. Shakespeare finds a revolutionary way to escape from the clutches of wordplay. This enables him to enter into the spirit of the preverbal child and presents the whole play as a series of dreams for which the poet serves as mouthpiece. The play can then be experienced as a dream-image of the infant working through the weaning process to a new internalised relationship with its mother.

The map

It has been noted that although there is an absence of literal mothers in the play, the idea of the mother is all-pervasive.[2] The play opens with an almost farcical situation in which the baby Lear makes known his intention to master the emotional conflict of weaning in his own terms: 'let me unburthen'd crawl towards death' (I.i.41). He will abdicate, but will continue to rule the kingdom of his mother. Weaning is the growing point in human mentality at which there is a seismic shift in the relation between the mouth and the world; the infant's use of mouth, tongue, and teeth is diverted from feeding into oral exploration and, in particular, learning to speak.[3] Bion uses learning to walk as an example of alpha-function,[4] and there is a secondary theme in the play of learning to walk. But in the post-Kleinian view, neither speaking nor walking are automatic achievements; they are a feature of object relations. As such they are bound up with the ambivalent emotionality of the aesthetic conflict – simultaneous love and hate of the object spurring the self towards imagining its hidden meaning, the container for knowledge of a new state of being.

The turbulent situation of weaning is one which for some babies and mothers could have been handled with a gentle humour, but there is something about Lear's intensity which makes this impossible: 'Come not between the Dragon and his wrath' (I.i.121). He must be the one who divides and distributes, yet ultimately retains all his previous benefits. The interfering nipple-daughters Goneril and Regan are placated with part of the kingdom so that he can 'rest' in the 'kind nursery' of Cordelia, the feeding or containing breast.[5] Thus he 'maps out' his 'darker purpose' (I.i.36). The charade of dividing up the kingdom is a baby game based on a certain primitive but

80 The turbulence of aesthetic conflict: *Lear*

correct perception of adult politics and use of language. He believes this is the way the adults talk. For the infantile elements of the personality are 'propelled by jealousy, envy and competition for the pleasure which the child believes the parents to enjoy in private and which are denied to him' (Harris, [1975] 2018, p. 280). Goneril and Regan's flattery (split away from Cordelia) becomes associated with self-indulgent sensuality – greed, lies, and lechery. They make words heavy and indigestible ('I love you more than word can wield the matter' [I.i.54]). The language, mannerisms, and 'furred gowns' of the court signify hypocrisy, manipulation, lust, and greed.[6] The search for a language that can symbolise the true needs of the infant, 'unaccommodated man' requires going beyond the ordinary limits of language to find what Wittgenstein (1922) termed 'the unspeakable' – the roots of language in preverbal symbolisation. Such is the map of Lear's kingdom: his first dream of splitting his mother.

The bad mothers equivocate, but it is the truth-telling mother who creates a situation that the baby finds indigestible and unspeakable: there will be 'nothing' left in the breast.[7] Cordelia (previously 'cordial' like the milk) is consequently banished for her 'little-seeming substance' (I.i.198); her 'price is fall'n', and this distinguishes her true husband as France, not Burgundy, who was only interested in her dowry. Saying 'my love's more ponderous than my tongue . . . I cannot heave my heart into my mouth' (I.i.78, 91), she reflects her empathy with the baby's panic when tongue supersedes nipple, but she cannot contain his anxiety in reverie at that point (this feeling only finds expression later through the Fool). The baby 'banishes' this hated aspect of the mother, together with his loyal counsellor Kent, who in disguise, reflects something of the father's supportive role. The mother is helpless in the face of this passionate baby's intensity and stubbornness; responsibility for dealing with aesthetic conflict is left to the cruel sisters, split-off objects for her also.[8] They do not only magnetise bad feelings but also draw attention to Lear's lack of self-knowledge (he 'hath ever but slenderly known himself' [I.i.293]), which they suspect is liable to cause trouble. Hence they plan their campaign in advance: 'Let us hit together' (l. 303). First he is allowed a hundred knights (sucks), then fifty, then twenty-five, then one, then none. When the anticipated storm arises, 'wisdom bids fear' and they simply close the doors, resulting in an explosion of fierce and cruel animal imagery that appertains to them, but most especially expresses Lear's feelings about them.

In the Kleinian view, the infant's sexuality begins with

> the introjection of an appreciative and appreciating object in infancy . . . and identification with the mother as part-object: with the parts of her body which receive and hold the parts of his body, and the quality of understanding of his needs which is expressed in the meeting between the two.
>
> (Harris, [1975] 2018, p. 281)

The turbulence of aesthetic conflict: *Lear*   81

This reciprocity (termed by Bion 'container-contained') is the basis for adult sexuality and for symbol-formation. Infantile values, at whatever phase in life, are governed by the egocentricity of 'the pleasure principle modified by the reality principle – at best, enlightened self-interest . . . and are characteristic of what [Klein] termed the paranoid-schizoid position, where egocentricity and narcissism take precedence over love and gratitude to good objects' (Harris, p. 280). Lear's splitting represents his attempt to control his mother-map and eject her non-pleasurable aspects whilst denying the reality of his situation. His quest, once he sets out, is to discover the adult part within his infant self and its depressive orientation of love and concern for his object.

Poetry of the preverbal

Cordelia has been banished by the baby's ego, yet in a sense she has not left. Just as Kent changes his outward appearance but carries on his old course at Lear's side (helping Lear to 'see better' [I.i.158]), so Cordelia retires 'over the bourne' to France with her husband. In terms of play-action she is away for one night, a space for thought and emotional recuperation. She influences the course of the action even at the times when Lear appears to be most alone; internal communications by symbolic means are carried on quietly and sub-terraneously. The part of himself represented by Kent is the first to receive a message or 'letter' from her in the 'shameful lodging' of the stocks, where he has been put as a result of a fight with Oswald, servant of Goneril and comical caricature of polite speech and mannerisms. Kent, perceiving the man beneath the mask, employs the language of sincerity, and threatens to put Oswald 'in Lipsbury pinfold' (II.ii.8) – clamped between his teeth – in other words, to bite him. Pinned in the stocks himself, like a baby in its cot, actually facilitates contact with Cordelia, for in the darkness he can 'read a letter' from her that sheds light on her 'obscured course' (II.ii.168). The confinement and the separation create space for reverie and aid symbol-formation. Kent is thus the first to find a language for Lear's feelings, shortly to be superseded by the Fool.

The Fool has been 'pining' since Cordelia left. The parting from Cordelia has resulted in the Fool being unusually 'full of songs', stimulating his creativity owing to the need for introjection. He begins to put Lear in touch with his feelings about the absent object, in primitive lalling sounds: 'Can you make no use of nothing, Nuncle?' he asks (I.iv.136), echoing Cordelia's keyword which had originally made Lear explode. When Lear 'made his daughters his mothers', says the Fool, and 'pull'd down his own breeches',

> Then they for sudden joy did weep,
> And I for sorrow sung,
> That such a king should play bo-peep,
> And go the fools among.
> (I.iv.179–185)

82 The turbulence of aesthetic conflict: *Lear*

Pulling down the breeches suggests toileting, often in the play associated with being whipped (humiliated), something that the Kent aspect helps to overcome, demonstrating that it is not deadly.[9] But the Fool also implies that now Lear has acknowledged that his daughters are his mothers, they will appear and disappear at their own will, not at his command – as in the favourite baby game of 'peep-bo'. This makes the baby who believed he was omnipotent into a mere shadow of a king: when Lear asks, in bewilderment, 'Who is it that can tell me who I am?' the Fool answers, 'Lear's shadow' (I.iv.238–239). It is a revision of Richard and Bolingbroke, the shadow being the identity that is being cast off.

The Fool warns him against confusing his heart with his 'toe' – the baby comforting himself excessively or omnipotently by toe- or thumb-sucking, only to wake in 'woe' and start crying when the illusion no longer satisfies:

> The man that makes his toe
> What he his heart should make,
> Shall of a corn cry woe,
> And turn his sleep to wake.
> (II.ii.31–34)

The little toe-penis, like a 'shell'd peascod', has no 'house' for its 'head'; the mouth has no nipple, only a tongue. The element of comedy in these trans-actions adds poignancy to Lear's suffering (as Keats observed); it spices rather than relieves it. The first step in self-knowledge is the expression of his own helplessness, the other side of his omnipotence:

> *Lear.*   I will do such things,
> What they are, yet I know not, but they shall be
> The terrors of the earth.
> (II.iv.281–284)

He is not yet consciously aware that he is a 'poor, infirm, weak and despis'd old man' (as he soon will be), but already it has become symbolised in the tragicomic way that Wilson Knight termed '*Lear's* comedy of the grotesque'. The baby is seen from the adult perspective and the infant's at the same time.

Lear blames the storm at first on the 'unkindness' of his daughters: Goneril is one of these 'parings' peeled from the breast-apple (says the Fool [I.iv.196]), and Regan – Lear implies – is a cruel dark nipple that

> Look'd black upon me; struck me with her tongue
> Most serpent-like, upon the very heart.
> (II.iv.161–162)

They are preventing his access to the 'golden one', as the Fool calls Cordelia (I.iv.170). It is the heroic endeavour to hold in mind the cruel and kind aspects of his mother at the same time that brings on the storm, creating a tension (aesthetic conflict) that he knows will drive him 'mad'.[10] '*Hysterica passio!* down, thy climbing sorrow!' (II.iv.57) indicates his inchoate feeling-introjection of Cordelia's 'heavy heart' that she could not 'heave into her mouth'. Now his own sobs heave his body:

> I have full cause of weeping, [*storm heard*] but this heart
> Shall break into a hundred thousand flaws
> Or ere I'll weep. O Fool! I shall go mad.
> (II.iv.286–288)

Yet it is Lear himself, not his daughters, who actively conjures and invokes the storm:

> Blow, winds, and crack your cheeks! Rage! Blow! . . .
> Singe my white head! And thou, all-shaking thunder,
> Strike flat the thick rotundity o'th' world!
> (III.ii.1–7)

As a universal force of nature, it is a welcome symbolic expression of his feelings; it enables him to recognise the vulnerability of his houseless white head and the uselessness of the 'lendings' that are his egocentric outer coverings, left over from the time when as a newborn baby, he was a king whom everyone obeyed and who could flatten the breast's rotundity – its O-shaped nothingness, the empty container. The cracking of the heavens is a relief, a widening of perspective, and a step toward self-knowledge.

At this point the idea of the baby on the point of catastrophic change bifurcates into the persons of Lear and Gloucester with their parallel, interweaving stories. The two old men are like non-identical twins, their characters complementing one another. Lear (who feels he is a dragon) is driven by the great fire of his wrath, convinced of his righteous royal heritage; Gloucester (who is compared to a fox) vacillates and stumbles, hoping for a cunning political compromise until the very moment when his eyes are put out. He is deeply uncertain of the legitimacy of his feelings and of his own powers of conception, as expressed through his confusion of Edgar and Edmund – the true and bastard sons – and the 'dark place' where they were begotten. The old men represent different types of babies, as in Martha Harris' differentiation:

> Some babies at first only want peace, a return to the womb, and to shake off the disturbances of life. Some do seem to 'know', through their seeking, searching mouth, that there is something to be had from it, that satisfaction has to be looked for, when it isn't there.
> (Harris, [1975] 2011, p. 14)

84 The turbulence of aesthetic conflict: *Lear*

Lear is a 'searcher' (and an active splitter-and-idealiser); Gloucester is nostalgic for the womb (yet uncertain whether it was good or bad). Despite their differing qualities however, in this play the Lear-Gloucester baby is essentially a single entity: the aspect of the personality whose heartfelt goal it is to pass onwards to the next phase of life in which 'ripeness is all'. In this pilgrimage, two roads are open to them: to become like Edmund, or like Edgar.

Edmund is often regarded as an alienated romantic-style hero, owing to his declaration of allegiance to the goddess Nature: 'Though, Nature, art my goddess' (I.ii.1). In fact he is not fuelled by genuine emotion; he lives in a world of status, hierarchy, and masturbatory excitement, rather than of relationships. For him language is a means of manipulation, of himself as well as others. Working himself up through words (drumming on 'base'), he cries excitedly:

> Why brand they us
> With base? with baseness? bastardy? base, base?
> Who in the lusty stealth of nature take
> More composition and fierce quality
> Than doth, within a dull, stale, tired bed,
> Go to th' creating a whole tribe of fops,
> Got 'tween asleep and wake?
>
> (I.ii.9–15)

He constructs a mythical romantic identity under Nature's banner, as a baby who was abandoned for spurious reasons of compliance with respectability. His self-idealisation culminates in masturbatory climax, linking abuse of words with abuse of hands:

> I grow, I prosper;
> Now gods, stand up for bastards!
> (I.ii.21–22)

His envy of 'legitimate Edgar' takes the form of attacking his status via a fake communication – a treacherous letter supposedly written in his hand: 'It is his hand, my Lord; but I hope his heart is not in the contents' (I.ii.69). His letter is the kind of action that is a substitute for communication, an anti-thought (Bion's minus K). It then becomes clear that his real god is the delinquent 'whoremaster man' with his 'divine thrusting on':

> My father compounded with my mother under the dragon's tail, and my nativity was under *Ursa major;* so that it follows I am rough and lecherous. Fut! I should have been that I am had the maidenliest star in the firmament twinkled on my bastardizing.
>
> (I.ii.131–140)

Despite the superficial contempt of witchlike superstition, this passage effectively conveys Edmund's dream of the meaning of his conception: this is his identity – the dragon's-tail penis that Lear later compares to a 'shell'd peascod'. Whereas Edgar, he believes, is guided by creative internal parents – with their fertile 'tribe of fops'. Edmund, by nature, lacks the essential innate preconceptions that Money-Kyrle postulated as necessary to enable a thinking function in the infant: the phantasy of a good breast and of creative internal parents. The other preconception, death, is what will finally exorcise the Edmund mentality.

For Edmund is essentially empty of vitality. He is an aspect of baby Lear – the little dragon – that has become useless to the nascent adult. Although gratified to be the object of Goneril and Regan's possessiveness he cannot reciprocate their lust, and at the end of the play he fades away almost unnoticed. His pathetic illusion 'Yet Edmund was belov'd' (V.iii.239) throws into sharp relief the real capacity to love and be loved that is embodied in the main protagonists. Edmund is merely Edgar's shadow, and his non-existence makes his passionless death a matter of no moment: "Tis past, and so am I' (V.iii.164).

The philosopher

Edgar's acting on the other hand is a dreamlike exploration. 'Edgar I nothing am', he says as he enters into the guise of Mad Tom (II.iii.21). His is the same kind of 'nothing' as Cordelia's: a vehicle waiting for meaning. His simulated madness is a form of poetic expression, distinguishing him from the civilised liars of the court and allying him with the Fool and the 'true voice of feeling' (as Keats put it). He will teach both the old men to 'see feelingly' rather than through projective identification with adult politician figures. It is the Fool, and Lear's own feeling of madness, that lead Lear to the hovel. After embracing the storm and its symbolism, Lear's next step forward is marked by a new solicitude for the Fool – the most babyish part of himself, who has only a 'little tiny wit' (III.ii.74). He enters the depressive position:

> My wits begin to turn.
> Come on, my boy. How dost, my boy? Art cold?
> I am cold myself. Where is this straw, my fellow?
> The art of our necessities is strange . . .
> (III.ii.67–70)

Throughout the play runs the theme of need versus greed; and it is only when Regan forces him to 'Reason not the need' (II.iv.266) that Lear *does* attempt to reason the need: to distinguish what he needs and what he does not. It comes as a 'strange' idea at first that he is not the world-mother's only needy baby; understanding this psychological reality is an art, and key to his successful weaning. The concept of 'shaking the superflux' (III.iv.35) marks a more sophisticated view of the inner world as well as the outer: it marks a widening perspective, a sense of wonder, and a glimpse of the possibility that there may be life beyond possession of the breast, not only for those other babies but also for himself. There is a sense in which 'age is unnecessary' (II.iv.156), and prolonged breastfeeding leads to becoming a 'superfluous and lust-dieted man' allied with the poisonous Goneril-and-Regan nipples who are obsessed with their sexual self-satisfaction.

Lear's encounter with Edgar in the hovel of the unconscious marks the beginning of his learning to think. For as Bion has pointed out, 'we need to tap these communications before they reach conscious thought' (Bion, 1987). The hovel is the place where the new container for knowledge, the one beyond the breast, is taking shape. This dream-sequence is central to the play. 'Lurk, lurk' is how Edgar describes his habitation, which is also associated with Plato's cave, the cave of Merlin the prophet-magician, and with the haunt of many chthonic deities in primitive religions. The Fool is urged by Lear to enter the hovel to shelter from the storm, but runs out again instantly, terrified of the strange 'spirit' he has glimpsed inside. As with all new ideas, the new spirit appears monstrous to the existing personality. Edgar is destined to supersede the Fool as Lear's personal 'philosopher' (III.iv.158), and Lear decides to stick close to this 'learned Theban' or 'good Athenian' while together the little group 'anatomise' the cruel aspects of the weaning mother in a rational manner.

Inside the hovel-mind a court hearing is conducted. 'What is the cause of thunder?' (faeces), Lear had asked Edgar (III.iv.159). Now Edgar, elevated from naked beggar to 'robed man of justice', says, 'Let us deal justly' (III.vi.37). The baby's fears and guilt about soiled nappies, wetness, and soreness are likewise anatomised. Edgar understands what it is like to be an 'angler in the Lake of Darkness', attacked by fiends with 'red burning spits', 'back biting' the bottom ('the foul fiend bites my back' [III.vi.7, 17]). His refrain is 'Tom's a-cold'. The part of Goneril, in their little play-within-a-play, is represented by a 'joint-stool' and associated with forked fiends and faeces (stools; also with gonorrhoea).

Edgar puts destructiveness in proportion: he speaks to the adult aspect of Lear, the shepherd of his internal sheep:

> And for one blast of thy minikin mouth
> Thy sheep shall take no harm.
> (III.vi.43–45)

Lear's 'minikin mouth' (and anus) with their 'blasts' are not as big and destructive as he fears. His attacking devils then modulate into more familiar or recognisable 'little dogs' with household names:

> *Lear.* The little dogs and all,
> Tray, Blanch and Sweetheart, see, they bark at me.
> *Edgar.* Tom will throw his head at them. Avaunt, you curs!
> (III.vi.62–65)

The fiendish quality of the cruel biting black nipple (Goneril) is transmuted into a more plaintive, almost nostalgic relation with three 'little dogs' (daughters) who were once his friends – 'Sweetheart' being a synonym for 'Cordelia'. Tom/Edgar dispels the terror by means of a humorous interpretation: 'For, with throwing thus my head, / Dogs leap'd the hatch, and all are fled' (l. 73). The unpleasant feelings have all gone away. Lear, quieter now that his inchoate feelings have been given symbolic expression by his 'philosopher', adopts the voice of his internal mother to hush his baby-self to sleep:

> *Lear*: Make no noise, make no noise; draw the curtains; so, so. We'll go to supper in the morning.
> *Fool*: And I'll go to bed at noon.
>
> (ll. 85–87)

These are the Fool's last words; after this, his role as nascent poet who can speak the truth of feeling is taken over fully by Edgar. The dream inside the hovel constitutes a type of handover period.

A new way of seeing

While Lear is sleeping soundly, Edgar tackles the vacillating qualities embodied in Gloucester, Lear's fellow pilgrim. In the next dream-sequence, Gloucester is tortured by Regan in his own house for having directed Lear towards Dover (Cordelia-land). He tries to evade this admission of fellow-feeling – seen as treachery – and stay on both sides of the fence (here Regan, herself a 'fox', accuses him of being a 'cunning fox'). But he has his own need for knowledge: he has to know what eye-nipples are really for, and what is true seeing. Infantile cunning cannot help him here, any more than the map-game could help Lear at the beginning. So he finally commits himself to the pain of knowledge: 'I am tied to th' stake, and must stay the course' (III.vii.53). He says he hates the idea of the cruel nipple-nails plucking out Lear's 'poor old eyes', so Regan plucks the nipple from his own mouth: 'Out, vile jelly!' It is a cruel but logical response, showing she understands what he is most afraid of, and therefore what he needs to overcome – his defective internal support (courage). The 'stones' of eyes and 'bleeding rings' of sockets (V.iii.189) suggest the teeth and bleeding gums of teething, so often associated with weaning, and the baby's guilt at the new capacity for fiendlike 'biting', projected back via the nipple being withdrawn.[11]

Gloucester recognises now that he 'stumbled when [he] saw' (IV.i.19), and is eager to learn a new way of seeing: a new symbolic mode based on touch, smell, and hearing, to be known as 'seeing feelingly'. As Auden (1962) pointed out, the ear (music's organ) cannot be shut voluntarily, which makes it more open to the abstracting processes of true symbol-formation and less prone to concrete representationalism, whose forms the omnipotent ego can more easily

88 The turbulence of aesthetic conflict: *Lear*

manipulate.[12] Thrown out of the house to 'smell his way to Dover' (as Regan put it [III.vii.92]), he finds Edgar on the path, just as Lear found Edgar in the hovel. Unconsciously, Gloucester recognises his son, demonstrating he now has a good sense of psychic smell. Standing next to him, he says:

> Might I but live to see thee in my touch,
> I'd say I had eyes again.
>
> (IV.i.23–24)

He is, in effect, gaining renewed eyes, in the same way that Lear learned about the facts of feeling, from his Fool and from becoming naked 'unaccommodated man'. Gloucester's new identity is glimpsed in his dreamlike memory of the meeting with Tom in the storm:

> I' th' last night's storm I such a fellow saw,
> Which made me think a man a worm. My son
> Came then into my mind; and yet my mind
> Was then scarce friends with him.
>
> (ll. 32–35)

Even then, at a deep (mythological) level of consciousness, he knew that Tom was Edgar; but only now can he symbolise it in a dream, a feature of the emotional storm. His son has 'come into his mind', a 'worm', like an embryo implanted in the womb; and this worm-like creature – a new 'friend' – will replace the 'vile jelly' of his previous eyesight.

We remember that during the storm, when Gloucester came over the heath looking for Lear and carrying a torch, the Fool described him as a 'walking fire', the kind of little fire that flickered in 'an old lecher's heart' (III. iv.115). His inner fire is still wavering, by contrast with Lear's sense of mission – 'Childe Rowland' going to the 'dark tower' (III.iv.172). Where Lear is a learner, Gloucester is a lecher: the Lear aspect of the baby is tempted to seek refuge in Oedipal control, the Gloucester aspect in sensuous indulgence. The solution to his weakness, Gloucester believes, is to seek punishment by a severe superego. He wants to go to Dover not to find Cordelia, but to find a formidable cliff with 'high and bending head' where he can throw himself down and put an end to his struggle. Edgar, intuiting his need, agrees to lead him to the cliff; however as they climb this purgatorial mountain together, his true intentions are revealed by a change in his language. Where previously he had used the language of 'madness' or childhood, using folksongs and riddles like the Fool, he now uses adult speech. Gloucester notices and says Edgar appears 'better spoken'. He moves from a primitive poetry to a sophisticated one: he is not just climbing uphill; he is growing up. From this new height, Edgar paints a haunting picture for him of the way he felt when a newborn infant, in terms of the huge distance from the clifftop down to the beach:

> How fearful
> And dizzy 'tis to cast one's eyes so low!
>
> (IV.vi.11–12)

The picture is of an infant dizzied by the unimaginable heights, yet not entirely trusting, fearful of being dropped, through cruelty or carelessness. Edgar ends by reminding Gloucester of his 'deficient sight' – the vision that misleads if it lacks the guidance of his internal object:

> I'll look no more
> Lest my brain turn, and the deficient sight
> Topple down headlong.
>
> (ll. 22–24)

Gloucester's 'bad thoughts', which cause his fears and dizziness, are symbolised and therefore become known and lose their destructive power. His internal witch-mother is caricatured as a demon on the clifftop, a Medusa-like figure with eyes like full moons, and 'horns whelk'd and wav'd like the enridged sea' (IV.vi.71). Gloucester is now sufficiently strengthened to 'bear affliction' until his time has really come – the time when 'ripeness is all' – for he is not yet quite 'ripe'. This moment comes when he recognises his son fully and consciously, and his heart 'bursts smilingly' at the acme of the aesthetic conflict: joy and pain together.

Weaning and introjection

Before either Gloucester or Lear becomes entirely ripe, they meet on the clifftop and exchange experiences. Lear sagely reminds Gloucester that they are both babies on a 'great stage of fools', and how at the caesura of birth they cried at the 'smell' of their new environment – a pattern for every catastrophic change that the personality must undergo:

> We came crying hither:
> Thou know'st the first time that we smell the air
> We wawl and cry . . .
>
> (IV.vi.180–182)

The picture of Lear running about on the high grasslands above the cliffs, alone for the first time in the play, suggests the tottering of the newly walking infant. Instead of being confined by tight swaddling bands ('stocks') or wet nappies ('lendings'), he is a nature-spirit like a faun or satyr, colourfully decked in flowers, playful 'weeds' in the middle of Cordelia's 'sustaining corn'. It is a picture of colour and fertility (Adelman, 1992 notes the association with Ceres). When Cordelia sends out her soldiers (arms) to catch him, there is another game as he

90 The turbulence of aesthetic conflict: *Lear*

shows now he can run away: 'Come and you get it, you shall get it by running. Sa, sa, sa, sa' (IV.vi.203–204). It is a comedic or romantic re-run of the earlier game of peep-bo, with its tragic aura. The game is called 'coming to Cordelia's eye', evoking 'tears and smiles together'. It contrasts with the furtive, manipulatory glances of Goneril and Regan – their 'strange oeillads and most speaking looks' in relation to Edmund (IV.v.25), a type of false art or false symbolisation based on titillation and seduction. The Lear-Gloucester baby is now in a position to ignore that mind-poisoning phantasy (that his position is to seduce the nipples). Instead, Lear puts his trust in Cordelia as the ultimate source of his good, saying he is prepared to 'drink poison' if she offers it – as in a sense she does, when she offers him one last feed.

In the final sequence, Lear is brought by 'servants' to Cordelia, exhausted from running about. Carried in arms or carrycot, he wakes from his bad dream to discover that his mother is in fact present, at a moment of eye-to-eye recognition: 'You are a spirit I know; where did you die?' (IV.vii.49). She appears a 'soul in bliss', he on a 'wheel of fire'.[13] There are smiles and tears together because the baby is growing up, and the sensuous intimacy of breastfeeding will be over. Cordelia says she too is 'cast down' (depressed), on account of this 'oppressed King'. They go to prison together for the final feed, at which the truth will become apparent.

> Come, let's away to prison;
> We two alone will sing like birds i' th' cage:
> . . .
> [We'll] take upon's the mystery of things,
> As if we were God's spies.
> (V.iii.8–9, 16–17)

Cordelia's husband, France, has withdrawn for the denouement; Cordelia is left with her personal 'army'. The implication is of privacy, not desertion. Lear is a baby who wants to die 'bravely, like a smug bridegroom'. But it would be an illusion to remain forever in the birdcage, singing with his mother (lalling, carried in arms). Lear recognises Cordelia is 'dead as earth', and hammers this knowledge home with his emphatic repetition:

> Thou'lt come no more,
> Never, never, never, never, never!
> (V.iii.307–308)

For Cordelia too is 'hanged', and the deluding eyes went out with Gloucester. The last feed affirms his suspicion of the flat and floppy breast, as he enters 'with Cordelia dead in his arms' – the 'nothing' that she had predicted now matched by his 'never'. It is his internalisation of the spirit of the breast that gives him the strength to bear what Edgar calls 'the weight of this sad time', something that must be 'obeyed'. Lear proudly asserts he killed the soldier who killed her; but his resurgence of physical strength is now a symbol for mental strength. He is infused not with milk but with spirit – the strange-smelling stuff that surrounds the newborn mind and that may or may not be poison. His transforming or 'abstracting' (James, 1967) aesthetic vision is recovered and breaks his heart, through equal measures of joy and sorrow, as with Gloucester. Like the ancient idea of Necessity, weaning is a stage in the history of man that must be 'obeyed'. It is time for Lear to become Edgar, walking and talking in the wide world.

Who is Edgar? On one level he represents the new, grown-up Lear. Also, however, I suggest he is the type of the inspired poet or playwright who recognises his role is to be a mere servant of the action, following the direction indicated by the mental lines of force known as 'characters'. He is 'nurse' to halting protagonists such as Gloucester, coaxing them to 'speak what they feel, not what they ought to say'. He sets them on whatever stage or scene is symbolic of the phantasy life that emanates from their interior and surrounds them (to use a phrase of E. M. Forster) 'like a thundercloud'.[14] Their emotional turbulence becomes visible, stained like a germ in a petri-dish – the 'worm' that 'comes into mind' and spreads apace. This vivid scene-painting on behalf of these needy characters is a burden, done almost against the poet's will: 'I cannot daub it further . . . and yet I must' (IV.i.51–53). He cannot 'take it from report', at second-hand; he has to project himself into this character's emotional experience (Coleridge), feeling it on his own pulses (Keats), painting himself in their colours (like Mad Tom daubed with mud), following their lead with negative capability and patience. Whatever his virtuosity with words, he may not use his talents for self-indulgent purposes, for display or manifesto; that would weaken the structure of the play, just as Edmund's motto 'stand up for bastards' results in the 'stumbling' vision of Gloucester. The playwright, like his protagonists, is engaged in a perpetual struggle between omnipotent control of phantasy and humility towards the muse. Edmund's 'I grow, I prosper' transmutes into Prospero; Lear-Cordelia into Ariel, whose free spirit must be relinquished. Edgar is a playwright who has successfully followed the dream, not the plot, and thereby repaired his relationship with his own muse. The old adage is that poets are born, not made. *King Lear* demonstrates also how poets are made as well as born. *Lear* is about the making of Shakespeare.

Notes

1 James Fisher (2000), considering the role of aesthetic conflict in *Lear*, sees the story as one of retreat or regression, as does Michael Jacobs (2008). However in terms of the poetic structure of the play, both protagonists advance through the emotional turmoil of aesthetic conflict towards self-knowledge; even Gloucester does not retreat despite his vacillation.

2 See for example Lisa Miller (1975), Coppelia Kahn (1986), and Janet Adelman (1992). Miller was the first to write about *Lear* as a weaning story.

3 Martha Harris writes: 'Weaning, for the baby, is the prototype of many situations that the child or adult encounters in later life which involve separation, giving up, changing and developing or branching out in new directions' ([1975] 2018, p. 38).

4 In *Learning from Experience*, Bion writes: 'A child having the emotional experience called learning to walk is able by virtue of alpha-function to store this experience' (1962, p. 8). According to philosophers such as Cassirer and Langer, symbol-making begins in the mythological consciousness expressed in the song, dance, and ritual which articulate the relations between humans and their gods. These social origins have their equivalent in the childhood of the individual, finding their first expression in the somatic experience. Integrating this with Bion's theory of thinking, a similar pattern may be postulated underlying the evolution of each idea.

5 Splitting between good and bad parts of the self, and object, being an essential developmental mechanism for the infant (Klein). For a summary see Meltzer, 'From Pain-and-Fear to Love-and-Pain', in *Sexual States of Mind* (1973): 'The capacity for sacrifice emerges – babies bear separation despite worry' (p. 39).

6 Lear's mother, very split in his eyes, avoiding his rage and passion, has not 'held' his greedy parts until it comes to the crux of weaning.

7 Philippa Berry (1999) points out Cordelia's 'nothing' is healing as well as destructive; David Willbern (1980) includes, in his survey of the idea of the 'O' or nothing, the roundness of head, egg, breast, and eye sockets.

8 See Miller's (1975) analysis of the complexity of the baby's picture of the weaning mother in *Lear*.

9 Klein recognised that 'Every area of [small children's] daily life – eating, sleeping, playing, urinating, defaecating, learning, being bathed, dressed, or treated for physical ills – each was seen to be molested with anxieties of a type seen with adults only in the most severe mental disorders' (Meltzer, 1973, p. 36).

10 Miller (1975) and Adelman (1992) write of the sexual connotations of the storm imagery (though not of how this links with speech).

11 Teething and speaking are also sexual, since the unconscious phantasy of container-contained focuses on the mouth in the oral stage.

12 Wes Folkerth (2002) describes the feminine qualities associated with acoustic perception in Shakespeare's day.

13 To be released from psychic and somatic persecution, resulting from projections, 'The baby depends on the mother's capacity to return to it parts of the self, divested of persecutory qualities, by means of the feeding relation to the breast', which is then internalised (Meltzer, 1973, p. 78).

14 One of the types of emotional representation described by E. M. Forster in *Aspects of the Novel* (1927).

Chapter 7

Love and the evolution of thought:
*Antony and Cleopatra**

Like *Lear*, this is a dream-play that symbolises the unconscious working through of the ambivalent emotions of aesthetic conflict in pursuit of knowledge of the other, and thus of the self – the meaning of 'new heaven and new earth'. Where *King Lear* established the meaning of the mother-baby relationship through its two 'old men' protagonists, *Antony and Cleopatra* tackles the question of what is a marriage of true minds. The play is a dramatisation of falling in love on the basis of identification with an internalised 'combined object' whose demands shake the structure of the personality. At the same time however it is an investigation into the nature of thought and thinking, and its dependence on this internalised object. The word 'thought' appears frequently at key moments, sometimes unobtrusively, but always asking us to consider what it means at that point. Is love antagonistic to thought, as commonly assumed, or does it underpin thinking as an evolutionary process, owing to the internal object relations?

As the play opens, Antony and Cleopatra are on the point of expanding out of their native groups – the predominantly single-sex societies of Rome and Egypt associated with early adolescent mentality. Rome's military might, spanned by its 'triple pillars of the world', interdigitates with Egypt's richness in treasures and natural fertility governed by the overflowing Nile. The action of the play flashes from one side of the world to the other in a multitude of short scenes; battles are fought and dismissed in moments, in characteristic Shakespearean disregard of the classical unities of time, place, and action. The effect of this, together with the exalted world-imagery, is to evoke a sense of cosmic scale, both geographically and in terms of the abundance of powerful energies. Yet on another level, the entire drama takes place within Cleopatra's bedroom: the impact of the poetry ensures that everything that happens in the play sheds some light on the developing sexual relationship between the hero and heroine, in an intense microcosmic way.

---

* An earlier version of this chapter appeared in *The Vale of Soulmaking* (2005). Quotations are from *Antony and Cleopatra*, ed. M. R. Ridley (1965). London: Methuen.

94   The evolution of thought: *Antony and Cleopatra*

There is hate, ugliness, and humiliation in the play, but there are essentially no enemies to love. All the main characters in the play are lovers of some type. Octavius Caesar (the 'scarce-bearded'), seen by Antony and Cleopatra as 'the Roman boy', 'the young man', is no Iago with power to undermine; he is a great admirer of the older-brother figure who 'like a stag' ate 'strange flesh' on the Alps (the strange food of the female sex). He sees himself as Antony's competitor but not yet in the field of the high mountain pastures. The only comic figure who cannot imagine what love is, is Lepidus; but then he can't imagine a crocodile either ('What manner of thing is your crocodile?') – a creature with predatory features both phallic and female (II.vii.41).

In *Antony*, uniquely in Shakespeare, the idea of physical feminine beauty is given a secondary role, in the person of Octavia, in order to focus on the mysterious beauty of internal forces that operate through the protagonists. Cleopatra is never described as conventionally beautiful, either in person or in behaviour, but rather as a force of nature: associated like Othello with an exotic alienness (a 'tawny front', the 'serpent of old Nile') and with ancient divinities like the goddess Isis. Enobarbus' famous speech, 'The barge she sat in', puts into words the image that he sees, but also the image that he intuits in the mind of Antony:

> I will tell you.
> The barge she sat in, like a burnish'd throne
> Burn'd on the water: the poop was beaten gold;
> Purple the sails, and so perfumed that
> The winds were lovesick with them; the oars were silver,
> Which to the tune of flutes kept stroke, and made
> The water which they beat to follow faster,
> As amorous of their strokes. For her own person,
> It beggar'd all description . . .
> Her gentlewomen, like the Nereides,
> So many mermaids, tended her i' the eyes,
> And made their bends adornings.
>
> (II.ii.190–208)

The baroque picture, foreshadowing Milton's 'burnish'd serpent', is not a description of Cleopatra's person but of her sexual attraction in the form of invisible airwaves 'burning', 'beating', 'stroking', and 'adorning'. The purple sail, like a pulsating heart/vagina at the body's core, directs the symphony played by air, waves, oar-strokes, and the 'adorning' (like the religious adoring) feminine bends, all prefiguring the play's final tableau of Cleopatra and her 'mermaids'.

Antony, sitting in the marketplace, does not see the picture, but he feels its emanations in the air's disturbance ('whistling to the air'). It is Shakespeare's version of Helen's invisible beauty in the *Iliad*. Antony, with eyes averted, still believes he is married to Octavia for his 'peace', but Enobarbus, on the basis

The evolution of thought: *Antony and Cleopatra* 95

of his own poetical impression, can state emphatically that it is not possible for Antony to be separate from Cleopatra – they are fitted to one another:

> *Maecenas*: Now Antony must leave her utterly.
> *Enobarbus*: Never; he will not:
> Age cannot wither her, nor custom stale
> Her infinite variety.
>
> (II.ii.233–236)

At this point, therefore, Enobarbus' knowledge is in advance of Antony's. Like Horatio, he is the analytical observer, a 'considerate stone', whose role is to speak the truth even – or especially – when it seems 'I had forgot that truth should be silent' (II.ii.110). He is the first incarnation of the poet, and admires Cleopatra as 'a wonderful piece of work', keeping his emotional distance whilst relaying his impression to Antony. He finds her 'puzzling' (III.vii.10), a significant and unusual term which Shakespeare uses also in Hamlet's 'To be or not to be' soliloquy; it suggests a special type of disorientation aroused by the first sensing of an unknown (new) thought. The ambivalent feeling may find a container or it may, as with Hamlet, be retreated from. The enigmatic object arouses both admiration and distrust – aesthetic conflict. Enobarbus awakens Antony's curiosity just as Horatio alerts Hamlet to the Ghost and his Oedipal suspicions.

There will come a point in this play, as in *Hamlet*, when thought in the limited sense of rationality needs to go 'beyond' philosophy and become dream-thought, generated by love. Like Othello, Antony's nobility is not interfered with by intellectuality, as if Shakespeare – owing to his suspicion of virtuoso wordplay and specious argument – wanted to separate the language of poetry from that of persuasion and debate, just as in *A Midsummer Night's Dream* he separated the workman from the ruler before reuniting Bottom's prose poetry with Theseus' imagination. Othello, like Bottom, was transported out of his element; and Antony too is seen at a vulnerable point of transition in the stages of man as he moves from the soldier's to the lover's sphere, in the sense of committing to one woman – relieved to be rid of Fulvia, regretful to lose Octavia, but he had to choose.[1]

From Enobarbus to Eros

The partnership between Antony and Enobarbus continues through the central body of the play like a bass-and-tenor duet on the lines of thought-and-feeling. It underlies Antony's attempt to digest the thought of Cleopatra, realising that it is not containable by the Roman worldview or mind-space, except in defensive caricature. She seems 'cunning past man's thought', outside the range of the analytical qualities of his Enobarbus-aide. Enobarbus' viewpoint needs expansion. Antony therefore plays out in public a subterranean, intimate

96 The evolution of thought: *Antony and Cleopatra*

dialogue with Cleopatra – a test of her sincerity and of the rationality of his potential commitment, which comes to the proof in the battle scenes.[2]

So long as the worlds of Rome and Egypt follow their own rules and maintain a balance of power, their psychological perspectives are 'commensal', in Bion's term. This state is unsettled by the deepening relationship between Antony and Cleopatra. Antony is the first to move his centre of gravity into the domain of the opposite sex, via a series of tests or trials. Jealous rages and whippings of messengers by both partners alternate with pivotal moments of trust:

> *Cleopatra*:   Not know me yet?
> *Antony*: Cold-hearted toward me?
> *Cleopatra*:   Ah, dear, if I be so,
> From my cold heart let heaven engender hail . . .
> Dissolve my life; the next Caesarion smite
> Till by degrees the memory of my womb,
> Together with my brave Egyptians all,
> By the discandying of this pelleted storm,
> Lie graveless . . .
>
>   (III.xiii.157–167)

After Cleopatra's passionate avowal, Antony declares 'I am satisfied'. From this point, each tiny shift in their relationship reads like a dream episode, changing with lightning speed. Through the series of emotional blows (military defeats) Antony pursues, intuitively and unconsciously, a strategy of testing Cleopatra's love and his own capacity to tolerate the apparent disgrace and humiliation that accompanies the metamorphosis in his image of himself.

In the tempestuous mixing, exchanging, and 'melting' of roles and elements that begins with Antony resigning his generalship to Cleopatra and following her whims – to fight at sea against all military sense – Enobarbus sees only Antony's loss of this military capacity, which he calls his 'brain', his capacity to think. Antony does not try to explain his actions to himself or his friends; he just says 'Well, well, away!' He is fighting a different war, unconsciously but deliberately following a different line of dream-thought, to the point at which he will say to Cleopatra: 'my heart / Makes only wars on thee.'

These emotional blows or battles are really dreams, like the battle in *Lear*. Their purpose is to 'hammer out' his emotional situation (to use Richard's phrase from his soliloquy). The military defeats are enshrouded in misty imagery of home-building – cows, sails (like women's garments), and nesting swallows:

> The breeze upon her, like a cow in June,
> Hoists sails, and flies.
>
>   (III.x.14–15)

It is a situation which, from the soldier's point of view, violates 'experience, manhood, honour'. It is in line with this insidious domesticity that they together send their 'schoolmaster' as ambassador to Caesar when in the past either Antony or Cleopatra, on their own, would have sent 'superfluous kings'. They unconsciously seek a family space, an outrageous notion to the value-systems of either Rome or Egypt.

Going beyond Enobarbus now, Antony pursues his intuitive, non-analytical tactics in his personal 'war' with Cleopatra. Through the seriousness of the first defeat, Cleopatra becomes aware of Antony's seriousness toward her:

> *Cleopatra*: Forgive my fearful sails! I little thought
> You would have follow'd.
> *Antony*:   Egypt, thou knew'st too well,
> My heart was to thy rudder tied by the strings,
> And thou shouldst tow me after.
> (III.xi.55–58)

She 'knew too well', says Antony; but in a sense she had not known before; indeed she had believed that he might use his freedom to get away. Her earlier fantasy with Antony (as with previous Roman lovers) had been one of 'betraying' 'tawny-finn'd fishes' with her 'bended hook':

> and as I draw them up,
> I'll think them every one an Antony,
> And say, 'Ah, ha! y'are caught.'
> (II.v.13–15)

After the defeat, because he has risked his status in order to follow her, the momentum of their relationship subtly changes. Cleopatra begins to take responsibility for her behaviour, reawakens the soldier within Antony, and ultimately follows his courageous example in 'death' (commitment to love), sealed in the simple and haunting repetition of the words 'I am dying, Egypt, dying' (IV.xv.18).[3]

'Authority melts from me', said Antony when he unjustly ordered the whipping of Thidias in his jealous rage. Then the music of the god Hercules plays beneath the stage to signify that Antony's martial god 'now leaves him': and his soldiers feel he has lost his spirit and become unrecognisable. But when he recovers his innate sense of honour, he in fact (as Murray Schwartz writes) displays the same 'steady authority he seems to his Roman soldiers to have abandoned' (1980, p. 30). He takes his inherent qualities with him to the new state of existence, the internal restructuring by the thought of woman which makes him appear 'womanish':

> That which is now a horse, even with a thought
> The rack dislimns, and makes it indistinct
> As water is in water.
> (IV.xiv.9–11)

98 The evolution of thought: *Antony and Cleopatra*

The infiltration of this new female 'thought' melts his 'visible shape' as he appears to others; his known features vaporise like a cloud, 'discandying', reshaping his identity through a change of state.

This transformation of thought is embodied most movingly in Enobarbus himself. In one sense the seasoned soldier deserts to the enemy, but in another he simply migrates into another body – that of Eros, the young squire whose very name means love. Antony's 'bounty' becomes internalised when Enobarbus' treasure chest is sent after him, in a kind of dream that turns into a full-blown thought and strikes him dead with its light of understanding:

> This blows my heart:
> If swift thought break it not, a swifter mean
> Shall outstrike thought, but thought will do't, I feel.
> (IV.vi.34–36)

An early taunt of Cleopatra's, on Antony's leaving the room, had been: 'A Roman thought hath struck him' (I.ii.80). That idea of thought-as-command is here reversed, by a Roman. Thought kills by revelation, not by dictate. Cleopatra respects Enobarbus and could always converse with him, and interestingly at that very point she calls 'Enobarbus!'

Now that Enobarbus has become Eros, Antony's aide in the war of love, Cleopatra reciprocates this mingling of roles and begins to enter into the spirit of Rome as a helpmate rather than subverting Antony's efforts. She becomes his internal soldier, buckled within his breastplate rather than flying loosely after her sails, restoring his masculinity from within. Introjecting her faith in him, he goes to war 'a workman', giving her 'a soldier's kiss', for the first time uniting his own qualities as soldier and lover, and is rewarded with the day's victory, the heart beneath the harness:

> O thou day o' the world,
> Chain mine arm'd neck, leap thou, attire and all,
> Through proof of harness to my heart, and there
> Ride on the pants triumphing!
> . . . My nightingale,
> We have beat them to their beds.
> (IV.viii.13–19)

The plain soldier Scarus (he of the scars), who had once called her a 'ribaudred nag', is honoured by her on that day of victory with a suit of king's armour. She is the 'great fairy' (according to Antony) who will dress his wounds.

Far from being effeminate, as he confusedly appeared to others and himself, Antony proves he is still the best fighter and he too has earned his scars, although a more intense and decisive internal battle is yet to come. In his final aesthetic conflict which explodes with renewed suspicions of the treacherous 'foul Egyptian', the tension between love and hate resolves into the recognition that whatever the truth about her allegiance, he can no longer hold off 'the battery from my heart'. He is on the verge of commitment to love; then comes the dream of Cleopatra's supposed death (meaning, his belief that she is prepared to commit to him), upon which he enters the state of becoming a 'bridegroom in death':

> Unarm, Eros, the long day's task is done,
> And we must sleep. . . .
> Eros! – I come, my queen: – Eros! – Stay for me,
> Where souls do couch on flowers, we'll hand in hand,
> And with our sprightly port make the ghosts gaze.
>
> (IV.xiv.35–52)

In this movement the presence of Eros, the spirit of love, merges into that of Cleopatra, as indicated by the interweaving of his calls to each of them. The aesthetic object is internalised.

Cleopatra's dream-play: internal object evolution

Antony has introjected the Egyptian spirit of Cleopatra and died into his new identity; this was his dream, and it was based on a mutual testing of reality as they both evolve in the direction of commitment to love. Cleopatra's 'dream' or analytic introjection of Antony is an even more complex thought process that comprises the entire last act of the play. It begins with bearing the 'weight' of Antony's dying body as she and her girls lift it into her monument, revising the early 'fishing' metaphor. Her faint, after he dies, is a foreshadow of death ('She's dead too') and symbolises her new responsibility, the introjection of the weight of Antony.

When she awakens from the faint, she has undergone a profound change. Iras calls, 'Royal Egypt: Empress!' But Cleopatra corrects her; now she sees herself as being

> No more but e'en a woman, and commanded
> By such poor passion as the maid that milks,
> And does the meanest chares.
>
> (IV.xv.73–75)

We remember how Octavia rid herself of the unwanted pomp of her situation and returned 'a market-maid to Rome'. Something of Roman Octavia with her previously reviled 'patience' and endurance now enters into Cleopatra. She sheds the tyrannical and hysterical aspects of her regal role and begins to explore a new definition of queenliness. Her new royalty will fulfil itself, not in the mere

100   The evolution of thought: *Antony and Cleopatra*

fact of her death but in its manner. Unlike Portia, she does not impulsively swallow fire as her message to Brutus. Her absorption of masculinity is more complicated than Antony's melting into femininity, and is associated with the place or space into which associations are gathered. Her 'monument' is the female space in which Egyptian energies are concentrated: it is womb, tomb, and was also, in Shakespeare's day, a common term for a poem.[4] It is the 'cave of Nile' in which mysterious procreativity takes place, marked by the 'aspic's slime' like the fig leaves in the farmer's basket, or the place where fish are hooked or heaved in from the river. It contains the long history of the race of Ptolemy and their gods; Cleopatra is descended of 'many royal kings', and like a poem, it will contain the meaning and memory of her death to be transmitted to future generations. Her internal objects, in their ancestral richness and fertility, have expectations of her, and they have now been joined by Antony in his Romanness.

Antony has left the last act to Cleopatra, the conversion of love into thought Her need to *know Antony*, to match up to the quality of his death, becomes in fact her means to knowledge of herself, the new regality. The new, thoughtful Cleopatra asks:

> Then is it sin,
> To rush into the secret house of death,
> Ere death dare come to us?
> > (IV.xv.80–82)

Cleopatra has a duty not just to Antony but to her sex, race, and religion, to enter the house of death poetically, at the moment which will make it meaningful not 'sinful', sinful being connected with 'rushing' – the overflow of powerful feeling, grief, or desire. When she becomes 'fire and air', what will be her image, her reputation; what idea of love does she embody and continue to embody after death? Her progress towards death is the evolution of a thinking process and comes to symbolise the knowledge that is contained within the Shakespeare play itself.[5]

First the idea of the false play has to be exorcised; this is the idea pictured by the Roman triumphal procession:

> The quick comedians
> Extemporally will stage us, and present
> Our Alexandrian revels: Antony
> Shall be brought drunken forth, and I shall see
> Some squeaking Cleopatra boy my greatness
> I' the posture of a whore.
> > (V.ii.215–220)

This is sometimes taken as proof of Cleopatra's egocentricity and fear of disgrace. Actually it is the desecration of art that is being guarded against. Her

The evolution of thought: Antony and Cleopatra 101

'greatness' is that of the artist aware of the responsibility to 'play' truthfully. In this, her enemy is Octavius Caesar, the patron of gladiatorial showbiz, the 'universal landlord' (III.xiii.72). He appears to hold all the cards, finances, and promotion; he has messengers and managers to fly back and forth; his legionaries guard the stage door. ''tis paltry to be Caesar', says Cleopatra; she knows that for the sake of 'a better life' for everyone, he needs educating; it is not enough for her just to exit the stage in a flourish, as she would have done a short time before.

In her personal battle with Caesar, she follows not Antony's advice but Antony's example. Antony had told Cleopatra to trust 'none but Proculeius' (IV.xv.48); but despite all his knowledge of Rome and Romans, he was mistaken. In the midst of their negotiation, Proculeius' gang of soldiers rush in and seize her from behind ('O Cleopatra – thou art taken, queen!' her women cry out [V.ii.37]). Thus she learns from experience that exchanging courtesies with a smooth-tongued politician is no defence against surreptitious rape. Proculeius' task is to prove Cleopatra is a whore as she is 'named in Rome', which he does by means of physical violence. But as she tests them out as individuals, Cleopatra discovers one Roman who is capable of imagining otherwise, and she transfixes him with her dream. 'I dreamt there was an Emperor Antony', she says to Dolabella:

> His face was as the heavens, and therein stuck
> A sun and moon, which kept their course, and lighted
> The little O, the earth . . .
>
>   For his bounty,
> There was no winter in't: an autumn 'twas
> That grew the more by reaping: his delights
> Were dolphin-like, they show'd his back above
> The element they lived in . . .
> Think you there was, or might be such a man
> As this I dreamt of?
>
> *Dolabella*:   Gentle madam, no.
> *Cleopatra*: You lie up to the hearing of the gods.
>   But if there be, or ever were one such,
>   It's past the size of dreaming: nature wants stuff
>   To vie strange forms with fancy . . .
>   (V.ii.79–98)

Structurally in the play, this is the equivalent of Theseus' speech on the imagination with its unconscious foundation in Bottom's Dream. It is a dream of internal reality, 'past the size of dreaming' in the sense of fancy.[6] The sun and moon represent the internal combined object that guides the 'little O' of her own mind. Contact with truth or reality is a complex process of object relations and identification; Cleopatra needs not only the dream itself, but a fitting recipient, to fulfil her destiny. It is the truth of the dream versus the lie of the triumph. Only when she accuses Dolabella of lying does he in fact tell the truth – that Caesar plans to lead her in triumph. This is because his heart has been struck like that of Enobarbus:

> I do feel,
> By the rebound of yours, a grief that smites
> My very heart at root.
>
> (V.ii.103–105)

He is now a dreamer, able to identify with Cleopatra's passion. He doesn't have to believe in Antony but he does have to believe in Cleopatra and the vision of Antony that she houses in her mind – her 'monument', as it is visualised in the stage play. Dolabella participates in the love story by reflection and becomes Cleopatra's agent, making a truthful link with her and thereby ensuring that Caesar loses the match.

This link between parts of the self that can make contact with a truthful object strengthens Cleopatra's strategy, and she has no difficulty dismissing Caesar's politic protestations (which imply, wouldn't she do better as a whore after all):

> He words me, girls, he words me, that I should not
> Be noble to myself.
>
> (V.ii.190–191)

While Antony's nobility consists in showing that love is a real thought, Cleopatra's consists in evolving a thinking function. She is her own monument. She is a thinker; Caesar is a manipulator, a showman. By returning worthless 'words' to him whilst she makes her preparations (sending Charmian for the asp at that very moment), she exorcises the Roman end which she is about to make from the taint of conquering and submission:

> My resolution's placed, and I have nothing
> Of woman in me: now from head to foot
> I am marble-constant: now the fleeting moon
> No planet is of mine.
>
> (V.ii.237–240)

She selects out the worthwhile aspects of masculine Rome (courage, resolution) and discards the political hypocrisy, together with the fable of female vacillation, whilst retaining its poetic associations: she is both moon and marble.

The evolution of thought: *Antony and Cleopatra* 103

When the point comes at which she can declare: 'Husband, I come', she is ready to marry, which she experiences as shedding her previous identity:

> Husband, I come:
> Now to that name, my courage prove my title!
> I am fire, and air; my other elements
> I give to baser life.
>
> (V.ii.286–289)

She has not been rushed or pushed into this 'secret house of death'; she has thought it through and resolved to revisit Cydnus 'to meet Mark Antony', while her girls complete the wedding preparations. Charmian is given leave to 'play till doomsday', a metaphor which she faithfully pursues:

> Your crown's awry,
> I'll mend it, and then play.
>
> (ll. 317–318)

'It is well done', says Charmian as she falls into Roman arms sighing, 'Ah, soldier!'

The myth of 'great Caesar' is untied by the asp: he is an 'ass, / Unpolicied!' (V.ii.306–307). Policy can be left to Proculeius. And at the end of the play there is a hint that even Octavius may one day become an ordinary soldier, his colonial omnipotence discandied and melted away by the dream of love attained by his older brother, stag-like Antony:

> She looks like sleep,
> As she would catch another Antony
> In her strong toil of grace.
>
> (V.ii.344–346)

There is hope for Octavius because he can see the beauty of the idea: the grace entwined in the serpent of love, symbol of eternity and of 'new heaven, new earth'. Octavius' heart is 'struck' by this 'high event'. Thanks to the infiltration of Roman mentality via Dolabella (the analyst-figure), this pubertal boy is set to potentially grow out of the school of Rome.[7] Caesar the wordster has been outmatched, and indeed he appreciates the 'solemnity' of the fact: he has discovered his internal combined object and noted its strength – the 'strong toil'. In acknowledging that his omnipotence has failed to triumph, he can enter the depressive position. Octavius is the boy who transfers the play over to us as audience, as once Puck offered to take hands. We see the ultimate play-image through his eyes, and this is the way in which we become potential dreamers.

Curiously, feminist interpretations generally believe Cleopatra loses empowerment and Egypt succumbs to the domination of imperial Rome.[8] But this

104 The evolution of thought: *Antony and Cleopatra*

is a play, not history. Cleopatra outgrows her girlish playing at power when she introjects masculinity, and through a mysterious internal linkage she then becomes a thinker. Wars worth fighting are won through education not through conquest – ''tis paltry to be Caesar' – and education is always a mutual link between the self and the inspiring object. Perhaps Cleopatra's New Rome embodied Shakespeare's hope for a more enlightened Britain – and insofar as that developed in subsequent centuries, he was the prime impetus behind it.

The bisexual object

Shakespeare, in his exploration of the sexuality behind falling in love in *Antony and Cleopatra* – female sexuality in particular – has gone far beyond the mutual self-idealisation of *Romeo and Juliet* and now also beyond the cross-dressing tomboys of the comedies, though these represented an initial way of blurring the rigid boundaries between male and female (indeed Antony and Cleopatra engage in cross-dressing at one stage). As playwright he relinquished caesarean control in order to draw on dreamlike identifications with internal objects both male and female: rewriting the 'serpent of old Nile', the crocodile of love foreshadowed in the fairy monsters of *A Midsummer Night's Dream* (Cleopatra herself being a 'great fairy', another Titania). The interaction of characters in a pattern of projection and introjection is the way plays are made, their elements bound into a new 'knot intrinsicate' – Melanie Klein's 'combined object'.[9]

While Cressida was crushed between the heavyweight discourses of the Greeks and Trojans in their self-important clamour, Cleopatra re-plays Cressida and at the same time redeems the idea of the play as a vehicle for truth when she becomes her own monument-poem. Her sexuality finds reciprocation and is able to develop, finally laying to rest Freud's myth about the masochistic nature of female sexuality. Martha Harris writes:

> One may distinguish [adult sexuality] from infantile sexuality, which is essentially concerned with getting pleasure and gratification for the self in omnipotent ways, by bodily manipulation or phantasy. It follows from this that sexual intercourse between grownup people may have the meaning of masturbation, or be contaminated by the masturbatory elements.
>
> If we assume that adult sexuality in both man and woman is based on an identification with two internal parents, we imply that each human is bi-sexual, having both a masculine and a feminine orientation; and this I imagine is generally acknowledged.
>
> (Harris, [1975] 2018, p. 281)

Although Cleopatra and her girls begin in a state of infantile sexuality, dominated by the pleasure-principle under the aegis of extravagant 'royal' parents,

The evolution of thought: *Antony and Cleopatra* 105

they end in the depressive position with a sense of responsibility, derived from a different picture of the internalised combined object, imaged in the serpent at the breast. After the internalised dream of Antony, the monument of the Ptolemies with its new and ancient idea of womanhood becomes a different kind of playhouse.

Shakespeare's mature picture of the interdigitation between male and female seems to be that it is not enough to fall in love at first sight. A complex and apparently, sometimes ugly, process of interdigitation is required in order to establish a real reciprocity, proceeding in steps towards the final leap of faith. Someone has to be the first to commit, and in his view that is the man or masculine part (though not without some rational grounds for the belief that faith will be reciprocated); the second phase, in which the container-contained is formed and sealed, is conducted by the complex female type of commitment, founded essentially on the container as womb or space for ideas/babies to germinate and develop. Shakespeare conducts a remarkable and innovative exploration of adult female sexuality. The dream-play (by contrast with the superficial plotline) demonstrates that love is not antagonistic to thought, as commonly assumed, but provides a fertile space for the type of unconscious and exploratory thinking that strengthens character. Like *Lear*, the play as a whole becomes a symbol of 'catastrophic change' in Bion's developmental sense, despite or because of the political catastrophe in the sense of disaster.

This insight was heralded by Richard in 'My brain I'll prove the female to my soul', but perhaps Shakespeare could not have produced the magnificent analysis of adult sexuality in this play without first investigating infantile sexuality in *Lear*, with its potential either to stultify in self-indulgence like Edmund or to transform into adult sexuality and a new type of kingship in Edgar. It is a conflict which has to be burned through time and again, but the infantile roots are always there, with the reciprocal fitting of bodily parts on which mother-infant communication is based. This is repeated with sexual maturation, though the psychic significance of the act is dependent on the accompanying phantasy. Adult sexuality in the Kleinian sense (with its mother-infant basis) is the model for the thinking process Bion denoted 'container-contained':

> Bion has used Melanie Klein's theory of projective identification to conceptualise this primary relationship to an object, and has employed the conventional symbols for masculine and feminine to represent the relationship between contained and container: that which is projected, and the object that receives the projection.
>
> (Harris, [1975] 2018, p. 281)[10]

Because essentially, thought is an *internalised* sexual activity; and therefore, Bion says, 'first you have to do what bisexual animals do'. In his autobiography Bion asks, regarding dread of sexuality and its consequences ('dreadful sex'): 'Could that gratifying world of sadomasochism ever be invaded by thought?'

(1985, p. 22). Sadomasochism is an evasion of reality: seeking relief in pleasure, pain, and domination. Contact with reality depends on the three basic preconceptions listed by Money-Kyrle (1968): the good breast, the creative internal parents, and death, all three of which need to be activated each time there are intimations of a new thought or thinking process.

Notes

1 G. Wilson Knight (1931) saw the play in terms of 'transcendental humanism', in which the core relationship is progressively cleansed of ugly elements or themes: a 'sport' in which Antony's sensuousness is 'pure as boy's pranks, the tragic agony of Cleopatra cleansed by girlish merriment' (p. 254).
2 Murray Schwartz (1980) observes 'the interpenetration of opposites' whose interplay 'allows for metamorphosis, active transformation of the self' (p. 30).
3 It is sometimes considered that the deaths of Antony and Cleopatra represent the failure of their relationship rather than its triumph (Michael Jacobs, 2018; Janis Krohn, 1986), but this is to disregard the poetic impact of the play.
4 It also has specific associations with the echoing cave-like space of female 'complaint' evolved from the medieval tradition (see several essays in Kerrigan, 1991).
5 Philippa Berry (1999) sees Cleopatra's death as an example of the 'thaumaturgic principle hidden within nature that tempers the tragic conception of death as terminus' (p. 24), surrounded by a host of humanist-religious echoes.
6 Here, Marjorie Garber points out, dream turns into 'a new form of reality which includes and transcends "shadows"'; Cleopatra's dream of Antony is 'a theogony in little' (1974, p. 136).
7 Harold Bloom (1999) says Octavius 'surpasses himself' (p. 574), which is literally accurate: he has in a sense become someone else in response to receiving Cleopatra's successfully conveyed vision. But we do not 'hope against hope there is one more Antony for her to catch' (p. 574); we hope she remains in the Elysian Fields as a model for the next novitiate from the neighbouring girls' school.
8 Julia Walker (1998), for example, sees Cleopatra as a victim of Shakespeare's powerful wordplay, the dramatist by analogy scoring over the audience; Christina Alfar (2003) as an example of Julia Kristeva's 'feminine abject' forced to subscribe to masculine ways of domination. By contrast, Evelyn Gajowski (1992) argues against the 'victimization by patriarchy' viewpoint, which fails to see the complex power of Shakespeare's heroines to give social status to private emotional and family life.
9 Berry (1999) points out that the name of Cordelia, owing to French *cordelier*, suggests the idea of a knot-tier. As with Cleopatra's monument and knot, femininity is associated with both containing space and linkage.
10 The male-female components are analogous in the good breast and the creative internal combined object.

Chapter 8

The organ of consciousness in *Cymbeline*

Cymbeline is the first of Shakespeare's final series of dream-plays and, like all of them, does not respond to being read in a character-analysis mode even where there is vivid characterisation. It is generally seen as a puzzling play because of its undefinable genre (history, tragedy, romance?) and the way it echoes previous plays (*Othello, Lear, Macbeth, Measure for Measure, As You Like It*), but in a more abstract and formalised way that invites allegorical interpretations about the regeneration of the soul or personality.[1] And even the fairytale mode does not help much as, unlike a fairytale, the plot is not only absurd but highly complicated three main plots rather than the usual plot and sub-plot.

As a protagonist, Cymbeline has been termed a 'cipher' (Bloom, 1999); it is impossible to identify or empathise with him; his nothingness seems empty rather than packed with ambiguities. There is certainly no chance of his becoming a hero. Shakespeare seems to be taking the dream-play into uncharted regions, in which the character directions, or plot patterns, may entwine in a 'knot intrinsicate' (in Cleopatra's phrase) around the non-hero in a way beyond his help, desire, or knowledge. Cymbeline is, in characterological terms, a non-hero, an empty vehicle for internal manoeuvres beyond his knowledge or control. If his internal world is still alive and not destroyed by his internal devils, it is not thanks to his own efforts but to his objects. When Cymbeline is seen as a dreamer bound up by his own dream (as does Stockholder, 1987), his emptiness, helplessness, and incapacity become the ground for allowing internal action to play itself out. Where *A Midsummer Night's Dream* concentrated on looking with the mind rather than the eyes, *Cymbeline* is concerned with vision in Freud's sense of an 'organ of consciousness' which can be directed outward or inward – a definition which corresponds to the earlier etymological correspondence between conscience and consciousness.[2] Meltzer writes, in *The Claustrum*:

> I am using the term 'consciousness' entirely in the sense of 'organ for the perception of psychic qualities' (Freud), therefore or 'attention' (Bion) or perception of phenomena (Plato). Fragmentation of the self being, to a greater or lesser degree, a universal attribute of the mental apparatus, the

108 The organ of consciousness in *Cymbeline*

'organ of attention' is highly prized and struggled over by the various parts of the self because of its direct access to motility (Freud), although it by no means holds a monopoly in this regard. The factors at play in this struggle for dominion over motility are a wide and fascinating area of study.

(Meltzer, [1992] 2018, p. 114)

The drama of *Cymbeline* revolves around which part of the personality is in control of this organ – constructive or destructive.

The drugged dream

If the key question in *Lear* is 'Who is it that can tell me who I am?', the key question in *Cymbeline* is 'Who is't can read a woman?' The questions mean much the same. Yet Cymbeline, unlike Lear or Antony, is not suffering from emotional turbulence but from confusion to a degree of mental paralysis. He falls into the category of Money-Kyrle's 'misconception', in which none of the three bases for thinking have found realisation. As he expressly tells us at the end, he has never had a clue about what Hamlet calls 'the difference between is and seems':

> Mine eyes
> Were not in fault for she was beautiful;
> Mine ears that heard her flattery; nor my heart
> That thought her like her seeming. It had been vicious
> To have mistrusted her.
>
> (V.v.63–67)*

It never occurred to him to look for the spirit behind the sensuous. In a kind of emotional lethargy, he allowed himself to be passively poisoned by the drugs his woman concocted in lieu of nourishing food. His infant part failed to confront the aesthetic conflict in relation to his object: the good and bad woman are split and the good one is dead. He then took refuge in belief in his own omnipotent status (his kingship), supposing that doling out exile or death to rebellious subjects would keep his house in order. He has banished all fear of jealousy, ambivalence, and other feelings difficult to tolerate. Where Lear is wrathful and passionate, Cymbeline is complacently bound in his own false security and typifies the state of a 'dull Briton' insufficiently penetrated by Latinate qualities either good or bad; they do at least have some colour.

Worse, he is oblivious to the perverted values in his own house, court, country, mind: a mind which unconsciously allows the loss or extermination of

---

* Quotations are from *Cymbeline*, ed. J. M. Nosworthy (1969). London: Methuen.

The organ of consciousness in *Cymbeline*   109

internal babies in fake scientific experimentation. The Queen is Lady Macbeth revisited, a fairytale witch. She deals in poison rather than in daggers, and in keeping with this, Cymbeline's mind is prey to creeping paralysis. The Queen is his anti-muse, a substitute object, the destroyer of low or mean 'creatures' (by implication foetuses, symbols, thoughts) that are 'not worth the hanging', as expressed in her dialogue with the doctor, Cornelius:

> *Queen*: Now, master doctor, have you brought those drugs?
>   . . . I will try the forces
>   Of these thy compounds on such creatures as
>   We count not worth the hanging (but none human) . . .
> *Cornelius*:   Your highness
>   Shall from this practice but make hard your heart.
>   (I.vi.4–24)

Cymbeline's precarious mental health relies on the presence of a 'master doctor' who disables evildoing by doctoring his own drugs and converting poisons to sleeping potions. But Cymbeline himself is oblivious to either aspect of his inner world, Queen or doctor. His family, his internal objects, are lost to him, not just consciously but unconsciously. His remaining child Imogen (the true muse) and her potential partner, his foster-son Posthumus, are motherless, their families having 'died' in various ways, lost to his active memory.

The image-maker

As a dream-play, the story begins when Cymbeline's locked state of mind is disturbed by news of a 'marriage' between these remaining vital internal objects. The first stirrings occur when he notices that Imogen has moved outside his restricted consciousness, making an internal link beyond his express permission, in the direction of becoming a creative combined object in his mind. She is his inner spark of life not yet extinguished, as proven by her demonstration that she is not his possession and will marry whom she chooses. Imogen, as her name suggests, is an image-maker (imagination) and has the strength to tolerate unknowing (her source name, Innogen, suggests innocence), hence represents his potential creativity which has been sadly depleted.[3] She is repeatedly highlighted for her perception and acuity of vision except at the key moment of seeing Cloten as Posthumus (though again, this has inner significance).

It begins to become apparent that Cymbeline cannot keep Imogen in his mind without Posthumus, who is considered too low in rank to be a suitable partner, so the king tries to superimpose Cloten, the fake prince who is like his mother the Queen in being superficially a 'worthy house' for inner qualities (as even Roman Lucius puts it) yet has a 'clot-poll' instead of a brain. The new awareness of loss, owing to Imogen's movement, is where Cymbeline's own regeneration begins, and that of Britain. The sense of absence begins to

110 The organ of consciousness in *Cymbeline*

awaken him from his psychically moribund state and he unconsciously questions, through a series of dreams (images) the possibility of restoration of a combined object capable of governing a fertile mind rather than a state of submissive dependency on a mother-turned-witch.

Both Posthumus and Imogen have moved outside the control of Cymbeline's anti-creative court-mind, but they have not yet made a marriage of true minds themselves, despite their history of being brought up together. As a couple they do not have the strength or understanding to rescue Cymbeline from his own blindness; for internal objects, also, need to evolve. First there must be turbulence (Bion, 1987). No sooner are Imogen and Posthumus together than they are separated. Although in plot terms this is at Cymbeline's command, in dream or poetic terms the story creates the impression that Posthumus has left for the Italian brothels, whether in actuality or in fantasy; it does not take long for Iachimo (little Iago) to insinuate himself into his mentality. Posthumous becomes tainted by a view of women that has always existed in his mind but never acknowledged, owing to his idealisation of the woman he believes he possesses. At the same time, Imogen strains her own vision to understand what is happening. The 'melting to air' speech has a fierce, almost violent intensity of focus, suggesting needle-vision that can pierce through the cloudiness of fog and air:

> I would have broke mine eye-strings, crack'd them but
> To look upon him till the diminution
> Of space had pointed him sharp as my needle;
> Nay, follow'd him till he had melted from
> The smallness of a gnat to air, and then
> Have turned mine eye and wept.
>
> (I.iv.17–22)

Posthumus has diminished himself; he becomes infiltrated by Iachimo-jealousy in one sense, and Imogen in another, as she 'turns her eye' and in effect invites Iachimo into her bedroom/body/trunk, by now well aware of his character. The organ of consciousness moves from outward to inward facing. Imogen knows what the loss of the bracelet means ('I hope it be not gone to tell my lord / That I kiss aught but he'; that is precisely the message she wants to send Posthumus). In this sense she differs from Desdemona with the loss of her handkerchief: for Desdemona, jealousy is foreign to her consciousness, almost unknowable. For Imogen, however, it is part of her fantasy about sex.

Iachimo is a more successful intruder than Cloten, who attempts to 'assail' Imogen through 'musicians' (fingers), fantasising in a masturbatory way about bodily protuberances: 'If you can penetrate her with your fingering, so; we'll try with tongue too.' Imogen is not penetrated by this level of intrusion, but Iachimo becomes part of her erotic dream-within-a-dream, and her closed eye opens like a flower in the form of the mole on her breast:

> On her left breast
> A mole cinque-spotted, like the crimson drops
> I'th'bottom of a cowslip.
>
> (II.ii.37–39)

(For the association of flowers with eyelids we can compare violets that are 'sweeter than the lids of Juno's eyes' in *Winter's Tale*.) As she dreams, there is a sense that the nipple-like mole is looking out, observing what is looking in. Imogen has specifically asked her maid to leave the taper burning (as if it wasn't usually), a kind of negative invitation to the intruder; the taper 'underpeeps her lids', the closure to sight (also, like the flower, with genital overtones):

> The flame o' the taper
> Bows towards her and would underpeep her lids
> To see th'enclosed lights . . .
>
> (II.ii.19–21)

The bending light, joining the enclosed light of her eyes, images a projective-introjective communication that is also a sexual union. Her eyes are shut in order to see feelingly better what being seen in this intrusive way feels like. She prays in advance for protection, and initially we assume that because Iachimo gets in, her prayer has failed. But perhaps it has not failed, as the psychological significance of bodily entry is multifold, and this dream seems like an adventure for Imogen, almost an investigation into the complexities of the fantasies behind sexual intercourse; for as Milton put it, 'I cannot praise a fugitive and cloister'd virtue'.

We later learn that her lost brother Guiderius (a not-yet-known masculine part) also has a mole, on his neck, that proves his lineage as a prince: 'a sanguine star, a mark of wonder'. The mole seems to indicate guardianship of the breast, as in the infantile combined object of breast-and-nipple described by Meltzer: in part-object terms, breast and nipple form complementary parts of a unit of phantasy in which 'the breast-is-the-world' and the nipple (the male component) in control of entry and quantity. Through the image of the mole, Imogen and Guiderius become linked as siblings in a dream or psychic sense whose validity goes beyond plot implausibilities.

The dream of the cave

As Meredith Skura observed, Cloten is Posthumus' 'alter ego', a parody of a husband, yet 'there is no way for him to find himself as husband until he finds himself as son' (1980, p. 207). Imogen's quest is to discover or reveal the real Posthumus behind the clottish exterior, the notion of dominance and possession that is another component in jealousy, expressed by Cloten with a primitive British brutishness that complements Iachimo's Italian subtlety ('To the court I'll knock her back, foot her home'). In order to do this, she needs to 'become' a man, to see as a man sees – perhaps as an actor or playwright needs to become a character. Pisanio (a type of analyst-figure, or perhaps playwright) warns her she will find it exhausting (and she says herself that 'I see a man's life is a tedious one'): that the journey to Milford to find Posthumus will be tiring, and that she won't manage more than twenty miles a day. But she jumps to it: 'I see into thy end and am almost / A man already', and she rebukes Pisanio for not understanding her passion:

> I see before me, man: nor here, nor here,
> Nor what ensues, but have a fog in them,
> That I cannot look through.
> (III.ii.79–81)

She is prepared to plunge into the 'fog' of unknowing that surrounds her route, clinging to her focus on the vision of Posthumus that she has retained since his leaving like a gnat fading into air. Pisanio also gives her a drug from the wicked Queen the internal understanding of wickedness; her horizons and identifications need to expand. Like an inoculation, the drug will in fact keep her safe, in a roundabout way; it has been detoxified. It enables her to move into the resilient world of the Romans.

She becomes 'cave-keeper' in Belarius' cell and cuts carrots into shapes to please her brothers, as if entering a repressed latency period, wanting to 'change sex to be companion' with the newfound friends of her tomboy identity.[4] The cave, like a kind of boarding-school, is a primitive enclosed substitute home but not a claustrum; all the young people are chafing at freedom. At the same time, she resurrects the role of their dead nurse-mother Euriphile; she is both brother and mother. In the cave section she becomes a more Rosalind-style heroine who finds that dressing in men's clothes does in fact change the nature or understanding of the person inside them: clothes are not merely external trappings but projections which can indicate introjections (though unlike Rosalind, Imogen is never a controller of the action, merely a subject).

In Cloten however, clothes represent in caricature the flesh without the spirit. He ruminates mindlessly and obsessively on Imogen's insult that he is not even the equivalent of Posthumus' 'meanest garment' before he inserts himself into those garments:

> How fit [Posthumus'] garments serve me! . . . why should his mistress not be fit too . . . I mean, the lines of my body are as well drawn as his . . . yet this imperceiverant thing loves him in my despite. What mortality is! Posthumus, thy head which now is growing upon thy shoulders, shall within this hour be off, thy mistress enforced, thy garments cut to pieces before her face . . .
> (IV.i.2–17)

He calls her an 'imperceiverant thing', and when she fails to distinguish between the two lovers (a familiar theme in Shakespeare), despite her sharp vision, we wonder if she is indeed unperceiving. Yet the confusion, or conflation, is less strange when seen as part of her own dream:

> The dream's here still. Even when I wake it is
> Without me, as within me; not imagined, felt.
> A headless man? The garments of Posthumus?
> I know the shape of's leg . . .
> (IV.ii.306–309)

In Imogen's dream Posthumus appears to lack an essential attribute, namely his head: his Cloten side does indeed appear to her a mindless body. Lying together with Cloten's bloody trunk in a tragicomic tableau, 'fitted' to Cloten in the way he suggested, we have a caricature of Titania and Bottom with his ass's head, and at the same time a fantasy of a violent, castrating sexual intercourse, with the penis itself turned to the bloody rag that eventually finds its way round Posthumus' neck in battle, like a lady's favour carried by a knight. It is Guiderius who has cut off the ambiguous head and emphatically twice confirms his responsibility: 'I did it . . . I cut off's head' – a surgical operation to revitalise a degenerate masculinity, sending the soulless head down the creek to the sea. It is also (as Simonds, 1994 points out) an inescapable reference to the fate of Orpheus who lost Eurydice through stupidity. Posthumus can never return as Cloten, nor Euriphile as the Queen; the poison is drawn, the blood let.

The action proceeds in a series of deaths and rebirths. 'What mortality is!' as Cloten put it, uncomprehendingly, before he discovered its meaning somatically. As in a country dance, Imogen changes hands as she supersedes her partners and what they represent; and in a certain sense it is a dance of developmental stages. In order to 'die' and thereby purge her fantasy of sex-as-death, Imogen has taken the Queen's drug, whose nature has changed in passing through the hands of the 'doctors', Cornelius and Pisanio. The Lethean drug is 'melancholy', a mysterious yet characteristic adolescent sickness, diagnosed by the paternal Belarius:

> O Melancholy!
> Who ever yet could sound thy bottom, find
> The ooze, to show what coast thy sluggish crayer
> Might easiest harbour in: Thou blessed thing!
> Jove knows what man thou mightst have made; but I,
> Thou diedst, a most rare boy of melancholy.
> (IV.ii.203–208)

(Lines evoked by Keats later, like other atmospheric or mood elements in the play.) Then the beautiful song 'Fear no more the heat o' th' sun' is spoken by

114 The organ of consciousness in *Cymbeline*

the two brothers, who say that it was originally sung for their mother and now 'Euriphile is Fidele'. Guiderius' forthrightness contrasts with Arviragus' sensitivity to the poetic resonance of words, which Guiderius considers too 'wench-like'. As a compromise, they agree to speak rather than sing: the first stanzas in unison and the others in stichomythia (single alternate lines), complementing one another.

> Fear no more the heat o' th' sun
> Nor the furious winter's rages;
> Thou thy worldly task hast done,
> Home art gone, and ta'en thy wages.
> Golden lads and girls all must
> Like chimney-sweepers come to dust.
>   (IV.ii.257–263)

Structurally the eulogy for Imogen recalls the fairy lullaby of *A Midsummer Night's Dream* ('Never harm nor spell nor charm / Come our lovely lady nigh') that occurs before the central tableau, since it has an implication of protection by the internal deity represented by the maternal legacy of Euriphile ('wide-loving'). In a shadowy way, Euriphile heralds the 'great creating nature' of *The Winter's Tale*, the universal nurse and closer of eyes who in the form of a godlike abstraction oversees the total action. When Imogen-Fidele, the boy-nurse, is carried out 'dead' in Arviragus' arms, there is a hint of the divine world behind the image (including, some critics have suggested, the pietà, as in *Lear*). Knowing mortality in this beautiful, ambiguous way (gold and dust, joy and sorrow together) effectively brings to life the internal family and its values, with the sharpness of aesthetic conflict; it is now Plato's cave of sun and shadow. Later Imogen admits, 'I was dead'. But she is protected from the harm that can follow from the 'melancholist's dream' (as Keats puts it) by association with the many golden boys and girls who have worked in a cave – in a way that she was not protected when we saw her first go to sleep in her palace chamber. She is left uncovered, other than by flowers, ready to reawaken and flower.

However unlike the sleeping beauty, she is at no point awoken by a prince: she is the one who has to fight her way through the brambles, up to the very last moment when Posthumus unknowingly strikes her down, 'killing' her yet again. This capacity to withstand death (catastrophic changes) is earned in relation to both British and Roman qualities that are discovered through masculine identifications. The good British qualities are not those of Cymbeline's court but of the cave, a sphere of natural nobility governed by the ancestral goddess with implications of the ancient roots of civilisation somehow lost or banished by the poisoned court. Imogen has experienced these and got herself adopted into this sphere of values, then feels the need to expand her knowledge further, hence her melancholic sickness. After the transition imaged by her 'death' in the cave, she links up with Roman masculinity when, on awaking, she engages herself to Lucius the Roman general with only the briefest of excuses muttered to herself ('If I do lie and do no harm by it'). Her life-force instinctively precludes being buried alive with the body of Posthumus. The new adventuring Imogen is developing a model of femininity that can supersede that of the wicked Queen.

A counterfeit mother-world

The Queen is already associated with baby-killing in the form of small creatures 'not worth the hanging'; this is then linked with the image of a mother-country or woman's body that is Charybdis-like, not merely well-defended but rocky and aggressive. As Bloom (1999) has suggested, her 'Neptune's park' speech is a parody of the 'little Eden' speech in *Richard II*:

> Remember, sir, my liege,
> The kings your ancestors, together with
> The natural bravery of your isle, which stands
> As Neptune's park, ribbed and paled in
> With rocks unscalable and roaring waters,
> With sands that will not bear your enemies' boats,
> But suck them up to the topmast. A kind of conquest
> Caesar made here; but made not here his brag
> Of 'Came' and 'saw' and 'overcame': with shame –
> That first that ever touch'd him – he was carried
> From off our coast, twice beaten; and his shipping –
> Poor ignorant baubles! – upon our terrible seas,
> Like egg-shells moved upon their surges, crack'd
> As easily 'gainst our rocks: for joy whereof
> The famed Cassibelan, who was once at point –
> O giglot fortune! – to master Caesar's sword,
> Made Lud's town with rejoicing fires bright
> And Britons strut with courage.
>
> (III.i.17–34)

Hidden behind this is Elizabeth I's speech after the defeat of the Armada, yet with an unexpected gloss. The beautiful, idealised mother-country turns out to have a brittle exoskeleton that doubles as a murderous trap. Shakespeare both invents the myth of nationalist self-sufficiency and demolishes it in advance, long before the British Empire came to dominance or its tail-end dissolved into Brexit. In this mindset, the model of femininity is one in which 'eggshell' babies ('poor ignorant baubles') are to be smashed against the body's rocks. London Town will glow with fires and heads on sticks as Britons strut in self-satisfaction (Belarius is afraid his sons' heads will end up like this for killing the king's son). It is in the context of this image of the mother-world as wrecker that Cloten makes the brag about his nose:

> Britain's a world
> By itself and we will nothing pay
> For wearing our own noses.
> (III.i.13–14)

This is, of course, before his nose-penis is cut off along with his head. It makes a caricatural contrast with Bottom being 'led by the nose' silently to Titania's bower wearing his ass's head.

The dream of the Roman invasion

Once the genuinely stupid Cloten has been despatched, what then is the model of manhood (and sex) being developed by the remaining male characters, to match the new Imogen? Iachimo repents; his guilt 'takes off [his] manhood'. Instead of Cloten's language of brutish 'fingering' and 'knocking back' or Iachimo's insinuating 'Italian brain' with its intruding taper, Posthumus now seeks to acquire or refind his Romanness in the internal family which had somehow got lost during his maimed education at Cymbeline's court. He begins by proving himself in the 'magical' battle alongside Belarius and the two boys who guard the 'narrow lane' (entry to the mother-country), thereby rescuing Cymbeline's kingdom, unknown to him as they are. It is a shadow-battle like that in *Lear*. Posthumus invokes the aid of his Latinate, lion-hearted ancestors in casting off his reliance on superficial signs (his exoskeleton):

> Let me make men know
> More valour in me than my habits show.
> Gods, put the strength of the Leonati in me.
> To shame the guise o' the world I will begin
> The fashion, less without and more within.
> (V.i.29–33)

Again the plot absurdity of the victory underlines the dreamlike quality of unconscious phantasy-as-action, and Shakespeare deliberately emphasises this by having a Lord question these unlikely events which appear to have been managed by 'angels'.

Posthumus' search for death is, like Antony's, a metaphor for commitment to love: 'For Imogen's dear life take mine' (V.iv.24). Having failed to find it in the battlefield, he seeks the 'welcome bondage' of a prison where he can 'speak to Imogen in silence' – a silence which is in fact filled by the dialogue between his ancestors (his internal parents or objects under the aegis of Jupiter, in the formal stilted verse of the old playwrights to indicate its separate reality). As

The organ of consciousness in *Cymbeline*   117

Skura puts it: 'Posthumus cannot find his parents in the flesh; he must find the idea of his parents' (1980, p. 212). At various points in the play speech has been equated with lies; so here it is substituted by a dream-language which, however strange or even mad-seeming, is yet like life, just as it is in plays:

> 'Tis still a dream, or else such stuff as madmen
> Tongue, and brain not; either, both, or nothing;
> Or senseless speaking, or a speaking such
> As sense cannot untie. Be what it is,
> The action of my life is like it, which
> I'll keep, if but for sympathy.
>
> (V.iv.146–151)

His sympathetic and admiring jailer wonders at his determined willingness to seek 'hoodwinking', the 'way of blindness'; for Posthumus is learning to see beyond external beauty and misleading oracular proofs. The jailer is the first to understand his attempts at integration (that is, responsibility for his own mistakes and projected bad parts): 'I would we were all of one mind, and that mind good.'

The final long recognition scene, a series of recapitulations and aftershocks, is a tour de force in its creation of the idea of an integrated mind from the disparate coincidences of the parallel plots. Cymbeline's vision is cleansed in stages, imaged first by his unconscious recognition of the boy-aspect of Imogen:

> Boy,
> Thou hast looked thyself into my grace
> And art mine own.
>
> (V.v.93–95)

It is really Cymbeline himself who is acquiring grace through being looked into by Imogen's eyes. Yet the vision of Imogen herself is still clouded in one respect: she rejects Pisanio, the 'dangerous fellow' who 'gave her poison' which we have seen, thus mediated, in fact operated as a type of dream-potion furthering insight; whilst Pisanio observes Posthumus reject Imogen yet again with a blow that echoes, harmlessly, the murder Pisanio did not commit: 'You ne'er killed Imogen till now.' Evil or poison is experienced at one remove, observed by an analytic part of the self. Recognition, as the organ of consciousness penetrates outwards and inwards simultaneously, takes place through a series of minute shocks, even when it is overall a dawning revelation (catastrophic change in the classical sense).

It is significant that Cymbeline himself remains helpless; everything is done for him by 'fairy hands', as Blake would put it. At times he comes out semi-automatically with vestigial threats of death (as when Guiderius is condemned for killing Cloten), but they have no power and fade away, just as the Queen has been fading away in the background, dying not from suicide like Lady Macbeth but from despair because her poisons have not worked; she no longer has a role in Cymbeline's inner world. Her illness began with the Roman invasion (the new masculinity), as if it were she who ingested the somatic ill effects of the potion given Imogen, whilst the knowledge or understanding of evil was separated off.

The return of the Romans – though some (for example, Adelman, 1992) see it as the reimposition of masculine authority at the expense of the feminine – is like the cleansing of the Augean stables, a dream myth figuring the release of the female body from internal damage caused by hostile projections (Meltzer's claustrum). The Queen gets ill at the moment the Roman invasion is made known. She becomes a nonentity, like Cymbeline's clumsy, abortive authority which she literally embodies and which dissolves with her like a clarified chemical solution. The anti-female or false nurture is shed, but at the same time Lucius' conventional Roman expectations require transformation:

> *Lucius*: I do not bid thee beg my life, good lad;
>   And yet I know thou wilt.
> *Imogen*: No, no: alack,
>   There's other work in hand: I see a thing
>   Bitter to me as death: your life, good master,
>   Must shuffle for itself.
> *Lucius*: The boy disdains me,
>   He leaves me, scorns me: briefly die their joys
>   That place them on the truth of girls and boys.
>   Why stands he so perplex'd?
>   (V.v.101–108)

The truth of girls and boys comes to dust and is replaced by another truth, as Imogen sheds her tomboy guise (or state of being) and claims the ring from Iachimo's finger: 'a thing / Bitter to me as death.' Her own vision is clarified; she becomes conscious of the poisoned pseudo-masculinity represented by Iachimo's theft. This introjected knowledge entails a deathlike feeling of internal catastrophic change – the peripeteia of classical tragedy. Even Lucius, after his brief stoical resignation, is instantly taken over by his curiosity, a feeling stronger than anxiety about his own life: tensions between love and hate are resolving in relation to knowledge about the aesthetic object.

Regaining the ring symbolises the moment at which Cymbeline newly recognises his live internal objects, like the rejointed 'lopped branches' of the 'stately cedar' dreamed by Posthumus. Instead of the tableau of faithful boy embracing headless trunk-body, Imogen and Posthumus unite in the form of the revitalised tree governing his inner world:

> Hang there like a fruit, my soul,
> Till the tree die!
>   (V.v.263–264)

The organ of consciousness in *Cymbeline* 119

We know that 'A Roman with a Roman's heart can suffer', and Cymbeline is not exempted from a small amount of distress in the process of mental rebirth, though he seems astonished to be told that he too may feel tortured when his mistakes are exposed to his own view: 'How? Me?' He barely has time to suffer much, since the recognitions (the new internal links) resolve the confusions in a series of flashes as the new knowledge is revealed. 'What am I?' he asks, 'A mother to the birth of three?' At last blind Cymbeline can see, through the lightning eyes of Imogen, his lost muse – a new type of striking:

> See,
> Posthumus anchors upon Imogen,
> And she like harmless lightning throws her eye
> On him, her brothers, me, her master, hitting
> Each object with a joy; the counterchange
> Is severally in all.
>
> (V.v.393–399)

The new friendship between ancient Britain and Rome is such a 'counterchange', just as Imogen and Posthumus have both been Romans as well as Britons. The counterchange is the passion of complex emotions and contradictory aspects of identity conveyed through aesthetic conflict.[5] Her lightning glance, powerful and capable not just of illuminating but of 'hitting', matches the prophecy about the Roman eagle soaring in the skies, and answers Posthumus' throwing her back when she was still Fidele. The kingdom as female body has been rescued from invasion not just by external force but by an introjected masculinity (Romanness) like that of Cleopatra. This enables Cymbeline to offer a willing tribute to the conquered – which to the common-sense eye is absurd, like Bottom's 'reason and love'; but in terms of dream logic it is fitting that 'imperial Caesar' and 'radiant Cymbeline', their male and female features transformed, become willingly – not forcibly – united 'in harmony of this peace'. The formality and artificiality of the deus-ex-machina link with the heavens is modulated by Cymbeline's moving, Keatsian image of the 'crooked smokes', pregnant with the suggestion of primitive contact with a benign world of higher knowledge (for the infant, the mother's face):

> Laud we the gods,
> And let our crooked smokes climb to their nostrils
> From our blest altars.
>
> (V.v.477–479)

They are his first poetic words in the play, spoken at the end. The non-poet has dreamed himself back to life by dint of doing nothing, accepting ignorance, and just waiting for the inner world to rearrange itself.

Notes

1 It can be convincingly read in contexts of early Christianity and Christian regeneration, neoPlatonism, and ancient mythical beliefs (Frye, 1965; Simonds, 1994; MacPhee, 2018; Garber, 1974); as well as about art and playwrighting (Rabkin, 1967; Shapiro, 1996). Cymbeline (Cunobelin) also embodies the semi-mythic origins of the history of England, set in the distant mists of time by contrast with the history plays proper.

2 Freud saw consciousness as a sense organ for the perception of mental processes that can be directed inwards or outwards, frequently cited by Bion from *A Theory of Thinking* (1961) onwards, as well as by Meltzer. Garber describes how the 'psychological dream' based on conscience as consciousness 'increasingly encompasses the entire world of the play' (1974, pp. 89–90).

3 Frye (1965) commented on the 'striking blindness' throughout the play and describes Imogen, framed by the two great songs of awakening and laying to rest, as 'surrounded by a kind of atmospheric pressure of unconsciousness' (p. 68).

4 Meredith Skura (1980) observes the plausible pun on the 'cutting of roots in characters' in the context of the play's search by its characters for their authentic origins (p. 215).

5 Wes Folkerth (2002) investigates a distinction between auditory and visual experience commonly assumed in Shakespeare's day, with audio being more inward directed and associated with femininity. In *Cymbeline* Shakespeare combines qualities to make the visual also inward directed.

Chapter 9

A dream of reparation:
*The Winter's Tale**

In possibly his most beautiful play, Shakespeare recovers the joyful optimism and humour of *A Midsummer Night's Dream* by means of a complex investigation of the turmoil aroused by the 'new baby', creating shockwaves of aesthetic conflict in the mind and its internal family. As has been his approach in most of the plays since *Hamlet* (though not *Lear* or *Antony*) he takes as protagonist an ordinary, unprepossessing character with little to recommend him. He has never had to struggle materially or emotionally; if there is anything of interest it is happening in his dream-world. Leontes of Sicily thinks he's a lion king and demands obedience from his courtiers, but in psychological terms he is a seven-year-old boy who has barely entered the latency period; his sexuality is still dormant and unequipped to face the emotional realities stirred by the new baby with its unknown origins – he can't believe he had anything to do with its engendering. Has it been brought by Polixenes ('many strangers')? The immature young father may identify with the first child (especially son) in a narcissistic, idealising way, 'as like as eggs' as Leontes puts it; they are identical twins, just as he and his alter-ego Polixenes are 'twin lambs frisking in the sun' (I.ii.67).[1] But the arrival of the next child constitutes a blow to the belief that actually he *is* the one and only child: creativity perhaps lies elsewhere, outside his tyrannical control.

In this play 'great creating nature' is the dominant goddess or internal object,[2] and the characters gradually align themselves with the magnetic concept by means of the dream-world of Bohemia, whose cleansed perceptions restore joy and fertility to the wintry narcissism of Sicily.[3]

The new baby

When the play opens, the baby has not actually arrived but its presence is indisputable and creating advance stirrings in the court: much is said about the roundness of the queen's belly, and about the devilishness of whatever has impregnated her.

---

* A shorter version of this chapter appears in *The Chamber of Maiden Thought* (Williams & Waddell, 1992). Quotations are from *The Winter's Tale*, ed. J.H.P. Pafford (1963). London: Methuen.

122 A dream of reparation: *The Winter's Tale*

Hermione jokes that she and Polixenes' queen are 'devils' for destroying the inno-cence of the twinned lambs and bringing temptation into their garden of Eden. Leontes' jealous tyranny will move them all 'to laughter', believes Antigonus, a father of three. The atmosphere of the court is that of an extended family trying to cope with a bad-tempered and anxious child: as Leontes says himself, if he were really a tyrant, 'where were your lives?' Indeed it all seems a joke until it becomes serious, wintry. In psychological terms, the child-tyrant's projections of his own paranoid confusion can have an effect as real as political beheadings.

Leontes' internal disintegration is mirrored in his strangulated language, deriving from his inchoate dreams:[4]

> Can thy dam – may't be?
> Affection! Thy intention stabs the centre:
> Thou dost make possible things not so held,
> Communicat'st with dreams; how can this be? –
> With what's unreal thou coactive art,
> And fellow'st nothing: then 'tis very credent
> Thou may'st co-join with something; and thou dost,
> (And that beyond commission) . . .
>
> > (I.ii.137–144)

He is confused about communication, joining, co-acting, in other words what is sexuality: is it something other than frisking in the sun with his innocent boyfriend? He can't understand how the child came into being, since from his point of view, Mamillius is really himself:

> Looking on the lines
> Of my boy's face, methought I did recoil
> Twenty-three years, and saw myself unbreech'd . . .
> > (I.ii.153–155)

His is not an adult jealousy like Othello's but a child's fear of loss of control of his mother, being ousted by a substitute. The pregnant belly is a container for monsters, its 'gates opened, / As mine, against their will':

> No barricado for a belly. Know't,
> It will let in and out the enemy,
> With bag and baggage . . .
> > (I.ii.204–206)

The woman's body (belly, infiltrated by sex) is the cup of poisoned knowledge in which he sees the spider-baby, a miscreation of his own envy:

> I have drunk, and seen the spider . . .
> And I

A dream of reparation: *The Winter's Tale*   123

Remain a pinch'd thing; yea, a very trick
For them to play at will. How came the posterns
So easily open?

(II.i.45, 50–53)

He suspects he was not party to this creative 'play' ('Thy mother plays') and that he is a 'pinch'd thing' playing a 'disgraced part', his omnipotence punctured. Like Iago, it is the implications for his own ugliness that affect him. Polixenes (like Cassio) has a creative penis, not a pinched spider. So long as he was ignorant of this – his 'knowledge . . . not infected' he could believe in Hermione's 'without-door form' (l. 69), until Polixenes presented this 'abhorred ingredient' 'to his eye'. His idealised relationship, founded on projective identification with the 'real' father, has been threatened with new knowledge: in his unresolved aesthetic conflict, the woman's external beauty contrasts with his suspicions of what is inside. The postern gates of the city are confused with easy entry to the woman.

Hermione tried a policy of appeasement (enacting the flirtation with Polixenes that Leontes demanded), but this exacerbated the situation; as Paulina recognises, what Leontes needs is a firm hand, but his male courtiers are too passive and 'will never do him good'. Paulina as analyst-figure comes the nearest to parental discipline, evoking Leontes' little-boy sulkiness:

Away with that audacious lady! Antigonus,
I charg'd thee that she should not come about me.
I knew she would.

(II.iii.42–44)

The wintry superego

Winter comes when mother and child are separated; it is the link that is destroyed by Leontes' envy, despite his belief that he can separate the two parts of this emotional unit: when they are separated, the child dies. The mother-and-child scene when Mamillius tells his 'winter's tale' is the most realistic in Shakespeare; the child, unlike the king, has a real relationship with Hermione. It begins with Hermione asking her ladies to relieve her: 'Take the boy to you: he so troubles me / 'Tis past enduring'. Hermione's tiredness (repressed in the previous scenes as society hostess) finds a space in this female environment, as does the child's jealousy of the new baby. When the ladies tease Mamillius about transferring their attentions to the new prince, Hermione, after her short break, calls him to her: 'I am for you again: 'pray you, sit by us, / And tell's a tale'. She asks for a merry one but understands when the child says 'A sad tale's best for winter', and he has one ready of 'sprites and goblins'. Mamillius does not have to pretend he is happy when he isn't:

Hermione: Let's have that, good sir.
      Come on, sit down, come on, and do your best
      To fright me with your sprites: you're powerful at it.

Mamillius: There was a man —
Hermione: Nay, come sit down: then on.
Mamillius: Dwelt by a churchyard: I will tell it softly,
    Yond crickets shall not hear it.
Hermione: Come on then,
    And giv't in mine ear.

(II.i.26–32)

The ladies ('crickets') support Hermione in a way that her husband does not, and one imagines, never has. She is then able to gather her resources and pay attention to her child's dark feelings, which focus on the figure of his father – a man dwelling by a churchyard beset by goblins. It is Leontes who is really troubling her, more than Mamillius.

It is at this moment that Leontes enters with his contingent of male courtiers to sweep Hermione off to prison, a highly visual and dramatic violent separation equivalent to the death of the Macduff child on stage, followed by his attempt to justify himself in a council meeting. It is an inspired transition; Shakespeare suggests it is dreamed in advance by the child. The contrast is stark between the intimate female space of authentic feelings and the male politic space where propriety has to be observed. Here Leontes, the tyrannical child, speaks a different language, a bombastic pastiche of the 'truth':

> Our natural goodness
> Imparts this; which if you, or stupefied,
> Or seeming so, in skill, cannot or will not
> Relish a truth, like us, inform yourselves
> We need no more of your advice.
>
> (II.i.164–168)

This is the point at which Antigonus says, in an aside, they will be raised 'to laughter'; but the constraints of courtly behaviour mean that they have no means of containing Leontes' absurdity, and there is no Fool – or rather, the role of the Fool will be distributed amongst others.

The Trial of Hermione is also a kind of dream, in which Leontes demands obedient confirmation by his own paternal superego in the form of Apollo's oracle, convinced that his message will uphold his male authority. By contrast, Hermione in her defence speech says that she is standing up for her 'honour' not for her own sake but for that of her children:

> for honour,
> 'Tis a derivative from me to mine,
> And only that I stand for.
>
> (III.ii.43–45)

She dissociates herself from Leontes' 'language':

> *Hermione*: You speak a language that I understand not:
> My life stands in the level of your dreams,
> Which I'll lay down.
> *Leontes*:   Your actions are my dreams.
> You had a bastard by Polixenes,
> And I but dream'd it!
>
> (ll. 80–84)

By default, the truth is spoken (Leontes did indeed dream the 'bastard'), but Leontes cannot understand its language. When the oracle (his internal object) tells him he is a jealous tyrant he instantly denies its conclusion ('There is no truth at all i' th' Oracle' [l.140]). It is only the announcement of Mamillius' death, following immediately afterwards, that penetrates his tyrannical omnipotence. The child was not his but its mother's. The death has meaning for him owing to his identification with the child, suddenly more serious in nature, thereby enabling the veil to drop from his eyes regarding Hermione: 'I have too much believ'd mine own suspicion' (l. 151).

But the damage to internal objects is not so instantly repaired through a simple change of viewpoint; it requires a long process of reparation (sixteen years of analysis, according to the personification of Time at the centre-point of the play). Paulina, an avatar of Apollo (with a hint of the apostle Paul) is Leontes' analyst over this period in a three-dimensional dream called Summer in Bohemia, equivalent to a play production. He submits to becoming her patient:

> Once a day I'll visit
> The chapel where they lie, and tears shed there
> Shall be my recreation.
>
> (ll. 238–240)

Paulina is the link between Hermione and Leontes, though they never see each other, in preserving hope that the lost may be found (and putting this down to a message from Apollo). Leontes is merely observer of his own dream and is otherwise helpless, unable to do anything other than maintain his awareness of loss, whilst a group of internal characters, through the vitality of their relationships, reconstrue the structure of his mind.

Great creating nature

We have heard much about wombs, prisons, gates, exits, and entrances: the babe being a 'prisoner to the womb', 'freed and enfranchis'd' by 'great nature' (II.ii.59–61). Perdita is Leontes' lost creative spirit, which he has in a sense thrown out, yet not without ensuring a suitable container for the wanderer

126   A dream of reparation: *The Winter's Tale*

in the great wide world, as Miranda will set to sea with Prospero in a 'rotting carcass of a butt' or Thaisa was thrown to the waves in her coffin. Despite his threats to have the child burned, Leontes selects Antigonus very particularly as the most parental of his male courtiers, governed by his wife Paulina: 'You, sir, come you hither', he demands, making sure that Antigonus will venture his own blood to 'save this brat's life':

> As by strange fortune
> It came to us, I do in justice charge thee,
> On thy soul's peril and thy body's torture,
> That thou commend it strangely to some place
> Where chance may nurse or end it. Take it up.
>   (II.iii.178–182)

This is just before he sets Hermione to a trial 'past enduring', as she described Mamillius. It is necessary for this hopeful spirit to leave the prison of his own tyrannical dominion and find room for growth under the aegis of 'strange chance', following ancient Necessity as in *Oedipus*. Leontes thereby gives the child-spirit the best chance of survival, following a dream-route to recreation that begins when Antigonus is shipwrecked, eaten by a bear, and metamorphoses into the good Shepherd – with religious implications, like Bottom and the Ass.

The transition to the world governed by gods, not by men, is experienced by Antigonus as a type of initiation in which Hermione appears to him a dream robed in white, her eyes spouting tears:

> To me comes a creature,
> Sometimes her head on one side, some another;
> I never saw a vessel of like sorrow,
> So fill'd, and so becoming: in pure white robes,
> Like very sanctity, she did approach
> My cabin where I lay: thrice bow'd before me,
> And, gasping to begin some speech, her eyes
> Became two spouts . . .
>   (III.iii.19–26)

The baby has been snatched from its mother with 'the innocent milk in its innocent mouth' (III.ii.100), yet through this dream of spouting milk from the eye-nipples, first on one side then another (breast), the white 'sanctity' of motherhood is transferred to Antigonus, as in Bottom's 'translation' in *A Midsummer Night's Dream*. He then lays down his courtly identity, which has become a prison to his better self, become contaminated by the obsession with bastardy that prevailed in Leontes' court owing to his inner insecurity. Discarding these restraints (basic assumptions) thanks to the Bear, he can now fulfil his

A dream of reparation: *The Winter's Tale* 127

feminine potential in the new, caring role of Shepherd: 'thou met'st with things dying, I with things new-born', he exclaims to his son (III.iii.113) – two sides of the transitional movement of catastrophic change, death and rebirth. The Clown puts the tempest and the devouring together: 'I have seen two such sights, by sea and by land! . . . the ship boring the moon with her mainmast . . . And then for the land-service, to see how the bear tore out his shoulder-bone' (III.iii.83–85). The change of direction appears instantaneous, but the psychic work of reparation – Leontes' recreation – takes much longer, although yet again, it is a dream-measurement of Time which is in a sense timeless:

> I turn my glass, and give my scene such growing
> As you had slept between.
> (IV.i.16–17)

Is it sixteen years or a midwinter's night? In the dream-world, omnipotence sleeps while 'great creating Nature' (a phrase of Perdita's) is the ruling goddess and 'grows the scene', starting afresh with 'things new-born'.

Bohemia, as well as the world of dreams, is also the play-world which governs the audience's response and relation to the dreams of the playwright, mediated subterraneously by Paulina the analyst-figure. In the Bohemian pastoral everyone is allowed to dress up and 'play' without retribution, by contrast with the disgraced 'playings' fantasised by Leontes ('go play boy play . . . thy mother plays'). Piece by piece Leontes' misconceptions are set right. The overriding abundance of Nature allows scope for all sorts of harmless naughtiness and trickery amongst the children, epitomised by Puck-like Autolycus the aspiring poet or playwright (as MacNeice saw him)[5] – entertainer, jester, and songster in Nature's court, stealing purses for his services and at times being an actor too. He even echoes, in play, 'my shoulder blade is out' – the eating of Antigonus – thereby ensnaring the Clown; but neither bones or feelings suffer real injury, and his defrauding or purse-cutting is itself a form of play which emphasises the general richness and good nature that cannot be marred by such minor flaws, and is far exceeded by delight in the songs that he peddles. The glorious sheep-shearing festival is heralded by Autolycus singing:

> When daffodils begin to peer
> With heigh! The doxy over the dale,
> Why then comes in the sweet o' the year,
> For the red blood reigns in the winter's pale.
> (IV.iii.1–4)

The 'winter's pale' indicates the rewriting of the winter's tale; the 'red blood' the new vital spirit that replaces Leontes' threats of fire, a theme reiterated throughout the festival. Like Ariel or Orpheus, Autolycus charms the primitive senses with his songs: 'no hearing, no feeling, but my sir's song, and admiring

128 A dream of reparation: *The Winter's Tale*

the nothing of it.' He gaily brings in the gods that Paulina said would never look Leontes' way: 'let him approach singing', they say, for he sings his songs 'as if they were gods or goddesses' (IV.iv.214). Changing clothes and changing tunes, even at the expense of honesty, are necessary to the life of the society that will engineer the unfreezing of Leontes' mind. Mopsa and Dorcas willingly suspend disbelief in ballads that are 'pitiful, and as true', preluding the ultimate restoration of Hermione's family 'like an old tale'.

It is significant that during the period that Hermione herself is 'stone', there is no queen in either court or country; Polixenes' wife is never mentioned and the Shepherd's wife is dead. This means that the mother figure must be imagined, dreamed, introjected, intensifying the association with Nature or with Ceres the goddess of harvest, in particular (via Perdita) with the Ceres-Proserpina myth, taken by Milton and Keats and other poets to be the story of poetry and the muse. Aspects of the muse are represented by the Shepherd's wife in her absence, indicating the values of warmth and hospitality inculcated in Perdita via her shepherd-father:

> Fie, daughter! When my old wife liv'd, upon
> This day she was both pantler, butler, cook,
> Both dame and servant; welcom'd all, serv'd all;
> Would sing her song and dance her turn; now here
> At upper end o'th'table, now i'th'middle;
> On his shoulder, and his; her face o' fire
> With labour, and the thing she took to quench it
> She would to each one sip.
>
> (IV.iv.55–62)

It is an alternative view of queenliness from that of the court with its fake hospitality (that Hermione connived in when she tried to appease Leontes). 'Red with mirth', 'on fire with labour', are associated with the idea of equal distribution, serving all in turn (so 'distribution should undo excess', as Lear discovered, 'and each man have enough'). Complex ideas of justice and generosity infuse the prevailing thread of red colouring: Perdita's blushes, or the 'true blood which peeps fairly' through Florizel's person to prove him an 'unstain'd shepherd', not a courtly wooer of false words. Perdita can see through his external princely guise to the shepherd spirit beneath (and whose clothes he is in fact wearing):

> *Florizel*: When you do dance, I wish you
> A wave o'th'sea, that you might ever do
> Nothing but that, move still, still so,
> And own no other function. Each your doing,
> So singular in each particular,
> Crowns what you are doing, in the present deeds,
> That all your acts are queens.

Perdita: O Doricles,
Your praises are too large: but that your youth,
And the true blood which peeps fairly through't,
Do plainly give you out an unstain'd shepherd,
With wisdom I might fear, my Doricles,
You woo'd me the false way.

(IV.iv.140–151)

'All your acts are queens' echoes Leontes' 'Your actions are my dreams', but it brings out the reality in the dream: Florizel's words are a fair description and a world away from the strained dialogue between Leontes and Hermione. In enacting Apollo, the 'fire-rob'd god' who became, for love, 'a poor humble swain / As I seem now', he is in fact becoming an avatar of Apollo, just as Perdita is Flora-Proserpina, 'goddess-like prank'd up' but also sensing a change in her identity: her robe 'Does change my disposition' (IV.i.135).

The motif throughout this act is that true blood shows through, and sometimes because of, disguise – whether words or clothes. But true blood does not mean aristocratic heritage; it means sincerity of feeling – something which had no place in Leontes' court, except in Hermione's secluded room with her ladies. However this insight is now being dreamed on his behalf. Narcissistic idealising and the Platonic ideal are being differentiated: one based on controlling projective identification and the other on trust in the object which has nonetheless to be founded on reality, not delusion.

Perdita in her goddess-guise proves her inner worth, beyond her physical beauty, through her inspired introjection of the mother-figures she never met but has nonetheless imagined, a mysterious innate identification nurtured by the Shepherd and his values (his true education). This is where nature and nurture meet. He knows of her noble origins but he also reminds her of her obligations as hostess, and in performing these in her own way she becomes a vehicle of 'grace', filling out the Platonic ideal. Her distribution of flowers, like the Shepherd wife's distribution of ale, is an expression of her inner mother, in response to Florizel's discovery of her with his 'falcon' eyes (IV.iv.15). Identifying with Proserpina, she offers to all the maids a vision of the potential beauty in marriage, opening their 'virgin branches' to the sun-god:

O Proserpina,
For the flowers now that, frighted, thou let'st fall
From Dis's wagon! Daffodils,
That come before the swallow dares, and take
The winds of March with beauty; violets, dim,
But sweeter than the lids of Juno's eyes
Or Cytherea's breath; pale primroses,
That die unmarried, ere they can behold

Bright Phoebus in his strength (a malady
Most incident to maids) . . .

(IV.iv.116–125)

It appears to be a lament but is in fact a celebration, a manifestation of Nature's generosity in the role of her priestess.

The other key proof of her inner worth is the famous 'art is nature' debate with Polixenes, whose intrusion echoes the original one in Leontes' apparently happy marriage, a shadow here to be reworked and reformed. Accompanied by Camillo, both disguised in wintry hoods, he enters the scene as an avatar of dusky Dis, the dark deathlike shadow at the heart of Arcadia. It is a darkness that always has to be confronted and understood, *for knowledge is the key that underpins the resolution of aesthetic conflict*; and significantly the Shepherd welcomes these unknown strangers, for 'unknown friends' are 'a way to make us better friends, more known'. In the famous 'art is nature' debate, Polixenes clearly wins the argument but Perdita refuses to concede defeat, suspecting intuitively that he is trying to dub her one of nature's 'bastards'. She rejects the insinuations that lurk beneath his rhetoric:

I'll not put
The dibble in earth to set one slip of them;
No more than, were I painted, I would wish
This youth should say 'twere well, and only therefore
Desire to breed by me.

(IV.iv.99–103)

His words are right, but his intentions are wrong. In spiritual terms, Perdita wins because she won't be bullied by this smooth-tongued Hades-tempter; she sticks to mother Nature and rejects his accomplished sophistry.[6] She sees her beauty as real, not painted, and this is not vanity but identification with her mother's 'honour', which Hermione said was 'derivative from me to mine'.

Then when Polixenes' disguise is thrown off and his threats erupt to scratch her beauty with briars and boil the old Shepherd in oil, she declares with characteristic directness that the sun surveys all mortals equally:

I was not much afeard; for once or twice
I was about to speak, and tell him plainly,
The selfsame sun that shines upon his court
Hides not his visage from our cottage, but
Looks on alike.

(IV.iv.443–446)

A dream of reparation: *The Winter's Tale* 131

Yet there is a sense in which Polixenes is acting as devil's advocate to both Perdita and Florizel, becoming a feature of the inquiry into Leontes' own confusions. His name, as well as 'many strangers', echoes that of Paulina and Apollo, the sun-god whose light was withdrawn from Leontes when he doubted the truth of the oracle. He is a dark tempter whose real function is to reveal sunlit reality. Just as *Antony and Cleopatra* was a play in praise of love, *The Winter's Tale* is in praise of truth, and all the characters promote its discovery, even when like Autolycus they believe themselves mighty liars. Polixenes is provoked by the realistic adolescent insults directed at him by Florizel as an 'ancient sir' who has 'sometime loved'; he replies:

> Pray you once more,
> Is not your father grown incapable
> Of reasonable affairs? Is he not stupid
> With age and alt'ring rheums? Can he speak? Hear?
> Know man from man? dispute his own estate?
> (IV.iv.397–401)

As always in such circumstances, we suspect the son recognises his father unconsciously. The crescendoing mutual irritation between them pushes Florizel into a position in which his oath is put to the test: is he really willing to give up his royal inheritance for the sake of a pretty country girl, as he protests? He has two minutes to grow up. To prove his inner worth he needs to both acknowledge his father and deny his worldly inheritance:

> From thy succession wipe me, father; I
> Am heir to my affection . . .
>   I am put to sea
> With her whom here I cannot hold on shore.
> (IV.iv.481–482, 499–500)

Insofar as the sheep-shearing feast is a betrothal ceremony,[7] conducted by a 'meeting of the petty gods', this point of commitment is fundamental to the durability of a marriage. The couple need to shed their borrowed godlike garments, 'put to sea', and weather the turbulence.

Gentlemen born

As in *A Midsummer Night's Dream* (and other comedies), the action reverts back to the place of origin for an awakening, via the transition of the sea-voyage and its accompanying seasickness. The key point is that Polixenes sweeps offstage without carrying out any of his threats, and finds himself arranging for a boat to Sicilia like everybody else in the lemming-like rush to go and watch the final scene of the drama for real. By now 'flaying' has come to mean stripping clothes

132 A dream of reparation: *The Winter's Tale*

rather than the 'wheels, racks, fires and flaying' of which Paulina accused Leontes; the emotional violence is being digested, and instead of betraying, characters become 'advocate' for one another. We have seen that clothes reveal and create identity as well as hiding it, so the multitudinous exchanges mark intercommunication between facets of the self: they see and feel in an expanded way, laterally and vertically – not just crossdressing, but crossing ages and social status.

Camillo, like Kent with Lear ('See better, Lear') has 'a woman's longing' to 're-view Sicilia' – the name of both the country and the king; he wants to see if Leontes can now see better. Autolycus brings 'these two moles these blind ones', the Shepherd and his son, aboard ship, blind himself to what will be revealed outside his agency, but echoing the two spouts seen by Antigonus in his dream of Hermione on the previous voyage. He is eager 'to smell out work for the other senses' and dresses accordingly: 'Seest thou not the air of the court in these enfoldings?' he inquires of the Clown in a gentle parody of the poet's social status. His plotting becomes increasingly irrelevant as he finds himself a mere onlooker; but he too is received within the all-embracing new family, where no less than everybody is acknowledged to have played a useful role, whatever their omnipotent intentions. Under the aegis of great creating Nature, love is not true unless everyone is included in the picture. In this play there is no Malvolio or Shylock outcast, no Mercutio skewered in the interests of egocentric privileged lovers.

The groundwork is thus done in Bohemia's dream-world for the denouement back in the land of the waking. The characters awaken from their sea voyage, and Leontes from his wintry sleep, to find themselves restored to something greater than they were: in this rebirth, they discover they are all 'kindred', all 'gentlemen born' in the same family:

> *Clown*: See you these clothes? Can you see them not and think me still no gentleman born: you were best say these robes are not gentlemen born: give me the lie, do, and try whether I am not now a gentleman born.
> *Autolycus*: I know you are now, sir, a gentleman born.
> *Clown*: Ay, and have been so any time these four hours.
>
> (V.ii.131–137)

Meanwhile the Clown, though he knows Autolycus is a rogue (but a harmless one), vouches for him as a 'friend' – that is, not out of stupidity but because in essence he is a gentleman – a concept which the play has redefined and taken back to its roots in gentility.

Leontes has awoken to discover in Florizel and Perdita the two children he had lost, and thereby the person he 'might have been', capable of wonder and touched with the grace of spring:

> I lost a couple, that 'twixt heaven and earth
> Might thus have stood, begetting wonder, as
> You, gracious couple, do: . . .

> Welcome hither,
> As is the spring to the earth.
> (V.i.169–185)

The loss but also the link between Florizel and Mamillius ('born within a month') is emphasised in such a way that we feel one does literally restore the other. Only when the lost is found can Leontes rediscover his queen. Initially he makes the attempt through a mistaken recognition, seeing the younger Hermione in Perdita and, in his old way, wanting to possess her for himself (the incest theme in the late plays, here hinted at, is a type of upside-down Oedipus complex; the lion king was always confused about the issue of begetting). The new couple, 'begetting wonder', are for him a combined internal object who will lead to rediscovering his own wife. It is Paulina, his analyst-figure, who keeps an eye on him, and ensures that he does not lose direction.

The revelations about identity are conveyed in the second scene indirectly, which has the effect not just of modulating the emotional intensity – distancing it like an 'old tale' – but of ensuring the peripheral and low characters have a voice; they are part of the family scene even if not the protagonists:

> They looked as they had heard of a world ransomed, or one destroyed: a notable passion of wonder appeared in them . . . such a deal of wonder is broken out within this hour, that ballad-makers cannot be able to express it.
> (V.ii.14–23)

At that moment, their faces are so 'distracted' that only garments identify the participants: 'they were to be known by garment, not by favour'; and garments are interchangeable as we cannot escape noticing. Even those who were 'most marble' in countenance 'there changed colour', infused by the red thread of Bohemia. Those who were not there have 'lost a sight which was to be seen, cannot be spoken of' (V.ii.43). This is one way of expressing the inexpressible – through distance and disguise; but of course in the final scene Shakespeare achieves the representation of what even he feared could be seen as 'unlawful magic', the bringing of the dead to life. So real has the play become that it approaches hubris on the part of the playwright.

The Clown announces: 'Hark! the kings and the princes, our kindred, are going to see the queen's picture' (V.ii.173). His understatement, concluding the narrated recognition scene, heightens by contrast the forthcoming realism of the statue that becomes infused with life in response to the receptiveness of the onlookers. The scene works because of its carefully timed naturalism, with Paulina as ministrant managing the music and tempo of the revelation, mediating between Hermione-as-statue and the family in tentative stages:

> Prepare
> To see the life as lively mock'd as ever
> Still sleep mock'd death.
> (V.iii.18–20)

134 A dream of reparation: *The Winter's Tale*

On the basis of the analogy between sleep and death, the play-within-a-play is presented as an awakening of a dormant Hermione, rather than a giving of life:

> That she is living,
> Were it but told you, should be hooted at
> Like an old tale; but it appears she lives . . .
> (V.ii.102–117)

But Hermione's numbness can only fall from her if the family 'awake their faith', which is the final stage of Paulina's gradual unveiling:

> 'Tis time; descend; be stone no more; approach . . .
> Bequeath to death your numbness; for from him
> Dear life redeems you.
> (V.iii.99–103)

The recognition scene is long drawn out, to stress its solemnity and the delicacy, even tenuousness, of psychic reality as distinct from wish-fulfilment. Hermione steps down and embraces Leontes, but even this has a sense of unreality, like a dumbshow within a play, a visual pageant: 'it appears she lives', Paulina comments ambiguously, attentive to the reaction of the others. It does appear, in the sense of coming forth; but is appearance part of art's well-known illusionism or 'mockery'? It is only when Paulina directs the final 'turn' from back to front that Hermione becomes fully real to us, the audience, linking our dream to that of Leontes: 'Turn, good lady, / Our Perdita is found' (V.iii.121). Only now does Hermione speak, and she speaks only to Perdita:

> Tell me, mine own,
> Where has thou been preserv'd? where liv'd? how found
> Thy father's court? For thou shalt hear that I,
> Knowing by Paulina that the Oracle
> Gave hope thou wast in being, have preserv'd
> Myself to see the issue.
> (V.iii.123–128)

The reawakening culminates in the restoration of the crucial emotional link between mother and child, the model for all internal reparation of damaged objects (in the Kleinian sense) on which the life of the mind relies, analogous to the creative relation between poet and muse on which the life of the play or poem depends.

Notes

1 A 'retrospective idealisation of boyhood', as Schwartz (1973) points out; he observes the infantile quality of Leontes' jealousy in relation to his mother figure.

A dream of reparation: *The Winter's Tale* 135

2 Perdita's phrase, used by G. W. Knight as the title of his essay on the play (in *The Crown of Life*, 1932), expanded by N. Frye as the antithesis of magic, offering 'only a sense of a participation in the redeeming and reviving power of a nature identified with art, grace, and love' (1965, p. 116).

3 The withdrawal of projective identification cleanses perception: see Money-Kyrle, 'On Aesthetics' ([1960] 2015), p. 127; a formulation also characteristic of William Blake.

4 M. M. Mahood (1957) observes how Leontes' puns on words such as neat, cleanly, dear, apparent, play, and issue 'erupt like steam forcing up a saucepan lid' (p. 216).

5 Louis MacNeice, 'Autolycus' ([1966] 1968), pp. 232–233. Marjorie Garber (1974) writes of his 'dramatic role as poet-observer' and suggests a connection with Autolycus, father of Odysseus: 'to a certain extent he is transformation itself and not merely a practitioner of it' (p. 179).

6 A. D. Nuttall (2007) points out that when Shakespeare reverted to myth in the last plays he 'stopped thinking in an explicitly philosophical manner' (p. 345). Perhaps standard terms of debate were no longer sufficient.

7 As Northrop Frye (1965) pointed out. According to Meltzer, the 'adult organisation' of both the family and the community depends upon the sense of being governed internally by a 'combined object' based on 'the integration of masculine and feminine attributes of mind' (Meltzer & Harris, 2013, p. 28).

Chapter 10

The birth of ideas:
The Tempest

Emotional turbulence and catastrophic change are at the heart of *The Tempest*, just as in post-Kleinian theory they are at the heart of psychoanalysis and personality development. Of emotional turbulence, Bion writes:

> I have described 'emotional turbulence' as a state in which there is this kind of churning going on [elements 'seeping up' into consciousness] and all kinds of elements keep on obtruding . . . From time to time the individual is aware of this kind of turmoil and aware that there is some development which is striving to take place; the pressure which arises in a particular area is feared as being likely to break out and destroy his accepted method of behaviour.
>
> (Bion, [1978] 2019, p. 7)

The pressure relates to the presence of an idea that is trying to be born, and the personality instinctively reacts against it. Conflicting emotions congregate at a 'caesura' which brings them to unconscious attention, disturbing the existing state of knowledge:

> That is an example of the caesura: it is hard to penetrate what we 'all know' and to suggest that there may be something that has *not* yet emerged from the turbulence, just as there may be something – we do not know what – that led to the turbulence. Are we then to inhibit the turbulence? Or are we to investigate it?
>
> (Bion, 1987, p. 231)

The art-symbol is such a caesura: it brings unconscious conflicts to a place where they become visible and where different directions and links interact.[1]

Perhaps more urgently than any of his plays so far, *The Tempest* dramatises through a sea-story the process of giving birth to an idea, amidst conflicts of love and hate on the one hand and the negativity of philistinism on the other. With its allegorical flavour and abstract format, *The Tempest* seems to pair with the family story of *The Winter's Tale* in a way that prefigures

Bion's description of the psychoanalytic quest, at the end of *Attention and Interpretation*:

> What is to be sought is an activity that is both the restoration of god (the Mother) and the evolution of god (the formless, infinite, ineffable, non-existent).
>
> (Bion, 1970, p. 129)

The two plays are in a sense complementary: *The Tempest* could be seen to dramatise the principle of evolution that underlies all the recognisable manifestations of psychic life, as generated by the poetic muse or its model, the internal mother-baby relationship, in *The Winter's Tale*. It has the quality, Anne Righter suggested, of being (paradoxically) a cultural or created myth, susceptible to multiple interpretations;[2] and is perhaps Shakespeare's most influential or inspiring play, to judge by the linguistic echoes found in subsequent poets. It has an integral sense of a 'existence beyond itself' (to adopt Emily Brontë's phrase in *Wuthering Heights*), that is, of giving shape to a principle of evolution that hovers beyond the human kaleidoscope of elements. In that sense it focuses on the introjection of the *thinking principle*, not just the *thought* (in Money-Kyrle's, 1968 formulation).

Indeed, all the late plays explore explicitly the death-to-birth motif underlying the transition to a new world or new mentality, often by means of sea-voyages that bear the 'bark' of the human vehicle containing the idea.[3] The 'sea-change' – the catastrophic change generated by the sea – is more radical and less bounded than that of the green dreamworlds such as the wood of *A Midsummer Night's Dream*. The sea has no edges; it moves to its own unearthly music, sometimes harsh, generated by humming whales and hushing winds whose enhanced Pythagorean associations link dreaming with the music of the spheres. The sea has infinite potential for the genesis of life, as Shakespeare with pre-Darwinian imagination intuited; and at some point threw up this island of the mind, where the primitive and the unearthly mingle breath. Our window is opened by Miranda to the faculty of 'wonder', leading us after the manner of Marvell's *Garden* to 'far other worlds, and other seas', or Emily Brontë's eternity (both among the many metaphysical offspring of Shakespeare's play):

> Held backward from that tempting race,
> Gazed o'er the sands the waves efface,
> To the enduring seas –
> There cast my anchor of desire
> Deep in unknown eternity.
> (Brontë, 1941, p. 232)

We realise that no shore is stable for more than a short period: the anchorage is far beyond in the infinite and ineffable. The sands of Prospero's island have a

138   The birth of ideas: *The Tempest*

fluid, evanescent quality impressed by movements of the undersea world on its fringes, with its aura of prenatal life, forever lapping at consciousness.

The Tempest is a birth-story, less literally than *Pericles* but more analytically: its island not the 'teeming womb of royal kings' of John of Gaunt's England (which was an illusion) but teeming instead with a mixed bag of aspects of personality (like Aeolus' bag of winds). Set to roam on the island, they each find their role in forming the thing that ultimately emerges as the play itself. This is in a sense true of any play, but as readers have always observed, *The Tempest* elevates the mythical, preverbal quality of their interaction to an intensified focus on the nature of the play itself and its making. And when the island has served its purpose of giving birth to the 'brave new world' it becomes, like Milton's cast-off Eden (the new world's placenta), an 'island salt and bare'. We cast it off, or we are cast off from it. The new home of the idea is in the minds of the audience.

The roarers and the wreckage

The play begins with the realistic storm that appears to provide its title, though as we discover later, the real tempest is an internal 'beating', for Prospero and all the characters who are capable of receiving an emotional impression. Only the cynics Antonio and Sebastian, who cannot tell the difference between their conscience and a chilblain, have no such capacity, and this is their role in the play: they are the vestigial remnants of minus K, and Shakespeare has little interest now in this deprived mindset other than to record its existence on the map. The main function of the shipwreck is to dramatise the intrusion of emotional reality onto the basic assumptions of everyday life and its established social hierarchy: for 'What cares these roarers for the name of king?' (I.i.16).* The switch from a protomental to a mental mode is disorienting (Brontë's 'tempting race' of worldly values, versus the 'anchor of desire' impelled by an unknown goal).

It is the ship of Miranda's puberty that has brought 'all his enemies' to the shore of Prospero's mind. The wreck is a type of chaotic birth, spilling out assorted specimens of humanity whom only the innocent Miranda could imagine to be good, fraughting souls. Once Hamlet said he could be 'bounded in a nutshell' were it not for his 'bad dreams'; now the bad dreams are brought by the Boatswain, whom Gonzalo with gallows humour declares is not destined for drowning, 'though the ship were no stronger than a nutshell, and as leaky as an unstanched wench' (I.i.46). The party have been brought to the island by Providence – not Prospero – on their return from a marriage celebration, and

---

* A shorter version of this chapter appears in *The Chamber of Maiden Thought* (Williams & Waddell, 1991). Quotations are from *The Tempest*, ed. F. Kermode (1964). London: Methuen.

The birth of ideas: *The Tempest* 139

now Prospero realises it is time for Miranda (leaking the blood of womanhood) also to board the ship of humanity in all its variations, beyond his protection and control. These features include his own internal 'darkness' which he only acknowledges, reluctantly, at the end of the play, in the form of Caliban. His love for Miranda is his saving grace:

> I have done nothing but in care of thee,
> Of thee, my dear one; thee, my daughter, who
> Art ignorant of what thou art.
> (I.ii.16–18)

Miranda is, in his story, associated with the 'Providence divine' that rescued him from that earlier shipwreck in 'a rotten carcass of a butt' that symbolised his dilapidated state of mind:

> There they hoist us
> To cry to th' sea that roar'd to us; to sigh
> To th'winds, whose pity, sighing back again
> Did us but loving wrong.
> (I.ii.147–150)

She is the spirit of wonder or awe which has always modulated his dry or academic curiosity, 'rapt in secret studies' in his library, writing plays and casting spells. She led him out to sea to learn from experience:

> O, a cherubin
> Thou wast that did preserve me. Thou didst smile,
> Infused with a fortitude from heaven,
> When I have deck'd the sea with drops full salt,
> Under my burthen groan'd . . .
> (II.ii.152–156)

As the 'cherubin' Miranda is also his route to discovery of Ariel, who he releases from his tree-trunk prison on the island, in a movement reciprocating his own rescue from the wooden butt. Although there is no direct dialogue between Miranda and Ariel, there is unconscious or dream communication.

But now the twelve-year latency period is over, and once again a shipwreck is on the horizon. On Miranda reaching puberty, the quiescent educational link in the Oedipal triangle of Miranda, Prospero, and Caliban has turned sour, owing to the upsurgence of uncontrollable forces that demand a new kind of resolution. With Caliban this takes the form of wanting to possess his Miranda-mother and 'people the isle with Calibans'. He becomes ugly to her and she no longer 'likes to look on him', while he accuses her of seducing him with false pretences:[4]

You taught me language, and my profit on't
Is, I know how to curse. The red plague rid you
For learning me your language!

(I.ii.517–519)

The promising child feels rejected – 'a born devil on whose nature / Nurture will never stick', says Prospero later, a 'hag-seed'. But we shall see there are flaws in his educational methods; only the Ariel faculty of the mind can educate Caliban, and their meeting is first embodied within Ferdinand.

Caliban reminds them of his previous mother, the 'hag' Sycorax who in effect created the island in the first place: 'This island's mine, by Sycorax my mother, / Which thou tak'st from me' (I.ii.333–334). They are all in effect still in Sycorax' womb, sensing the need to break out – a concatenation of prenatal voices that Prospero tries to keep in hierarchical order. It becomes apparent that not only Prospero's punitive methods but also his feelings derive like Caliban's from this ancestral enchantress, the primordial ambivalent mother who arouses love and hate:

Caliban: As wicked dew as e'er my mother brush'd
   With raven's feather from unwholesome fen
   Drop on you both! A south-west blow on ye
   And blister you all o'er!
Prospero: For this, be sure, tonight thou shalt have cramps,
   Side-stitches that shall pen thy breath up; urchins
   Shall, for that vast of night that they may work,
   All exercise on thee; thou shalt be pinch'd
   As thick as honeycomb . . .

(I.ii.323–331)

Caliban is a Kleinian child rather than a romantic noble savage. The rich, imaginative language of torment and curses comes straight out of *Lear*, with the intense somatic pains of childhood feelings associated with hunger and defaecation.[5] The all-powerful witch-mother is split into male and female components, and in this context Prospero's old rigid omnipotence comes to the fore again.[6] Prospero's methods of keeping Caliban in a state of profitable servitude are no different from Sycorax's black magic.

It is the male superego figure who is deemed responsible for the child's nightmares when he 'needs must curse', calling down the spirits that frighten, pinch, prick, pitch him in the mire, mow and chatter like apes:

   Then like hedgehogs which
Lie tumbling in my barefoot way and mount
Their pricks at my footfall; sometime am I
All wound with adders who with cloven tongues
Do hiss me into madness.

(II.ii.10–14)

The birth of ideas: *The Tempest* 141

Consequently his language of hatred and violent attack on his erstwhile father-figure ('paunch him with a stake', etc.) has an authentic validity; the somatic sensitivities of this creature of 'earth' have been abused, and like unaccommodated man, he respects basic necessities: 'I must eat my dinner.' Language itself, we suspect, when unintelligible, sounds like the hissing of adders to a preverbal Caliban. Prospero's education is 'lost' on him because his teaching methods are, like his art, a form of authoritarian vanity (a precursor to colonialism as a mental as well as a political condition, in which domination precludes communication).

Where Miranda and Prospero teach Caliban how to name the sun and moon, and how to 'know his own meaning' thereby (I.ii.358), he teaches them the 'qualities of the isle', that is, the innate riches of the island mind:

> and then I lov'd thee,
> And show'd thee all the qualities o'th'isle,
> The fresh springs, brine-pits, barren place and fertile:
> (I.ii.338–341)

Significantly, the philistine and cynical aspects of the mind (Antonio and Sebastian) or depressed ones (Alonso) are unable to see these fertile qualities, and regard the island projectively as hostile and deserted, sterile. Caliban is a 'moon-calf' who embodies childlike instinctual vitality, together with a sense of beauty and of awe that ties him to his Miranda-mother: the nascent mentality of aesthetic conflict. He leads the foolish children, Stephano and Trinculo, to the sound of Ariel's voice: 'calf like, they my lowing followed' (IV.i.179). Thus in Caliban's ugliness and primitiveness resides the babylike beauty of developmental potential, but it requires reciprocity, not derision as 'hag-seed'. He is as much a feature of creativity as is Ariel: according to Ted Hughes, 'the enigma from which in a sense [Shakespeare] had wrestled his whole creation' (1992, p. 488).[7] The key is musical sensitivity, the dreamlike song which is presented as something quite distinct from discursive language:

> *Caliban*: Be not afeard; the isle is full of noises,
> Sounds and sweet airs, that give delight, and hurt not.
> Sometimes a thousand twangling instruments
> Will hum about mine ears; and sometime voices,
> That if I then had wak'd after long sleep,
> Will make me sleep again; and then, in dreaming,
> The clouds methought would open, and show riches
> Ready to drop upon me; that, when I wak'd,
> I cried to dream again.
> (III.ii.133–141)

Miranda is his adored 'mistress', associated in his dream-memory with her showing him the 'Man in the Moon', the breast as combined object, dropping riches from the cloud-face – an education he can understand. But she has

142 The birth of ideas: *The Tempest*

somehow become contaminated by the male principle. All this contributes to Caliban's confusion and makes him vulnerable to the comical perversities of Stephano and Trinculo and their substitute-breast, the bottle of liquor.

Breast and bottle: the music of the rabble

Insofar as the Caliban-Prospero-Ariel trio has some similarity to a Freudian id-ego-superego structure, Caliban is primitive in the sense of both instinctual and authentic, but owing to the mind's imbalance his judgement is easily perverted and enslaved by a fake value system, governed by imagery of faecal smells and skewed vision, all misconstrued by Caliban in terms of his original man-in-the-moon religion. In a caricatural birth image, Stephano (the pseudo-Prospero) discovers Caliban (the slave-child) wrapped up with Trinculo (the pseudo-Miranda) in a gabardine (perhaps Shylock's):

> This is some monster of the isle with four legs, who hath got, as I take it, an ague. Where the devil should he learn our language? . . . He's in his fit now, and does not talk after the wisest. He shall taste of my bottle.
>
> (II.ii.66–76)

He is 'a most delicate monster' with two voices, oral and anal – the forward to 'speak well', the backward to 'utter foul speeches'. He emerges 'fish-like', a sea-monster. Just as Prospero's talent for contriving torments derives from a common source with Caliban, so the comic sub-plot turns on common elements between Prospero and the clowns. Stephano, the 'man in the moon', 'wondrous man', drops neatly into the god-shaped hole which Prospero has created and vacated in the mind of Caliban:

> *Stephano*: How now, moon-calf! How dost thine ague?
> *Caliban*: Hast thou not dropp'd from heaven?
> *Stephano*: Out o' the moon, I do assure thee: I was the man in the moon when time was.
> *Caliban*: I have seen thee in her, and I do adore thee:
>   My mistress show'd me thee, and thy dog, and thy bush.
> *Stephano*: Come, swear to that; kiss the book:
>
> (II.ii.135–142)

Stephano commands Trinculo to 'kiss the book' as he holds out the bottle, to keep him under control. The bottle-book is a container of magical properties pertaining to pseudo-divinity:

> *Caliban*: That's a brave god, and bears celestial liquor:
>   I will kneel to him.
>
> (II.ii.118–119)

The birth of ideas: *The Tempest* 143

As with any dictatorial system, the banner is 'freedom', rapped out to a democratic drum:

> Ban ban Cacaliban
> Has a new master, get a new man.
> Freedom, hey-day! Hey-day, freedom!
> (II.ii.184–186)

And Prospero's book as a container of powerful spells is not much different from their bottle; it is the similarity that impresses us, not the difference. The psychological function of the low characters' sub-plot is to exorcise these aspects of omnipotence that contaminate creativity and constrain the true freedom of the object, Ariel.

Prospero complained that nurture would never stick on Caliban's bad nature; but it is, rather, mis-identification which creates this comical tableau of misconception (in Money-Kyrle's sense of misconstruing the knowledge-filled breast). Insofar as he follows the book, Caliban remains in servitude, but he only succumbs to plebeian values when he is drunk. It is no accident that his words are always given in verse, not in prose, even if their argument is a mistaken one: the implication is of an innate contact with the poetic, the beauty of images. By contrast, for Stephano, being 'king' means 'getting his music for nothing' (III.ii.133–142) and trafficking Caliban as a showpiece back at the Naples fairground. Caliban preserves the idea of his moon-mistress and is led to his re-education by Ariel in the poetic passage where they traipse 'lowing, calf-like' to Prospero's cell. His internal image of beauty enables the restoration of his judgement as soon as he sees what 'trash' commands the clowns' attention – the clothesline of superficialities that diverts from genuine emotionality. No longer innocent, he has learned the distinction between the genuine emotions of love and hate and the stupidity of political allegiance. From that point he vows:

> I'll be wise hereafter,
> And seek for grace. What a thrice-double ass
> Was I, to take this drunkard for a god,
> And worship this dull fool!
> (V.i.294–297)

Grace devouring

While Caliban is engaged in his misconceived search for freedom, his alter-ego Ferdinand is busy modelling an alternative type of willing servitude:

> *Miranda*:　　　　My husband then?
> *Ferdinand*: Ay, with a heart as willing
> 　　As bondage e'er of freedom: here's my hand.
> (III.i.88–90)

144   The birth of ideas: *The Tempest*

The love story is the only thing Prospero cannot control; he can merely provide the stage-set. It therefore causes him great anxiety, but is also the potential ground for earning his own freedom from himself and his omnipotent designs. He can bring Ferdinand and Miranda together but cannot make them fall in love, though his 'soul prompts' it. Miranda expresses her freedom by instinctively and (as it were) innocently overriding all her father's commands as soon as Ferdinand appears: she gives her name before remembering she had promised her father not to, but is not therefore assailed by guilt; rather, her attitude to her father is always of solicitude. She first saw Ferdinand in a dream, listening to Ariel's description of the shipwreck; hence the sense of recognition when she awakes and then holds fast to her initial judgement that she has 'no desire to see a goodlier man', despite the fact she hasn't seen any others than her father and Caliban to compare him with. Indeed her choice of Ferdinand does not give the impression of an escape from Caliban but an assimilation: suddenly an 'abhorred slave' (a phallic part-object) reappears in the form of a handsome prince as in the fairytale of the frog and the princess. Vision is changing, as suggested by the unearthly, enigmatic quality of the phrase through which Prospero introduces Miranda to Ferdinand:[8]

> The fringed curtains of thine eye advance
> And say what thou see'st yond.
>
> (I.ii.409)

The new couple will constitute a work-group: not only does Ferdinand carry logs (Caliban's job) and become her 'patient log-man', but Miranda insists on helping him, believing her father is asleep at his books.

Ferdinand too undergoes a change of mind preparatory to meeting Miranda. He is both Caliban-transformed and Ariel-inspired: they are his emotional equipment, his assimilation of the island's native elements within himself. He is Arielised on shipboard by the spirit of 'flaming amazement' which energises his body like electricity:

> [The mariners] quit the vessel,
> Then all afire with me, the King's son, Ferdinand,
> With hair up-staring, – then like reeds, not hair –
> Was the first man that leap'd . . .
>
> (I.ii.211–214)

He is the key explorer, the knight on a quest, although he does not initially know where to turn his attention. He embodies genuine curiosity (Bion's K) – the only character to do so, other than old Gonzalo with his mild observations regarding the dryness of their clothes and the colour of the grass.[9] Ferdinand thought he was drowned, but instead his vision has been reborn; sitting with

The birth of ideas: *The Tempest* 145

his 'arms in a sad knot' (I.ii.224), he is disengaged from identification with a depressed and guilt-ridden father, by a dream of a transformed father. Amazement filters through mourning, 'cooling the air with sighs', and modulates to 'something rich and strange':

> Full fathom five thy father lies;
> Of his bones are coral made;
> Those are pearls that were his eyes:
> Nothing of him that doth fade,
> But doth suffer a sea-change
> Into something rich and strange.
>   (I.ii.396–403)

Ariel's music draws him upwards through the waves of depression or doubt, just as he 'beat the surges / Under him' and 'breasted / The surge' when he swam to shore (II.i.110).

Ariel's 'sea-change' song, as observed by Harold Bloom (1999), recalls Clarence's dream from *Richard III*, a passage which almost seems to exist outside its play like a recurrent nightmare of its author:

> O Lord! methought what pain it was to drown!
> What dreadful noise of waters in mine ears!
> What sights of ugly death within mine eyes!
> Methoughts I saw a thousand fearful wracks;
> A thousand men that fishes gnawed upon;
> Wedges of gold, great anchors, heaps of pearl,
> Inestimable stones, unvalued jewels,
> All scatt'red in the bottom of the sea:
> Some lay in dead men's skulls, and in the holes
> Where eyes did once inhabit, there were crept
> (As 'twere in scorn of eyes) reflecting gems,
> That wooed the slimy bottom of the deep
> And mocked the dead bones that lay scatt'red by.
>   (*Richard III*, I.iv.21–33)

The jewel of the soul (a traditional metaphor) is here perverted into the form of worthless money (no longer a working worldly currency) surrounded by dead debris. This is the meaning of shipwreck and drowning here: it is a 'mockery' of life-values and beauty, a 'melancholy flood' of unalleviated depression related to a perverted value system associated with tyranny, ambition, and worldly gain. This negative ethics (minus K) is represented in *The Tempest* by the cynical duo Antonio and Sebastian, whose lack of imagination and human feeling is epitomised by their inability to see beauty or to hear Ariel, consciously or unconsciously; they remain unaffected even by the drowsiness that Ariel induces. The

146   The birth of ideas: *The Tempest*

words 'imagination', 'riches', 'crown', and 'dream' are empty shells, dead skulls to them, employed to point to just one thing – worldly ambition:

> *Antonio*: My strong imagination sees a crown
>   Dropping upon thy head.
> *Sebastian*:   What, art thou waking?
>   (II.i.202–203)

The same words, elsewhere in the play, have a positive significance (for example, the 'blessed crown' dropped over Ferdinand and Miranda). For Antonio in his boredom, words are 'empty caskets' to be used as spurs to action rather than contemplation; he is Prospero's exoskeleton, the rival shadow of a playwright, the embodiment of envy and ingratitude.[10] Shakespeare revisits this nightmare of deadness through Ferdinand's eyes and converts it into a dream about developmental catastrophic change, where ugly becomes beautiful, 'dreadful noise' becomes unearthly singing, dead bones are living coral.

It is in the nature of artistic transformation to stimulate spiritual transformation, as in Milton's 'solemn music' which is 'Dead things with inbreath'd sense able to pierce', or as in Paulina's gradual mediation between life and stone in *The Winter's Tale*. Having understood this unconsciously, Ferdinand is ready to meet 'admir'd Miranda' (playing musically as well as etymologically on the name): 'O you wonder . . . be you maid or no?' he asks, and she replies, 'No wonder . . . but certainly a maid'; the ideal is reciprocally infused by direct homely realism. The naturalism of the nascent relationship makes a distinct contrast with the artificial illusion of Prospero's omnipotent art in the subsequent wedding masque.

Ferdinand is in the process of un-drowning, of being drawn out of dark melancholy waters into airy, musical wonder. 'What strange fish / Hath made his meal on thee?' asks Alonso, imagining his drowned son (II.i.108–109). Rather, Ferdinand has himself internalised both fishlike Caliban and the airy minister with 'grace devouring', as Prospero describes Ariel in the harpy speech which marks the turning-point in Alonso's own depression: 'You are three men of sin . . .' (III.iii.53). Alonso, in parallel with his son, though unbeknownst to each other, has his own dream in which he catches and echoes Ariel's sonorous rhythms, 'bassing his trespass':

> Methought the billows spoke, and told me of it;
> The winds did sing it to me; and the thunder,
> That deep and dreadful organ-pipe, pronounc'd
> The name of Prosper; it did bass my trespass,
> Therefore my son i' the ooze is bedded . . .
>   (III.iii.96–100)

His new sensitivity to the tempestuous qualities of the island where his sins have been 'belched up' awakens his sense of responsibility and leads to his son being restored and his inner world revitalised.

The reasonable shore

Ariel and Caliban represent two poles of the creative mind, the evanescent and the sensual, operating in an intimate dreamlike tension: at one point Prospero summons Caliban with 'Come, thou tortoise', and immediately Ariel enters (I.ii.318) as if on Caliban's cue. He hates one, loves the other, but they function in counterpoint and were both born on the island (Ariel from the cloven pine in which Sycorax imprisoned him, his groans revolving 'as fast as millwheels strike'). These early births and confinements form the matrix – the 'full poor cell' – from which Ferdinand and Miranda will be delivered to the brave new world and Prospero delivered to the audience.

Prospero's relinquishment of Ariel and Miranda, and acknowledgement of Caliban, constitute his own internal tempest. Giving freedom to his objects and renouncing his magical omnipotence entail the very 'heart-sorrow' that he tries to inculcate in the enemies who have landed on the shore of his mind. His personal crisis occurs at the hour when he believes he has at his mercy all his enemies. Significantly, it comes to his mind or memory in the middle of the wedding masque with its irrelevance and unreality – 'some vanity of mine art' supposedly to please the young lovers, although as usual, really a means of control (here of sexuality and the 'virgin knot'). They make polite compliments about his entertainment, 'harmonious charmingly', whilst evidently not caring at all about the nonsense which is designed as a time-filler before the wedding night. It is very different from the mechanicals' play in *A Midsummer Night's Dream*, which has meaning in itself and through the intentions of its workmen actors. Prospero dismisses the show with a 'strange, hollow and confused noise', since that is essentially all it is. It is no more real than the trumpery of the dressing-up clothes on the washing line outside his cell, set to trap the conspirators. Psychic reality, in the form of the anti-masque (of bestial emotion and musical hunting dogs) is impinging on the kind of artifice that serves escapism and wish-fulfilment. The conspiracy of Caliban and the clowns is absurd, but the feelings of murderous attack are real, and penetrate Prospero accordingly. Caliban cannot direct his fellow conspirators to the crucial business of seizing Prospero's book of magic and 'paunching him with a stake' – that is, to acknowledge genuine hatred.

The crisis, therefore, concerns having to differentiate between the kind of art that serves childish omnipotence (imaged by the courtly masque) and the art of the play itself, which imaginatively serves to present psychic reality and has a life beyond its author. As in Coleridge's distinction between fancy and imagination, Prospero is awoken from his self-indulgent fantasy of being a magician, in which his island cell is just another book-lined refuge like the one back in Milan. The life of the play means the death of the author:

> The cloud-capp'd tow'rs, the gorgeous palaces,
> The solemn temples, the great globe itself,

148   The birth of ideas: *The Tempest*

Yea, all which it inherit, shall dissolve,
And, like this insubstantial pageant faded,
Leave not a rack behind. We are such stuff
As dreams are made on; and our little life
Is rounded with a sleep.

(IV.i.151–158)

His stirring speech about 'bedimming the noontide sun' and creating artificial tempests and conflicts has a superficial power (perhaps because we know he is imitating Medea-Sycorax, his progenitor in stage-witchcraft),[11] but it does not have the profundity of this speech of renunciation which emphasises his own helplessness rather than his power, whilst drawing on all the cloud and tempest-imagery of the play. Like Antony on the point of catastrophic change, 'even with a thought / The rack dislimns', and the existing structure of identity seems to 'dissolve' – the price of creative dreaming rather than glamorous action.[12]

The internal tempest that results in Prospero's 'beating mind' is not his literal fear of death at Caliban's hands but his awareness that from now on, having given away 'a third of [his] life' (as he calls Miranda), 'Every third thought shall be my grave' (V.i.31). The price of the new world of creative thinking, founded on wonder, is the death or dissolution of the self in an insubstantial pageant. The condition of the new world's becoming real is that it should not be his. In the very process of giving it a habitation and a name, the playwright loses the egotistical solidity of his own identity, which is superseded and subsumed. As Keats was to say: 'A Poet is the most unpoetical of any thing in existence; because he has no Identity – he is continually informing – and filling some other Body.'[13]

In *The Tempest*, the omnipotent and the imaginative self coexist. The play presents the 'little world' of the essential Shakespearean mind which Richard II was struggling to cast as drama in Pomfret Castle; and the result of his success is, paradoxically, the slow death which represents the playwright's having to continue living with the insignificant identity of his mere self, as he acknowledges in the epilogue: 'what strength I have's mine own / Which is most faint.'

The final movement of the play has brought Prospero's 'enemies' back within the orbit of his own consciousness, a final test of strength:

Their understanding
Begins to swell, and the approaching tide
Will shortly fill the reasonable shore
That now lies foul and muddy.

(V.i.83–86)

The 'reasonable' tide is allowed to flow over the storm-befouled shores of mud. But the knowledge that the tide carries in over the brain's ridged sands varies

The birth of ideas: *The Tempest* 149

according to individual capacity. Those who cannot change, like Antonio and Sebastian, do not; those who can are turned inwards, to self-discovery, to find themselves (as Gonzalo observes) 'Where no man was his own' (V.i.213). But this includes the playwright himself. He has presided technically over the union of Ferdinand and Miranda, who will colonise the world of the future:

> *Miranda*: O brave new world,
>   That has such people in it!
> *Prospero*:   'Tis new to thee.
>   (V.i.184–186)

But he has no power over the actual relationship, as imaged in the little tableau in which he draws aside the curtains to discover them quarrelling amicably over a game of chess, in what Miranda calls 'fair play':

> *Miranda*: Sweet lord, you play me false.
> *Ferdinand*:   No, my dearest love,
>   I would not for the world.
> *Miranda*: Yes, for a score of kingdoms you should wrangle,
>   And I would call it fair play.
>   (V.i.171–174)

For them, kingdoms are chess pieces, just as Antony dropped realms from his pocket. Usurpation of thrones and dukedoms is a game, not a serious matter. The 'fair play' between them is a real play-within-a-play, by contrast with Prospero's illusionist masque. 'When did you lose your daughter?' asks Alonso; 'In this last tempest', Prospero replies (V.i.154–155). This loss is intimately connected with the parting from Ariel, the androgynous analyst-figure who can speak of love to Prospero (like the groom in *Richard II*):

> *Ariel*: Dost thou love me, master? No?
> *Prospero*: Dearly, my delicate Ariel.
>   (IV.i.48–49)

Ariel's 'feelings' are those evoked by others or breathed into others, in a transference relationship.

> Has thou, which art but air, a touch, a feeling
> Of their afflictions?
>   (V.i.21–22)

asks Prospero. He demonstrates how to feel, at the moment of parting. Miranda is one embodiment of Ariel on earth, as Ferdinand is an avatar of Caliban, those eternal principles that do not belong to the playwright's self but to his world of internal objects. They make his own existence redundant.

It is because of this that he bids farewell to Ariel and decides to drown his book 'deeper than did ever plummet sound' – back to the slimy depths strewn with bones. To follow 'virtue rather than vengeance' as Ariel suggests, rather than wreaking punishment on his enemies, is not so much an ethical decision as a recognition of reality and of the limits of technical competence. Indeed his reluctant concession to Ariel's advice is hardly a model of forgiveness, but at last he realises he is no longer the master of the play. It is not he, any more than it is Paulina in *The Winter's Tale*, who (despite appearances) can bring the dead to life, but great creating Nature, the inspiring force. In the depressive position, the object with creative potential is acknowledged to be free and independent of the self. The sea-change from bejewelled skull to pearls and corals – to the 'thing of beauty' that is the eternal work of art (Keats) – is not made on behalf of the playwright; it is made for us, his audience. As he sheds his magic robes, a minister to creativity, the playwright as Prospero is precipitated out of the airy cloud-shaped symbol and holds out his hands to the audience, asking for a response:

> Now my charms are all o'erthrown,
> And what strength I have's mine own,
> Which is most faint . . .
> Gentle breath of yours my sails
> Must fill, or else my project fails.
>
> (Epilogue)

Shakespeare is the servant of the play, not its master. The play is the aesthetic object that contains the baby, the brave new world of unknown shape; and we have been privileged to observe the playwright's aesthetic conflict in relation to its birth. But it is also up to his audience to breathe life into it, to make it their own dream-ship.[14]

Notes

1 A favourite image of turbulence, for Bion, is Leonardo's drawings of hair and water.

2 Anne Righter (Barton) lists some interpretive modes as a drama of various aspects of Prospero's mind; the nature of the poetic imagination; the three-part division of the soul; Renaissance science; and colonial responsibilities (1968, p. 21). She concludes, however, that the play 'cannot be about all these things' – but why not, so long as none of them is deemed complete or explanatory but is taken simply as an authentic response to the play as art-symbol. A. D. Nuttall (2007) calls the play 'pre-allegorical'.

3 Bark referring to both the human body and a ship. B. J. Sokol (1993) stresses the Kleinian implications of the ship 'splitting'.

4 It is not always clear in this section who is speaking, Prospero or Miranda, but our impression is that they both taught Caliban.

The birth of ideas: *The Tempest* 151

5 Norman Holland in 'Caliban's Dream' (1968b) discusses breast-milk and faecal symbolisations in Caliban.

6 B. J. Sokol points out that modern theorists such as cultural materialism, feminism, or new historicism are liable 'to assume the only human relations of significance are power'. Prospero himself struggles against this assumption and the play is about his 'dangerous inner rebellions' (1993, p. 181).

7 The name 'cauliban' means blackness (Kermode, 1964, p. xxxviii [fn]) and, as with Othello or Cleopatra, suggests the exotic and unknown; Ted Hughes (1992) associates it with the blackness of Dionysus or the blueness of Krishna, or the Boar (from the Adonis myth) who is a component of Shakespeare's goddess-muse. Sycorax came to the island from Algiers. Montaigne's essay 'The Cannibals' is considered a source for both the name and the colonial setup, as was pointed out by D. G. James:

> Prospero is not only the Virginia planter; and the time will come when he will say: 'this thing of darkness I acknowledge mine; as St Augustine in his *Confessions* knew well the darkness was in *him*, set over against the light before which he trembles in love and awe.
>
> (1967, p. 21)

Some critics dispute the colonial them just as they also dismiss the traditional view of Shakespeare's farewell to the stage.

8 A phrase noted by Coleridge for its strange beauty, spiritual rather than strictly human. The eye movement is the embodiment of nascent wondering curiosity (Bion's K-link).

9 Wendy MacPhee (2018) sees Ferdinand as the neophyte in a search for soul-knowledge in (additional to Christianity) the context of Shakespeare's knowledge of Ficino, the Cabala, Celtic arcana, and the alchemists.

10 The song about ingratitude, 'Blow blow thou winter wind', has an unusually personal flavour.

11 The renunciation speech 'Ye elves of hills, brooks, standing lakes and groves' is based on Ovid's Medea in the *Metamorphoses* (discussed by Brown, 1994, and others). Northrop Frye writes that 'drama is born in the renunciation of magic, and in *The Tempest* and elsewhere it remembers its inheritance' (1965, p. 59). The primitive origins are both linked with and transcended.

12 Shakespeare's characteristic dichotomy of words-as-power versus words-as-expression is here paralleled by the transcendence of magic to become contemplation rather than action.

13 Keats, letter to Woodhouse, 27 October 1818 (ed. Gittings, 1970, p. 157).

14 W. H. Auden in his essay on the play's music (1962) thinks it ends on a 'sour' note, in contrast to the other late romances. Perhaps it just makes the sharpest distinction between the benefits gained by the poet as a man, and the benefits potentially gained by the audience.

Epilogue

The play's the thing – but not in Hamlet's sense of a plaything for omnipotent intentions. The play is no transitional object, providing an escape from our conflicts and anxieties, but a container for psychic reality. Both we and Shakespeare learn from the play's existence, from the dream-knowledge trapped in its aesthetic form: just as in psychoanalysis, analyst and analysand learn from the analysis as an aesthetic object, something beyond themselves. The function of a play is not to catch the conscience of the king; that is the role of the lawyer or politician. If we try to trap the meaning like a mouse the mystery disappears, like Meltzer's metaphor of the light going out in the fridge in the face of intrusion into the aesthetic object:

> In [the Klein-Bion] model of the mind the locus of alpha-function is the combined internal object, in its primal form the breast-and-nipple, the nuptial chamber of Keats's 'Maiden Thought'. One could jokingly imagine that the 'prohibition' against intrusive voyeurism into this mystery and privacy would operate in the reverse of the fridge: if you open the door, the internal light goes out. This is a gentler view of these god-like objects than Oedipus' self-blinding would suggest.
>
> (Meltzer & Williams, [1988] 2018, p. 253)

The godlike objects of Money-Kyrle's 'innate preconception' of creativity – Melanie Klein's 'combined object' – shut the door on any form of conscience or consciousness that does not shine inwards and outwards at the same time: that is, inwards to the self and outwards to the external aesthetic attributes of the independent object, enabling imagination to operate. The interior is illuminated on a dream-level.

This drama of knowledge is presented in all Shakespeare's plays; it is the story that lies behind all the other stories of progressive or thwarted personality development. It is also the story of both the making of the play and of our reception of the play: are we to adopt a colonising explanatory attitude or a depressive learning one? Throughout his career Shakespeare was preoccupied with the idea of the play: not just its value and effectiveness in its social context, but its meaning in relation to his activity as symbol-maker. All the performance factors contribute to the art-symbol, but at its core is language, precipitating an internal war between mastery of words and service to the muse. The poet-servant working through inspiration pays close attention to his dreams and allows the muse to formulate them in poetic language. That is how psychic meaning is captured.

Wariness of language and its misuses is one of the most central preoccupations in Shakespeare: the question being, which is dominant – persuasion or expression, the wish to gain a point or the need to say what is meant. Language, especially in the case of those who can employ it with virtuosity, can be used as an exoskeleton, a dazzling facade, to the detriment of psychic exploration – Bion's 'language of substitution' rather than 'language of achievement'. The language of achievement evolves during analytic practice on the basis of dreamlike observation, just as it evolves during the writing of a poem or play; but in the latter case, owing to its poetic structure, it is of universal not private relevance.

In terms of originality, Shakespeare knew that nobody was going to come up with any mode of argument that had not already been deployed by the ancient Greeks and catalogued by Renaissance rhetoricians. But the job of the dramatist is to ask, what does this character mean by using this argument? The credo intended to ensure Tudor stability is brilliantly formulated in Ulysses' 'degree' speech, but Ulysses is a diplomatic shark. The Renaissance philosophy of music has never been more elegantly articulated than by Lorenzo, but Lorenzo is an opportunist parasite. The rhetoric of Brutus' hidden narcissism rouses the rabble beyond his best intentions. Richard, in relinquishing his narcissistic control to become a vehicle for poetry, has to undergo the 'death' of catastrophic change, from one use of language to another; he learns to hear the music of friendship behind the tones of an inexpertly played instrument. Poetic language does not mean persuasive or pretty – a feature only of debating chamber or drawing room. If anything it means the language of the wild wood, the heath, the sea – the dream-world. It does not always take the form of verse, often mistakes words in the effort to be sincere (represented generally by the low characters), and sometimes does not speak at all. Hippolyta's silence in response to 'What cheer, my love?' envelops Theseus like a mist and turns his questioning inward. Ophelia's speech is 'nothing', but the Queen's dream speaks for her. If any of Shakespeare's plays concludes with a moral it is *Lear*, with Edgar's 'Speak what we feel, not what we ought to say' – a complex problem in the simplest of words. But it is the poet who gives even the most cynical character the language that can express feelingly their inability to feel or think.

All these characters really represent abstract forces: not ones to which we need to give a name, but rather to allow a status, as aspects of our own mentality, creatures of light and darkness that we acknowledge ours. They are 'links' or 'valencies' in Bion's chemical metaphor of psychic directions seeking transformation, discovered on our behalf by Shakespeare and embodied in a form with which we can identify, somewhere between impulse and action. In the process the play becomes for its author an aesthetic object which he has a duty to present truthfully: not a plaything to display his own virtuosity. The author and the work have a container-contained relationship. Creating the play means, in psychic reality, mediating between his internal objects (muse) and the audience – which includes himself. His own language skills are governed by the 'underlying idea' (Langer), the equivalent of the 'underlying pattern' of a psychoanalytic session, its 'O' (Bion).

As audience, we follow the playwright's own journey through the play as these abstract links weave themselves into a new kaleidoscopic pattern. The play activates love, hate, and the desire for knowledge of its dreamlike interior, evoked by its exterior attractions. The hate comes from the ugliness of our own confusion, which can be temporarily dispelled by the impact of a powerful stage performance. But the temptation remains to cover the confusion with a theoretical treatise, to replace unassimilable ambiguities with complacent wordplay. The surface sign-language of debate and discourse treats the play as a colonial possession in the old patriarchal mode (even when nominally feminist); it is a retreat from the aesthetic conflict aroused by the mysterious interior. The play as aesthetic object contains the information that facilitates our own process of becoming; it is a ship to a brave new world. A subjective reading need not be a projection of the 'selfhood' (in Blake's term); on the contrary, it can model a process of identification and self-discovery, the 'evolution of O' in other minds. As we try to read both it and ourselves at the same time, our own existing identity is subsumed and sea-changed.

Appendix
Dream-life in the post-Kleinian model of the mind

The model of the mind founded on Melanie Klein's view of unconscious phantasy as expressing the reality of psychic events in a concrete inner world lends itself well to analogies with theatre, derived as it was from investigating the meaning of children's play. This is the model used in this book to link the playwright's self-analysis with the potential emotional conflicts of his audience. Shakespeare had a special ability to listen to his unconscious dream-world and translate it into the art-symbols of his plays in a way which constitutes creative thought. All his stories dramatise the struggle between omnipotent control and the subterranean knowledge lodged in dreams and accessed via the poetic muse or internal object. The appendix to this book summarises the main features of the psychoanalytic understanding of this psychic network. As they underlie the psychoanalytic process, they are employed probably by most psychoanalysts; but here I focus primarily on the post-Kleinian formulations of Wilfred Bion and Donald Meltzer, as they particularly stress how in dream-life, internal objects perform real functions in the mind. Conflictual emotions which are initially intolerable are worked on unconsciously through internal object relations; thus they acquire meaning and can be integrated into the personality. The transference evoked through the psychoanalytic setting is not simply a vehicle for emotional containment but for unconscious thinking, a quest for intimate self-knowledge. This moment of understanding involves an aspect of truth taking root in a specific earthly context, caught in the link of a relationship between two minds – something both exemplified and fictionalised in a Shakespeare play, where the story within the play is mirrored in the playwright's and the audience's relation to the artwork through their receptive dreams.

Donald Meltzer writes of dream life as 'a theatre for the generating of meaning' – not as day residue nor a means of seeking the equilibrium of instinctual impulses. The dream-world is a place where mental events take place, thoughts take root, are given birth, and developed through a series of stages of increasing complexity. In dream-life, internal objects perform real functions in the mind, including processing conflictual emotions which are initially intolerable but when worked on unconsciously, by internal object relations, acquire meaning and thus become integrated into the personality as part of its intimate knowledge felt on the pulses (Wilfred Bion's 'learning from experience', or Piers the Plowman's 'kyndely knowing'). Knowledge that has entered the mind through this processing of dream thoughts and images is of a different type from that which is acquired in the form of external information ('learning about'), although both have their role and of course interact unless the mind is intent on retreating from the pain and turbulence that accompanies self-knowledge. This is also the kind of knowledge dealt with in psychoanalysis: it is the truth of the transference, at that time, held by the container of the psychoanalytic setting, which Meltzer describes as a forcing-house for symbol-formation. Thus it is not simply emotional containment but thinking, as in the theory of thinking adumbrated on the basis of mother-baby communication. The moment of knowledge, or understanding, is termed by Bion 'intersection with O', meaning that an aspect of truth has taken root in a specific earthly context, caught in the link of a relationship between two minds.

Meltzer in his book *Dream Life* integrates Kleinian psychoanalytic approaches to symbol-formation with ideas about the origins and development of language derived from linguistic and aesthetic philosophy:

> Philosophers . . . have moved in a direction that alters the view of the senselessness of the emotive aspects of human mentality. The later Wittgenstein of the *Philosophic Investigations,* Cassirer of *Symbolic Forms,* Susanne Langer of *Philosophy in a New Key*, among others, have moved from the equation of word and symbol in a direction that views symbol-formation as the heart of the matter and its diverse forms as the prime object of study. This means that the problem of meaning has been widened from a view that placed it as a fact of external reality which had to be apprehended, to a more internal position as something to be generated and deployed, a neoPlatonic view. This move has accompanied the tendency away from the view that the mind is the brain, in favour of a vision that places human mentality at a different phenomenological level from animal neurophysiology, with symbol formation and the generating of meaning, and thus the possibility of discovering significance, as the central object of epistemological study.
>
> (Meltzer, [1984] 2018, p. 22)

Meltzer considers Ella Sharpe's view of a dream's 'poetic diction' in the light of its potential to build a 'bridge to the field of aesthetics' in general, and in addition to his own aesthetic picture of the psychoanalytic process, sets the symbol-making of a dream in the wider context of the 'deep grammar' of symbolic forms, as in Chomsky's 'universal generative grammar'. This is different from the common Freudian-Lacanian sense of symbol as a signifier or pointer. Meaning is contained in a way that is inextricable from the dream or artwork and its formal structure, and something equivalent takes place in a psychoanalytic session in which the analysis itself is the symbol-generator. The real, underlying meaning is not the same as its formulation in an interpretation, though the aim is to approximate as closely as possible.

Dream-life is the same as 'unconscious phantasy' as described by Susan Isaacs (1948), the real basis of psychic life, with many levels of complexity, unlike primary process. It lies at the heart of the mind's capacity to build itself through thinking thoughts and is considered to be a continuum within each developing mind or personality, for which remembered dreams are the tip of the iceberg. Intimate relations and art forms are parallel examples of the continuous, unconscious processing of dream-life. Subsequent to Bion's work, all these intimate areas can be seen to contrast with the protomental or adaptational forms of existence which represent the equivalent of language's lexical or surface grammar rather than its poetic 'deep grammar'. Language, as a symbolic mode, has two functions and two roots: one concerned with communication of information (the discursive), the other concerned with communicating states of mind (the presentational, including the poetic).[1] The latter originates in mother-baby communication and is therefore a feature of internal object relations, worked out through unconscious phantasy and dreaming, and resulting in the capacity for speech. It is dreaming that makes us what we are. Referring to Emily Brontë's 'wine through water',[2] Meltzer concludes: 'When such a dream has visited our sleeping soul, how can we ever again doubt that dreams are "events" in our lives?' ([1984] 2018, p. 101).

Dreaming is not wish-fulfilment, as is almost ubiquitously assumed in psychoanalytic criticism, but an expression of the psychic situation as it is: it represents the truth about the dreamer's state of mind. For this reason dreams may vary hugely in their poetic and condensation qualities. Although some dreams may give evidence of wish-fulfilment or the desire to escape from reality, the dream itself is not unreal but is the symbolisation of an emotional fact. As such the dream represents the first contact with an idea in representational form, after it has been inchoately sensed through 'the facts of feeling' (Bion). These 'facts' underpin the life of ideas and are the genesis of dream-life and symbol-formation in both the arts and the individual personality.

Meltzer describes the Kleinian model, founded on the mother-baby relationship, as a neoPlatonic, quasi-theological one in which the more advanced or knowledgeable parts of the mind are experienced as internal deities which nurture the familiar everyday self with its limited knowledge and understanding of its own condition. Money-Kyrle (1960) calls this model 'realist' as opposed to 'nominalist' – that is, emphasising psychic reality. In his paper on 'Cognitive Development' (1968) he lists three essential innate preconceptions on which all subsequent conceptions are based: a good breast (feeding); a good parental intercourse (creativity, imagined through the nipple-in-mouth experience); and the idea of death, which gives an awareness of time and absence, hence the need to mourn loss and internalise the object. The idea of a good breast (arousing love) logically precedes the idea of an absent breast (arousing hate).[3] The process by which preconceptions become conceptions or ideas is described by Bion as 'alpha-function': the symbiotic link between baby and mother in which anxiety is projected into the mother, digested through her reverie, and returned to the baby with a sense of meaningfulness and understanding.[4] The baby not only receives back the particular anxiety transformed into a thought but also introjects something of the mother's thinking process as an aspect of mental equipment, for future use. The mother is the first muse, and the power of poetry consists in its ability to access and express these otherwise inexpressible psychic events on behalf of readers.

Every situation of psychic growth entails 'emotional turbulence' (Bion)[5] owing to the 'aesthetic conflict' aroused in relation to the object (Meltzer, 1988). It is aesthetic because the primary response is to the beauty of the mother (or breast, or object),[6] which has immediate sensuous impact; but the mother's inside is unknowable and hence may have the meaning for the baby (or self) of absence or death. In the Platonic system, goodness, truth, and beauty are inextricably linked and point towards the ineffable, which Bion terms 'O'. The ambivalent emotionality stimulates the desire for knowledge of the object, and in particular the non-sensuous interior of the object, which can only be known through imagination.[7] Bion uses the formula L, H, K (love, hate and knowledge) to denote this aesthetic conflict and the direction of its resolution – towards knowledge, understanding, conceptualisation.[8] Aesthetic conflict thus derives originally from the baby's first learning experiences in relation to the mother, and then applies throughout life in terms of the unconscious phantasy behind all learning activities.

An analogous process of resolving the emotional tension between these basic links takes place in all creative learning experiences,[9] including the making of artwork and its appreciation. Where scientific discovery results from mapping the exterior of the object (the physically sensible), the art imaginatively explores the interior of the object and thereby creates a symbol of its nature. The symbol enables the reader to follow the voyage of discovery.

Alternatively, in cases where LHK fails to be dynamised in a developmental direction, and the emotional tension cannot be tolerated, a state of negativity may become entrenched, denoted by Bion through the negative links of 'minus L, H, K'. This is an extreme and fossilised version of a paranoid-schizoid state, which at its most entrenched can result in the type of intrusive unconscious phantasy described by Meltzer (1992) as living in 'the claustrum', the interior of the internal mother.[10] The aesthetic object is denigrated or colonised by the self's envy, possessiveness, or desire to control the object.[11] It takes the form of false or substitute knowledge based on a narcissistic phantasy of omnipotence. By contrast, the mental organisation that allows creative symbol-formation to take place is founded on Klein's 'depressive position', namely, dependence on the goodness of the internal object and its capacity to deliver truth. It is a 'reparation' of internal damage felt to be caused by infantile or envious destructiveness;[12] although as Money-Kyrle points out, the mechanism that the self is able to operate is simply the withdrawal of destructive projections; and Meltzer emphasises that the self cannot be creative in itself, only by means of ceasing from destructive actions, thus allowing the internal combined object to be creative and to repair itself.[13]

Having an idea entails a new contact with truth or reality, not of course the whole or absolute truth, but the truth of the psychic situation at that moment, known (however indirectly and incompletely) by 'intersection' with the essential or ineffable form of the idea (Bion's 'O') with a sensuous reality (Bion, 1970). We do not invent ideas, we discover them – by means of what the poets call inspiration, or psychoanalysts introjective identification: a dialogue between the self and the internal object or objects (the muse).[14] The truth which exists behind or beyond a sensuous manifestation is referred to by Susanne Langer, in aesthetics, as the 'underlying idea' of a situation, and guides the formation of the art-symbol or performance.[15] This reorganisation of unconscious phantasy is not simply expressed in dreams but also worked out in dreams – the new meaning of 'dream-work', which is, in post-Kleinian theory, not a disguiser but a revealer of truth. This is the type of dreamwork dramatised throughout Shakespeare's plays, whether or not the action is actually presented as a dream.[16] Thinking as dream-work is manifest as 'presentational' rather than 'discursive' form, in Langer's distinction: it contains, rather than states, its significance.

At the end of his final paper, 'Making the Best of a Bad Job' (1987), Bion cites Plato's *Theaetetus* on the difficulty of ensuring a young man's education fill his head not with 'phantoms' but with 'live thoughts'. How is it possible to 'become oneself' in a process of development without predetermined goals? Live thoughts will encourage an 'endoskeletonal' structure, whereas dead ones will confine the mind in a spurious exoskeleton – whether imposed by society's basic assumptions or by the existing self that, by default, will resist change. Bion describes the kind of real psychic change that is an integral feature of development as 'catastrophic change', owing to its associations with *peripeteia* in classical drama, the moment of knowledge achieved via the reversal of omnipotence. This is the point at which, in psychoanalytic terms, the infant's distress, received and mentally digested by the mother, is transformed into a dream-thought by means of alpha-function. In this the analyst, like Socrates, is a midwife or mediator to the birth of ideas, not a vial of wisdom. The analyst thinks by means of a 'countertransference dream' (Meltzer). Hence the psychoanalysis itself – the container for this process – takes on the reality of an aesthetic object, for both partners.[17]

The countertransference dream in literary criticism

When Bion writes that great minds such as those of Milton and Shakespeare could not only 'formulate the states of mind of the people among whom they lived' but also 'penetrate states of mind which did not then exist – ours' (1987, p. 232), he means poets can quite literally symbolise emotional states which have not yet become realised within a particular time or culture. They are not yet 'known' – they have not yet 'intersected with O' in Bion's neoPlatonic terminology – except within the poetic language itself, awaiting discovery by the future reader. This is in line with Shelley's 'unacknowledged legislators of the world', and explains how it is that psychoanalytic literary criticism does not need to confine itself to the culture of the era or exclude the possibility of any psychic understanding not formulated at the time.[18]

Bion borrows Keats' definition of 'negative capability' to describe the state of mind necessary for a 'man of achievement' – that is, a person who is engaged in the turbulent process of becoming themselves.[19] For the psychoanalyst, the turbulence is itself a healthy sign that 'valuable work is being achieved' (Bion, 1970, p. 124); and the same is true for the playwright, in relation to both his own activity as author, and to the evolution of the play's meaning via the interaction of characters. Technically he is the maker, but psychically he is the seer;[20] the play has to be allowed to become itself. As Meltzer puts it: 'Is the Muse a formal figure of speech or a psychological reality?'[21]

In psychoanalysis, the problem of observation is considered key to the psychoanalytic process. This implies that something exists that is capable of being observed – not invented. Bion adopts Freud's definition of consciousness as the 'organ of attention' that can look inwards and outwards at the same time, whether awake or asleep. Similarly, close reading, as a discipline, enables the critic to actually look at the work with the prospect of making discoveries rather than seeing only what he has put there himself.[22] The truth of a work exists objectively within its artistic structure even though it can only be accessed subjectively, though the same aesthetic conflict is aroused in the reader as in the author whose thought-process is being followed. Literary criticism too can be a presentational form, not simply a discursive one. The validity of a literary interpretation depends on establishing a symbolic congruence, psychically, with the aesthetic object, by means of a countertransference dream.[23]

The truth of the aesthetic object, in literary criticism also, can be understood in terms of the original mother-baby constellation. It arouses love and hate simultaneously owing to the enigmatic quality of its interior. Reading it, rather than inventing or playing with it, is strenuous and anxiety-producing, involving Bion's oscillation between the paranoid-schizoid and depressive positions. For the aesthetic object cannot be known by means of omnipotent projections but only by a receptive subjectivity, feeding from the artist's mind via the artwork which has trapped a particular emotional conflict in the cage of form.[24] This is far more strenuous, more confusing, and requires the same negative capability that Keats described and that Bion adopted in his proposal to seek a 'language of achievement' in psychoanalysis, by contrast with a 'language of substitution', the tedious wordplay of the anti-poetic that characterises linguistic behaviourism.[25]

Bion says of the evolutionary idea of psychoanalysis as a 'thing-in-itself' that it is promoted by each authentic analysis: meaning that not only the patient but the analyst must develop. Otherwise 'the future of his practice or of himself is

Dream-life in the post-Kleinian model 161

no part of psychoanalysis though it may be a part of the sociology of the practice of psychoanalysis' (1967, p. 137). Perhaps there is also literary criticism as a thing-in-itself, created by a series of authentic encounters between the reader's mind and that of the poet as embodied in the art-symbol. This is something different from a contemporary critical interpretation and explains why we still read the great critics of the past. While fashions in literary criticism merely reflect the sociology of their time, authentic subjective-objective readings can partake of the evolutionary idea of poetry by tracking the dream-thought that has the potential to develop the mentality of an individual or a culture, thereby expanding the container – which is in this case, the reception of poetry in the world.

Adrian Stokes wrote:

> The great work of art is surrounded by silence. It remains palpably 'out there', yet none the less enwraps us; we do not so much absorb as become ourselves absorbed.[26]

Basically, we have to remember that when we are absorbed in Shakespeare he is analysing us, not we him. Not Shakespeare as a person or man of his age but the other one who is 'for all time' – that is, the playwright who whilst conducting the play is in touch with an ethereal observer mediating with a world of expanded knowledge. Or is the play conducting him? In the Chamber of Maiden Thought, as Keats said, 'imperceptibly impelled by the awakening of the thinking principle within us' and seeking for symbolic congruence by means of our own countertransference dream, we have to 'follow in the steps of the author', who becomes integrated into our own internal object in the quest for self-knowledge.[27]

Notes

1 A distinction entirely absent in the Lacanian assumptions about language development that are so often quoted in psychoanalytic literary criticism (including the Kristevan or abjected feminist).

2 Catherine in *Wuthering Heights* speaks of dreams that have 'run through and through me like wine through water and changed the colour of my mind' (1992, p. 57).

3 Hence Meltzer's (1988) re-ordering of Klein's original formulation of the paranoid-schizoid position which she viewed as preceding the depressive position in the infant's development.

4 This is communicative projective identification, which functions in tandem with introjective identification as the developmental linkage between self and object, contained and container (Bion's container-contained).

5 The title of one of Bion's late talks (Bion, 1987).

6 Mother or breast as part-object may initially be taken in a literal sense, but in Kleinian thinking the external mother begins to become at a very early stage an internal object, with both maternal and paternal qualities (a 'combined object'). There is no such thing as a 'bad object' or 'bad mother', in *psychic* reality (which is not the same as external reality). The genuine internal object is by definition the most ethically advanced part of the mind, and a 'bad object' is really a self-object created by narcissistic projections when the self has

162   Dream-life in the post-Kleinian model

lost contact with the genuine object. Analogously, the preconception of a good parental intercourse clarifies Klein's original discovery of the 'combined object' in children's phantasy, which first manifest itself to her in a more troubled form. In both cases the clouded version only makes sense as a distortion of the real (good, beautiful, true) thing.

7   The Kleinian paranoid-schizoid position, based on projective identification, is ubiquitous and Bion describes its oscillation with the depressive position in terms of a formula with double arrows: Ps↔D.

8   The standard Kleinian concept is 'integration' of split parts of the object into a whole object. Bion specifies the developmental dynamic as the desire for *knowledge* of the object.

9   Bion calls this 'learning from experience', a common phrase used with a specialised meaning.

10 Meltzer maps out three types of intrusive identification into the head-breast, genital, or rectum of the object, the last being destructive of dream-life and the capacity to think. Logically, he points out, the child's own attacks imply an initial glimpse of the true or creative internal object, which is then distorted by these projections.

11 Meltzer terms this controlling and therefore anti-developmental link 'intrusive identification' to distinguish it from communicative projective identification as clarified by Bion. There are of course varying degrees of omnipotence.

12 Melanie Klein (1930) related symbol-formation to the child's need to process its earliest anxieties (Freud himself acknowledged his early theory did nothing to explain the artist's creativity). The link between 'reparation' and symbol-formation, in both personality structure and in the arts, was clarified by Hanna Segal in two seminal papers (1952; 1957).

13 The preconception of a good parental intercourse clarifies Klein's original discovery of the 'combined object' in children's phantasy, which first manifest itself to her in its troubled or monstrous form, something too overwhelming to be tolerable. Meltzer writes:

> The new idea in the end becomes the idea of the combined object, and this for Mrs Klein signified the advent of the depressive position. . . . Creativity does not require that there should be an integration of the self, but that there should be an integrated combined object well internalized.
>
> (2005, p. 179)

14 In 'Towards Learning from Experience in Infancy and Childhood', Martha Harris writes:

> Introjection remains a mysterious process: how do involvement and reliance upon objects in the external world which are apprehended by the senses (and, as Wilfred Bion has pointed out, described in language which has been evolved to deal with external reality) become assimilated and transformed in the mind into what he calls 'psychoanalytic objects' which can contribute to the growth of the personality? This is a process about which we have almost everything to learn.
>
> ([1978] 2018, p. 196)

15 Susanne Langer's (1942) theory of aesthetics is founded on music, which provides the clearest example of an underlying idea for which there is a notation. Composer, performer, and listener are focusing on the same underlying idea, inherent in the music's sensuous vehicle. Bion lamented that psychoanalysis had no such notation, and attempted to produce one in his (1963) Grid mapping the evolution of thoughts, though he later believed this experiment had been unsuccessful.

16 Marjorie Garber in *Dream in Shakespeare* (1974) made a deep and comprehensive evaluation of the many types of dream within the plays, in the context of the classical and contemporary view of dreams; she describes how Shakespeare's usage developed from monitory dream in the early plays, through dream as interior consciousness in the tragedies, to transformational dream as the 'pathway to transcendence and redemption' in

the late romances. Kay Stockholder (1987) observes that 'the denigration implied by the link between dream and art has . . . haunted literary criticism based on the psychoanalytic model' (p. 7). Building on Garber, she reviews Shakespeare's oeuvre in the light of dream-stories about family relationships structured around a single protagonist, an approach which yields many insights, although she still regards the activity of dreaming itself in the early Freudian light of wish-fulfilment rather than as exploration of psychic reality. I think that, other than *Hamlet*, the dreamer is more like a 'dreaming vertex' that switches between characters according to a particular sequence. Subsequent to these studies, the interest in dreams in Shakespearean criticism seems to have been overtaken by the anti-psychological approaches that began with postmodernism.

17 Bion insists (though it is not often noticed) that 'the personality has a container-contained relationship with psychoanalysis' (rather than with the analyst) (1970), an idea developed by Meltzer in *Studies in Extended Metapsychology* (1986). The psychoanalytic encounter forms and 'seals' a container that constitutes an aesthetic object, just as the play is an aesthetic object for both the playwright and the audience.

18 Stephen Greenblatt (1990) thought it anachronistic to use psychoanalytic concepts to discuss the early moderns as they were supposedly only beginning to have a psychology-centred conception of identity rather than a property-centred one. As a result, says Carolyn Brown, psychoanalytic theory as applied to early modern literature and Shakespeare became 'historicised' (2015, p. 3). It is actually not feasible to 'historicise' a Kleinian object-relations model, which is based on unconscious phantasy and the reality of the inner world. Brown's survey of psychoanalytic approaches does not mention the post-Kleinian.

19 Keats, letter to G. and T. Keats, 21 December 1817, cited by Bion in *Attention and Interpretation* (1970, p. 125).

20 The two complementary types of symbol-creator in classical theory.

21 Over-reliance on jargon constitutes a 'lie' in Bion's sense of an opaque covering of 'morality' (fixed ideas) that protects the self from the impact of new experience (1970, p. 27). Morality is a form of action – designed to persuade or dominate others – as distinct from contemplation which is inward-directed and dream-led (see Bion, 1970, p. 8).

22 Close reading and I. A. Richards' Cambridge school of 'practical criticism' was evolved in response to Coleridge's dictum 'Such is the life, such the form'. It demands precise observation of the deep grammar embedded in poetic diction. This kind of writing is an artistic practice rather than an explanatory or hermeneutic one, so relies on itself being translated by the reader in their own way.

23 Many theories of criticism have sprung up to justify the assertion that the artwork does not exist except when the reader is there to 'create' it. In '"Knowing" the Mystery: Against Reductionism' (1986), I suggested three categories of psychoanalytic literary criticism: linguistic behaviourism, softhumanism, and aesthetic criticism. The latter involves thinking with rather than thinking about the artwork, as in the art writings of Adrian Stokes with his emphasis on the rhythm of projection and introjection.

24 I refer to an ancient Chinese definition of poetry as 'trapping heaven and earth in the cage of form' (cited in MacLeish, 1961).

25 Bion (1970) means that a personal language needs to evolve between analyst and analysand that genuinely expresses the nature of their communication, not that there can be any ultimate theoretical language applicable to all analyses – indeed he considered this to be another 'lie'. Insofar as interpretations based on postmodern ideologies attain validity *as literary criticism* (rather than as sociology), this is always dependent on the individual critic's capacity to read the symbolic structure rather than to apply theory.

26 Stokes, 'The Luxury and Necessity of Painting' (1961), extracted in *Art and Analysis*, ed. M. H. Williams (2014), p. 32.

27 Keats, letter to Reynolds, 3 May 1818 (1970, p. 93).

References and bibliography

Quotations from Shakespeare's plays are from Arden editions.

Adelman, J. (1992). *Suffocating Mothers*. London: Routledge.

Alfar, C. L. (2003). *Fantasies of Female Evil: The Dynamics of Gender and Power in Shakespearean Tragedy*. Newark: University of Delaware Press.

Anson, J. (1969). Caesar's Stoic Pride. In: Ure, P. (ed.), *Julius Caesar: A Casebook*, pp. 207–219. London: Macmillan.

Auden, W. H. (1962). Music in Shakespeare. In: *The Dyer's Hand*, pp. 500–527. New York: Random House.

Bayley, J. (1981). *Shakespeare and Tragedy*. London: Routledge.

Berry, P. (1999). *Shakespeare's Feminine Endings: Disfiguring Death in the Tragedies*. London: Routledge.

Bion, W. R. (1962). A Theory of Thinking. *International Journal of Psychoanalysis*, 43, pp. 306–310.

Bion, W. R. (1967). *Second Thoughts*. London: Tavistock.

Bion, W. R. (1970). *Attention and Interpretation*. London: Tavistock.

Bion, W. R. ([1978] 2019). *Four Discussions*. London: Harris Meltzer Trust.

Bion, W. R. (1985). *All My Sins Remembered*. Abingdon: Fleetwood Press.

Bion, W. R. (1987). *Clinical Seminars and Four Papers*, pp. 224–233. Abingdon: Fleetwood.

Bion, W. R. (1989). *Two Papers: The Grid and Caesura*. London: Karnac.

Bion, W. R. (1994). *A Memoir of the Future*, 3 vols. Single-volume edition. London: Karnac.

Bion, W. R. (2018). *Bion in New York and Sao Paulo and Three Tavistock Lectures*. London: Harris Meltzer Trust.

Bloom, H. (1999). *Shakespeare: The Invention of the Human*. London: Fourth Estate.

Bradley, A. C. (1905). *Shakespearean Tragedy*. London: Macmillan.

Brontë, E. ([1847] 1992). *Wuthering Heights*. Ware: Wordsworth.

Brontë, E. (1941). *Poems*, ed. C. W. Hatfield. New York: Columbia University Press.

Brown, C. (2015). *Shakespeare and Psychoanalytic Theory*. London: Bloomsbury.

Brown, S. A. (1994). Ovid, Golding and the Tempest. *Translation and Literature*, 3, pp. 3–29.

Cassirer, E. ([1925] 1953). *Language and Myth*. London: Dover.

Coleridge, S. T. ([1816] 1997). *Biographia Literaria*, ed. N. Leask. London: Dent.

Cox, M. & Theilgaard, A. (1994). *Shakespeare as Prompter: The Amending Imagination and the Therapeutic Process*. London: Jessica Kingsley.

De la Mare, W. *Napoleon*. www.public-domain-poetry.com/walter-de-la-mare/napoleon-33514.

Empson, W. (1951). *The Structure of Complex Words*. London: Chatto & Windus.

References and bibliography   165

Fernie, E. (2005). *Spiritual Shakespeares*. Abingdon: Routledge.

Fisher, J. (2000). A Father's Abdication: Lear's Retreat from 'Aesthetic Conflict'. *International Journal of Psychoanalysis*, 81 (5), pp. 963–982.

Folkerth, W. (2002). *The Sound of Shakespeare*. London: Routledge.

Forster, E. M. (1927). *Aspects of the Novel*. London: Edward Arnold.

Frye, N. (1965). *A Natural Perspective: The Development of Shakespearean Comedy and Romance*. New York: Columbia University Press.

Gajowski, E. (1992). *The Art of Loving: Female Subjectivity and Male Discursive Traditions in Shakespeare's Tragedies*. Newark: University of Delaware Press.

Garber, M. B. (1974). *Dream in Shakespeare: From Metaphor to Metamorphosis*. New Haven: Yale University Press.

Greenblatt, S. (1990). *Learning to Curse: Essays in Early Modern Culture*. New York: Routledge.

Greenblatt, S. (2013). *Hamlet in Purgatory*. Princeton: Princeton University Press.

Gross, K. (2001). *Shakespeare's Noise*. Chicago: The University of Chicago Press.

Harris, M. (2007). *Your Teenager*. London: Harris Meltzer Trust.

Harris, M. ([1975] 2011). *Thinking about Infants and Young Children*. Perthshire: Clunie Press.

Harris, M. ([1975] 2018). The Early Basis of Adult Female Sexuality and Motherliness. In: *The Tavistock Model: Collected Papers of Martha Harris and Esther Bick*, pp. 279–294. London: Harris Meltzer Trust.

Harris, M. ([1978] 2018). Towards Learning from Experience in Infancy and Childhood. In: *The Tavistock Model: Collected Papers of Martha Harris and Esther Bick*, pp. 191–206. London: Harris Meltzer Trust.

Holland, N. (1968a). *The Dynamics of Literary Response*. New York: Columbia University Press.

Holland, N. (1968b). Caliban's Dream. *Psychoanalytic Quarterly*, 37 (1), pp. 371–381.

Hughes, T. (1992). *Shakespeare and the Goddess of Complete Being*. London: Faber.

Isaacs, S. (1948). The Nature and Function of Phantasy. *International Journal of Psychoanalysis*, 29, pp. 73–97.

Jacobs, M. ([2008] 2018). *Shakespeare on the Couch*. Abingdon: Routledge.

Jacobus, M. (2005). *The Poetics of Psychoanalysis: In the Wake of Klein*. Oxford: Oxford University Press.

James, D. G. (1967). *The Dream of Prospero*. Oxford: Oxford University Press.

Kahn, C. (1986). The Absent Mother in King Lear. In: Ferguson, M. W., Quilligan, M., & Vickers, N. J. (eds), *Rewriting the Renaissance: The Discourses of Sexual Difference in Early Modern Europe*, pp. 33–49. Chicago: The University of Chicago Press.

Keats, J. (1970). *Selected Letters*, ed. R. Gittings. Oxford: Oxford University Press.

Kermode, F. (1964). Introduction. *The Tempest*, pp. i–xciii. London: Methuen.

Kerrigan, J. (ed.). (1991). *Motives of Woe: Shakespeare and 'Female Complaint'*. Oxford: Oxford University Press.

Klein, M. (1930). The Importance of Symbol Formation in the Development of the Ego. *International Journal of Psychoanalysis*, 11, pp. 24–39.

Knight, G. W. ([1930] 1969). King Lear and the Comedy of the Grotesque. In: Kermode, F. (ed.), *King Lear: A Casebook*, pp. 118–136. London: Macmillan.

Knight, G. W. ([1930] 1989). The Othello Music. In: *The Wheel of Fire: Interpretations of Shakespearian Tragedy*, pp. 109–136. London: Routledge.

Knight, G. W. (1931). *The Imperial Theme*. London: Methuen.

Knight, G. W. (1932). *The Crown of Life: Essays in Interpretation of Shakespeare's Final Plays*. London: Methuen.

166 References and bibliography

Knights, L. C. (1979). *Hamlet and Other Shakespearean Essays*. Cambridge: Cambridge University Press.

Krohn, J. (1986). The Dangers of Love in Antony and Cleopatra. *International Review of Psychoanalysis*, 13, pp. 89–96.

Langer, S. (1942). *Philosophy in a New Key*. Cambridge: Harvard University Press.

Langer, S. (1953). *Feeling and Form*. London: Routledge.

Lianeri, A. & Zajko, V. (eds). (2008). *Translation and the Classic: Identity as Change in the History of Culture*. Oxford: Oxford University Press.

Mack, M. ([1966] 2005). *King Lear in Our Time*. Berkeley: University of California Press.

MacLeish, A. (1961). *Poetry and Experience*. London: Bodley Head.

MacNeice, L. ([1966] 1968). Autolycus. In: Muir, K. (ed.), *A Winter's Tale: A Casebook*. London: Macmillan.

MacPhee, W. (2018). *Secret Meanings in Shakespeare Applied to Stage Performance*. M-Y Books.

Mahood, M. M. (1957). *Shakespeare's Wordplay*.

Martindale, C. (2008). Dryden's Ovid: Aesthetic Translation and the Idea of the Classic. In: Lianeri, A. & Zajko, V. (eds), *Translation and the Classic: Identity as Change in the History of Culture*, pp. 83–109. Oxford: Oxford University Press.

Martindale, C. & Taylor, A. B. (eds). (2004). *Shakespeare and the Classics*. Cambridge: Cambridge University Press.

McAlindon, T. ([1969] 1976). Language, Style and Meaning. In: *Troilus and Cressida: A Casebook*, ed. P. Martin, pp. 191–218. London: Macmillan.

Meltzer, D. ([1967] 2018). *The Psychoanalytical Process*. London: Harris Meltzer Trust.

Meltzer, D. ([1973] 2018). *Sexual States of Mind*. London: Harris Meltzer Trust.

Meltzer, D. ([1978] 2018). *The Kleinian Development*. Book 3: Bion. London: Harris Meltzer Trust.

Meltzer, D. ([1986] 2018). *Studies in Extended Metapsychology*. London: Harris Meltzer Trust.

Meltzer, D. ([1992] 2018). *The Claustrum*. London: Harris Meltzer Trust.

Meltzer, D. (1982). Jacket Cover to M. H. Williams. In: *Inspiration in Milton and Keats*. London: Macmillan.

Meltzer, D. ([1984] 2018). *Dream Life*. London: Harris Meltzer Trust.

Meltzer, D. (1994). Sincerity. In: Hahn, A. (ed.), *Sincerity: Collected Papers of Donald Meltzer*. London: Karnac.

Meltzer, D. (2005). Creativity and the Countertransference. In: Williams, M. H. (ed.), *The Vale of Soulmaking*, pp. 175–182. London: Karnac.

Meltzer, D. & Harris, M. (2011). *Adolescence*. London: Harris Meltzer Trust.

Meltzer, D. & Harris, M. (2013). *The Educational Role of the Family: A Psychoanalytical Model*. London: Harris Meltzer Trust.

Meltzer, D. & Williams, M. H. ([1988] 2018). *The Apprehension of Beauty*. London: Harris Meltzer Trust.

Miller, L. (1975). A View of King Lear. *Journal of Child Psychotherapy*, 4 (1), pp. 93–124.

Money-Kyrle, R. ([1960] 2015). *Man's Picture of His World*. In: *Man's Picture of His World and Three Papers*. London: Harris Meltzer Trust.

Money-Kyrle, R. ([1968] 2015). Cognitive Development. In: *Man's Picture of His World and Three Papers*. London: Harris Meltzer Trust.

Nuttall, A. D. (1988). Ovid's Narcissus and Shakespeare's Richard II: The Reflected Self. In: Martindale, C. (ed.), *Ovid Renewed: Ovidian Influences on Literature and Art from the Middle Ages to the Twentieth Century*, pp. 137–150. Cambridge: Cambridge University Press.

References and bibliography 167

Nuttall, A. D. (2004). Action at a Distance: Shakespeare and the Greeks. In: Martindale, C. & Taylor, A. B. (eds), *Shakespeare and the Classics*, pp. 209–224. Cambridge: Cambridge University Press.

Nuttall, A. D. (2007). *Shakespeare the Thinker*. New Haven: Yale University Press.

Pater, W. ([1889] 2016). *Appreciations*. Torrance: IDB Productions.

Rabkin, N. (1967). *Shakespeare and the Common Understanding*. New York: Free Press.

Raffield, P. (2011). The Elizabethan Rhetoric of Signs: Representations of *Res Publica* at the Early Modern Inns of Court. *Law, Culture and the Humanities*, 7 (2), pp. 244–263.

Rank, O. (1992). *The Incest Theme in Literature and Legend: Fundamentals of a Psychology of Literary Creation*, trans. G. C Richter. Baltimore: Johns Hopkins University Press.

Righter, A. (Barton). (1962). *Shakespeare and the Idea of the Play*. Harmondsworth: Penguin.

Righter, A. (Barton). (1968). Introduction. In: *The Tempest*, pp. 7–52. Harmondsworth: Penguin.

Schanzer, E. (1969). The Tragedy of Brutus. In: Ure, P. (ed.), *Julius Caesar: A Casebook*, pp. 183–194. London: Macmillan.

Schwartz, M. (1973). Leontes' Jealousy in The Winter's Tale. *American Imago*, 30 (3), pp. 250–273.

Schwartz, M. (1980). Shakespeare through Contemporary Psychoanalysis. In: Schwartz, M. & Kahn, C. (eds), *Representing Shakespeare*, pp. 21–32. Baltimore: Johns Hopkins University Press.

Segal, H. (1952). A Psychoanalytical Approach to Aesthetics. *International Journal of Psychoanalysis*, 38, pp. 391–397.

Segal, H. (1957). Notes on Symbol Formation. *International Journal of Psychoanalysis*, 33, pp. 196–207.

Shapiro, M. (1996). *Gender and Play on the Shakespearean Stage*. Ann Arbor: University of Michigan Press.

Sheppard, A. (1993). Soiled Mother or Soul of Woman? A Response to Troilus and Cressida. In: Sokol, B. J. (ed.), *The Undiscover'd Country: New Essays on Psychoanalysis and Shakespeare*, pp. 130–149. London: Free Association Books.

Simonds, P. M. (1994). Myth, Emblem and Music in Shakespeare's Cymbeline. *Comparative Drama*, 27 (4), pp. 468–473.

Skura, M. (1980). Interpreting Posthumus' Dream from above and below: Families, Psychoanalysts, and Literary Critics. In: Schwartz, M. & Kahn, C. (eds), *Representing Shakespeare: New Psychoanalytic Essays*, pp. 203–216. Baltimore: Johns Hopkins University Press.

Skura, M. (1981). *The Literary Use of the Psychoanalytic Process*. New Haven: Yale University Press.

Skura, M. (1993). *Shakespeare the Actor and the Purposes of Playing*. Chicago: The University of Chicago Press.

Sokol, B. J. (1993). The Tempest, All Torment, Trouble, Wonder and Amazement: A Kleinian Reading. In: Sokol, B. J. (ed.), *The Undiscover'd Country: New Essays on Psychoanalysis and Shakespeare*, pp. 179–216. London: Free Association Books.

Stephens, L. (1993). 'A Wilderness of Monkeys': A Psychodynamic Study of *the Merchant of Venice*. In: Sokol, B. J. (ed.), *The Undiscover'd Country: New Essays on Psychoanalysis and Shakespeare*, pp. 91–129. London: Free Association Books.

Stockholder, K. (1987). *Dream Works: Lovers and Families in Shakespeare's Plays*. Toronto: University of Toronto Press.

Stokes, A. (1961). *Three Essays on the Painting of Our Time*. London: Tavistock.

Stokes, A. (1965). *The Invitation in Art*. London: Tavistock.

168 References and bibliography

Tennenhouse, L. (1980). The Counterfeit Order of the Merchant of Venice. In: Schwartz, M. & Kahn, C. (eds), *Representing Shakespeare*, pp. 54–69. Baltimore: Johns Hopkins University Press.

Walker, J. M. (1998). *Medusa's Mirrors: Spenser, Shakespeare, Milton and the Metamorphosis of the Female Self.* Newark: University of Delaware Press.

Wells, R. H. (2005). *Shakespeare's Humanism.* Cambridge: Cambridge University Press.

Wells, S. (1969). Introduction. In: *Richard II*, pp. 7–46. Harmondsworth: Penguin.

Willbern, D. (1980). Shakespeare's Nothing. In: Schwartz, M. & Kahn, C. (eds), *Representing Shakespeare*, pp. 244–263. Baltimore: Johns Hopkins University Press.

Williams, M. H. (1986). 'Knowing' the Mystery: Against Reductionism. *Encounter*, 67 (1), pp. 48–53.

Williams, M. H. ([1988a] 2018). Holding the Dream. In: *The Apprehension of Beauty*, pp. 187–210. London: Harris Meltzer Trust.

Williams, M. H. ([1988b] 2018). The Undiscovered Country: The Shape of the Aesthetic Conflict in Hamlet. In: *The Apprehension of Beauty*, pp. 89–140. London: Harris Meltzer Trust.

Williams, M. H. (1992). Macbeth's Equivocation, Shakespeare's Ambiguity. In: Meltzer, D. (ed.), *The Claustrum*, pp. 159–185. Perthshire: Clunie Press.

Williams, M. H. ([1997] 2014). *Hamlet in Analysis: Horatio's Story: A Trial of Faith.* London: Harris Meltzer Trust.

Williams, M. H. (2005). *The Vale of Soulmaking: The Post-Kleinian Model of the Mind.* London: Karnac.

Williams, M. H. (2008). A Post-Kleinian Model for Aesthetic Criticism. *Psyart*, online journal. www.questia.com/library/journal/1P3-1484530091/a-post-kleinian-model-for-aesthetic-criticism.

Williams, M. H. (2011). The True Voice of Feeling: Lear's Pilgrimage. *Psychodynamic Practice*, 17 (2), pp. 141–158.

Williams, M. H. (ed.). (2014). *Art and Analysis: An Adrian Stokes Reader.* London: Harris Meltzer Trust.

Williams, M. H. & Waddell, M. (1991). *The Chamber of Maiden Thought: Literary Origins of the Psychoanalytic Model of the Mind.* London: Routledge.

Wilson, R. (2003). Introduction. In: Dutton, A. R., Findlay, A. G., & Wilson, R. (eds), *Theatre and Religion: Lancastrian Shakespeare.* Manchester: Manchester University Press.

Wimsatt, W. K. & Beardsley, M. C. (1946). The Intentional Fallacy. *Sewanee Review*, 54, pp. 468–488.

Wittgenstein, L. ([1922] 2001). *Tractatus Logico-Philosophicus.* London: Routledge.

Name index

Adelman, J. 89, 91, 92, 118
Auden, W. 87, 151

Bayley, J. 53
Berry, P. 18, 45, 77, 92, 106
Bion, W. R. 4, 12, 19, 27, 60, 65, 76,
77, 86, 96, 107, 137, 157, 160; alpha-
function 9, 79; basic assumptions 2,
18, 32; beta-elements 64; catastrophic
change 105, 159; container-contained
81, 105, 161; emotional turbulence
110, 136, 150, 158; exoskeletonal
personality 52; language of achievement
153; learning from experience 22, 156,
162; LHK 78, 144, 151; on lies 61;
memory and desire 32; minus K 35,
43, 59, 84; morality 45; nameless dread
63, 66; O 154, 155, 158, 159; pain *vs.*
suffering 39
Blake, W. 117, 135, 154
Bloom, H. 13, 17, 18, 77, 106, 107,
115, 145
Bradley, A. C. 60, 76, 77
Bronte, E. 138, 157
Brown, C. 151

Cassirer, E. 92, 156
Coleridge, S. T. 27, 52, 66, 71, 77, 91,
147, 151, 163

De la Mare, W. 10

Empson, W. 70

Fernie, E. 48
Fisher, J. 91
Folkerth, W. 18, 23, 29, 45, 77, 92, 120
Forster, E. M. 91

Freud, S. 104, 142, 156; on dreaming 45,
163; organ of consciousness 107, 160; on
thought 21, 35, 63
Frye, N. 29, 46, 55, 58, 120, 135, 151

Gajowski, E. 77, 106
Garber, M. 12, 29, 30, 45, 76, 77, 106,
120, 135, 162
Greemblatt, S. 45, 163

Harris, M. 31, 80, 81, 83, 92, 104, 105, 162
Hazlitt, W. 32, 71
Hughes, T. 141, 151

Isaacs, S. 157

Jacobs, M. 91, 106
James, D. G. 91, 151

Kahn, C. 91
Keats, J. 10, 24, 82, 119, 128, 148, 150;
feeling on the pulses 91; maiden thought
152, 161; melancholist's dream 53, 113,
114; negative capability 160; true voice
of feeling 85
Kermode, F. 151
Kerrigan, J. 58, 106
Klein, M.: internal objects 104, 134, 152,
157; the positions 80, 158, 161, 162;
projective identification 105; splitting 92,
150; symbol-formation 162; unconscious
phantasy 155
Knights, L. C. 12, 61

Langer, S. 92, 154, 156, 159, 162

MacLeish, A. 163
MacNeice, L. 127

Name index

MacPhee, W. 151
Mahood, M. M. 17, 135
Marvell, A. 137
McAlindon, T. 58
Meltzer, D. 1, 31, 34, 43, 71, 92, 107, 111, 120, 152, 156, 160; aesthetic conflict 78, 158; claustrum 38, 59, 63, 118, 158, 162; countertransference dream 159; dream life 155–157; sincerity 73
Miller, L. 91, 92
Milton, J. 75, 94, 111, 128, 138, 146, 159
Money-Kyrle, R. 9, 22, 85, 106, 108, 135, 137, 143, 152, 157, 158

Nuttall, A. D. viii, 7, 14, 17, 25, 29, 54, 58, 135, 150

Pater, W. 2, 6

Raffield, P. 50
Richards, I. A. 163
Righter, A. (Barton) 18, 46, 58, 137, 150

Schwartz, M. 97, 106, 134
Segal, H. 77, 162
Shakespeare, W., plays: *A Midsummer Night's Dream* 19–29, 46, 68, 95, 104, 107, 114, 121, 126, 131, 137, 147; *Antony and Cleopatra* 14, 16, 32, 69, 93–106, 108, 116, 121, 131, 148, 149; *As You Like It* 49, 112; *Cymbeline* 107–120; *Hamlet* 30–45, 46, 52, 53, 57, 62, 95, 108, 121, 138, 152, 153, 163; *Julius Caesar* 10–17, 30, 35, 39, 43, 100, 153; *King Lear* 78–92, 93, 96, 105, 108, 114, 116, 121, 128, 132, 140, 153; *Love's Labour's Lost* 12, 29, 78; *Macbeth* 13, 59–69, 71, 72, 76, 109, 117; *Othello* 59, 69–65, 94, 95, 107, 122, 151; *Richard II* 1–10, 13, 22, 43, 48, 52, 68, 82, 96, 105, 115, 148, 149, 153; *Richard III* 145; *Romeo and Juliet* 25; *The Merchant of Venice* 46, 47–52, 79, 132, 142; *The Tempest* 35, 53, 70, 74, 91, 126, 136–151; *The Winter's Tale* 111, 114, 121–135, 137, 146, 150; *Troilus and Cressida* 52–58, 104
Sharpe, E. 156
Shelley, P. B. 160
Sheppard, A. 53
Simonds, P. M. 113, 120
Skura, M. 111, 117, 120
Sokol, B. J. 150
Stephens, S. 47, 58
Stockholder, K. 58, 107, 163
Stokes, A. 161, 163

Trilling, L. viii

Walker, J. 106
Wells, R. H. 29, 58
Wells, S. 5, 17
Wilson Knight, G. 12, 71, 82, 106
Wilson, R. 45, 58
Wittgenstein, L. 73, 80, 156

Subject index

adolescence/ adolescent 1–2, 21, 33, 35, 41, 93, 113, 131; central task 31, 43; gang/group 7, 42; isolated 10; and parents 36; worlds of 30

aesthetic: appreciation 27, 28, 91, 135, 156, 159, 160; criticism 163; false 20, 34–36, 38; object 50, 52, 53, 99, 118, 152, 160; and the play 37, 45, 58, 150, 154; psychoanalytic process 156, 163; speech 41

aesthetic conflict 24, 26, 31, 75, 77, 78–80, 95, 108, 114, 121–123, 141; contrary emotions 75, 79, 89, 93, 95, 99, 119; inside/outside object 24; and LHK 158; resolution of 130

ambivalence 32–33, 38, 75, 79, 95, 108; of aesthetic conflict 93; of mother 140

analyst figure 24, 30, 32–34, 39, 45, 67, 103, 112, 123, 125, 127, 133, 149; *see also* countertransference; psychoanalyst

anxiety 16, 37, 57, 78, 80, 118, 144, 152, 158; childhood 92, 162; of literary critic 160; nameless dread 63, 66

baby/infant, feelings 79, 141; aesthetic conflict 80; fears 86; and infanticide 62, 115; and mother 79, 137, 156–158, 160; new baby 39, 121–123; sensuality 88; weaning 83, 89; *see also* infantile values

basic assumptions 5, 10, 19, 20, 47, 48, 53, 55, 59, 72, 126, 138, 159; adolescent 2; fight-flight 11–12, 50; and hierarchy 2, 12, 47, 48, 54, 60, 64, 84, 138; messianic 12, 32, 75; protomental 18; three types 18

beauty: and aesthetic conflict 31, 34, 38, 59, 123, 141, 158; inner 70, 71, 94, 103, 117; and sincerity 73, 130, 143

birth, psychic 19, 61, 89, 113, 127, 132, 137, 138, 147, 150, 159; caricatural 142

breast, as object 9, 19, 79, 105, 111, 126, 141, 152; flattened 83, 90; innate preconception 85, 106, 157; substitute 142

catastrophic change 15, 17, 19, 25, 78, 83, 105, 114, 118, 136, 146; and birth/ rebirth 89, 127, 153; classical 117, 159

claustrum 38, 59, 61, 63, 69, 112, 118, 158

consciousness, as organ 107, 110, 117

container, psychic 8, 10, 33, 79, 86, 95, 125; analysis as 52, 156, 159; contained 9, 81, 92, 154, 161, 163; empty 83; false 36, 45, 60, 61, 63, 74, 142; play as 52, 152; poetry as 161

countertransference 33, 39, 42; dream 159, 160, 161; interference 32

creativity 9, 81, 100, 147, 158; as dream 30, 148, 155; false 55, 110, 143; of internal objects 10, 19, 22, 29, 86, 106, 109, 134, 141, 150, 152, 157, 162; lost 64, 125; *vs.* omnipotence of self 123, 159

curiosity *see* knowledge

cynicism/negativism 16, 58, 69, 71, 138, 141, 145, 153; minus K 35, 36, 43, 48, 59, 69, 84, 138, 146

death, as metaphor 3, 10, 17, 42, 44, 69, 71, 78, 97, 100, 114, 118, 134, 137, 147, 153, 157

depressive values 1, 63, 78, 81, 85, 103, 105, 150, 152, 158, 160, 161, 162; oscillation with paranoid-schizoid (Ps↔D) 78, 160, 162

dream-life viii, 20, 31, 155; destruction of 162; as work 10, 15, 19, 21, 29, 79, 96, 132, 155, 157, 159

172 Subject index

dream-world 9, 20, 29, 121, 127, 132, 153, 155, 162

emotionality 5, 12, 15, 24, 57, 60, 123, 144; of aesthetic conflict 26, 36, 75, 79, 91, 158; *vs.* basic assumptions 11, 96, 138; and form 160; humiliation 96; *vs.* language games 31, 41; of play audience 29, 37, 155; and thinking viii; turbulent 78, 88, 91, 108, 132, 136, 158

fake values 72, 84, 109, 128, 142
fantasy/phantasy 25, 29, 38, 61, 66, 72, 75, 90, 97, 110, 111, 127, 147; behind sexuality 104–105, 111, 113, 162; as innate preconception 85; intrusive 158; and playwright 91; unconscious 22, 155, 157; *see also* dream-life
femininity/feminine principle 12, 20, 40, 44, 49, 92, 94, 115; and masculine/male principle 98, 100, 104, 114, 118, 127, 135; perverse 60–62; projected 67; suspicion of 33; *see also* object, combined

hallucinosis 58, 63, 64, 66, 67, 76

idealisation vs. reality 2, 25, 33, 53, 84, 110, 115, 121, 123, 134; self- 70, 84, 104, 129; and splitting 84
identifications 6, 16, 24, 42, 61, 80, 112; actor's/poet's 22, 33, 148; adhesive 31; audience's 28, 32, 107, 154; complex 102, 119; introjective 5, 3, 80, 89, 98, 104, 118, 128, 130, 158, 159; misconceived 143; projective 49, 85, 105, 111, 123, 163
identity: adolescent 10, 31, 41, 129; clothed 132, 133; complementary 19; conceptions of 163; false/narcissistic 10, 43, 45, 49, 53, 121; group/social 1, 7, 57, 126; mythical 84–85; new 10, 70, 82, 88, 99, 103, 129, 148; split 7, 59, 69
imagination: as route to knowledge 26–28, 40, 44, 52, 101, 109, 152, 158; lack of 67, 68, 145, 146
infantile values 81
inspiration 153, 159
intrusive curiosity *see* knowledge, minus K

knowledge/ K: curiosity (K-link) 3, 34, 95, 118, 144; minus K 35, 52, 59, 68, 72, 84, 138, 145; of object (LHK) 78, 79,
99, 118, 140, 158; self- 4, 35, 59, 80, 82, 83, 155, 156, 161

language 4, 9, 22, 63, 81, 125, 140, 153, 156, 160; of achievement/creativity 9, 55, 60, 80, 88, 153, 160; deep grammar 156–157; of dreams 40, 117, 122, 156; false use of 5, 44, 50, 60, 69, 72, 84, 95, 153; games/ wordplay 31, 38, 48, 53, 57, 70, 78, 95, 154, 160; preverbal 23, 41, 79, 80, 81, 138, 141; *see also* symbol-formation
learning from experience 156, 162
literary criticism vii, 159–161; symbolic congruence 160

masochism 23, 25, 34, 41, 48, 50, 53, 104, 105–106
masturbation 64, 67, 72, 84, 104, 110
melancholy 45, 46, 53, 79, 113, 114, 145, 146
mother, internal 38, 39, 74, 79–81, 87, 90, 112, 123, 129; and muse 91; as part-object 80; restoration of 134, 137; witch- 60–63, 89, 110, 140; as world 11, 115; *see also* muse
mourning 145, 157
muse 24, 91, 119, 128, 134, 151, 153; anti- 109; as internal object 8, 154, 155, 159; mother as 137, 158
music, internal 3, 10, 16, 20, 23, 26, 41, 87, 97, 133, 137; false 48, 52, 110, 142–143, 145, 146

narcissism 1, 9, 10, 22, 56, 81, 121, 129, 153, 158
necessity, classical 5, 25, 91, 126
negative capability 19, 91, 160

object/s, internal 1, 21–22, 25, 30, 33, 59, 66, 73, 89, 107, 121, 129; absent 81, 157; bisexual/combined 9, 19, 42, 74, 93, 102–105, 110, 111, 133, 141, 150; breast/mother as 80; damaged/lost 46, 49, 56, 63, 109, 125, 134; evolution of 99; freedom of 143, 147; growth-promoting 59; part- 62, 80, 111, 144, 161; pseudo/substitute 74, 108; speaking 5, 10; transitional 152; *see also* aesthetic, object; creativity
Oedipal states 24, 88, 95, 126, 133, 139, 152

Subject index   173

omnipotence 19, 22, 25, 35, 52, 67, 87, 103, 108, 123, 140, 147, 158, 160; baby as 82; and infantile sexuality 104; struggle with 91, 127, 155, 159

paranoid-schizoid 46, 78, 81, 122, 158, 160, 161; oscillation Ps↔D 78, 160, 162
Platonism 26, 27, 29, 58, 86, 107, 114, 120, 129, 156, 157–159, 160
playwright as analyst 22, 30, 52, 71, 152
poet/poet figure 2, 10, 27, 45, 70, 87, 91, 95, 127, 132, 148, 153; anti-/ caricatured 15, 48, 51, 57, 69; and muse 128, 134, 159; and philosopher 86–87; and reader 78, 158, 169
poetry: and philosophy 19, 22, 31, 86, 95, 156; preverbal 81–85; in prose 95; *see also* language
projective identification 49, 62, 85, 105, 123, 129, 135, 141; communicative 161; and introjective 111; and paranoid-schizoid position 162
protomental 12, 18, 19, 20–21, 59, 75, 138, 157; and superstition 15, 74, 85; *see also* basic assumptions
psychoanalyst 32, 39, 45, 52, 152, 155, 160, 162; attitude of 33–34; and countertransference dream 159

reparation/restoration 67, 110, 121–135, 158; and mental evolution 137; and symbol-formation 162

school life 10–12, 20, 25, 37, 103, 112
sexuality 1, 5, 8, 13, 20, 22, 40, 46, 49, 70, 72, 74, 94, 147; and bisexual object 104–105; fantasies behind 38, 104–105, 111, 113, 122; female 105; infantile/ childish 80, 121
sincerity 69, 71, 73, 77, 81, 96, 129, 140, 153; *see also* language
splitting 5, 7, 10, 13, 25, 53, 59, 69, 80, 84, 92, 108, 140, 150, 162
symbol-formation 4, 21, 27, 31, 37, 41, 80, 87, 91, 100, 109, 118, 136, 150; as alpha-function 9, 19, 59, 79, 152, 158; in art/ theatre 136, 153, 155, 158, 159, 161; congruence in 160; false 33, 36, 59, 64, 75, 90; intersection with O 156, 159; preverbal 80; in psychoanalysis 156; *vs.* sign language 156–157; underlying idea 159

theatre: and inner world 9, 29, 53, 155
thought, creative 8–10, 31, 71, 79, 81, 93–106, 155–157; *vs.* action 21, 30, 35, 43, 60, 63, 70, 84; and catastrophic change 148; murder of 61, 65–66, 109; *vs.* non-thought 12, 55, 57, 59, 72–73; as sickness 37, 45; and thinking principle 137; unconscious 14, 19, 24, 26, 86, 96, 105, 110, 116, 136, 155
turbulence *see* emotionality, turbulent

work, mental/psychic 59, 69, 78, 95, 98, 114, 130, 153; -group 144, 147; of reparation 127